MS-100 Mic
Identity and Services
Exam

244 practice Questions and Answers

(New Edition 2020)

No Answers Spoiling
-Answers are found at the end of the book-

Microsoft 365 Identity and Services

By EXAM BOOST

The information contained in the book is provided for educational and informational purposes only

Pass Microsoft MS-100 Exam in First Attempt Guaranteed.

This book contains Real Exam Questions, Accurate & Verified Answers As Seen in the Real Exam.

Vendor: Microsoft
Certifications: Microsoft MS-100
Exam Name: Microsoft 365 Identity and Services **Exam Code**: MS-100
Total Questions: 244 Questions and Answers

These questions test your knowledge and skills related to:

- NOTE: The bullets that appear below each of the skills measured in the document below are intended to illustrate how we are assessing that skill. This list is not definitive or exhaustive.
- Design and implement Microsoft 365 services (25-30%)
- Manage user identity and roles (35-40%)
- Manage access and authentication (20-25%)
- Plan Office 365 workloads and applications (10-15%)

EXAM 1

Design and Implement Microsoft 365 Services

Question Set 1

QUESTION 1
Note: This question is part of a series of questions that present the same scenario. Each question in the series contains a unique solution that might meet the stated goals. Some question sets might have more than one correct solution, while others might not have a correct solution.

After you answer a question in this section, you will NOT be able to return to it. As a result, these questions will not appear in the review screen.

Your company has a Microsoft Office 365 tenant.

You suspect that several Office 365 features were recently updated.

You need to view a list of the features that were recently updated in the tenant. Solution:

You use the View service requests option in the Microsoft 365 admin center. Does this

meet the goal?

A. Yes
B. No

Section: (none)
Explanation

Explanation/Reference:
Explanation:
A service request is a support ticket. Therefore, the **View service requests** option in the Microsoft 365 admin center displays a list of support tickets. It does not display a list of the features that were recently updated in the tenant so this solution does not meet the goal.

To meet the goal, you need to use **Message center** in the Microsoft 365 admin center.

Reference:
https://docs.microsoft.com/en-us/office365/admin/manage/message-center?view=o365-worldwide

QUESTION 2
Note: This question is part of a series of questions that present the same scenario. Each question in the series contains a unique solution that might meet the stated goals. Some question sets might have more than one correct solution, while others might not have a correct solution.

After you answer a question in this section, you will NOT be able to return to it. As a result, these questions will not appear in the review screen.

Your company has a Microsoft Office 365 tenant.

You suspect that several Office 365 features were recently updated.

You need to view a list of the features that were recently updated in the tenant.

Solution: You use Dashboard in Security & Compliance.

Does this meet the goal?

A. Yes
B. No

Section: (none)
Explanation

Explanation/Reference:
Explanation:
Depending on what your organization's Office 365 subscription includes, the **Dashboard** in Security & Compliance includes several widgets, such as Threat Management Summary, Threat Protection Status, Global Weekly Threat Detections, Malware, etc. It does not display a list of the features that were recently updated in the tenant so this solution does not meet the goal.

To meet the goal, you need to use **Message center** in the Microsoft 365 admin center.

Reference:
https://docs.microsoft.com/en-us/microsoft-365/security/office-365-security/security-dashboard

https://docs.microsoft.com/en-us/office365/admin/manage/message-center?view=o365-worldwide

QUESTION 3
Note: This question is part of a series of questions that present the same scenario. Each question in the series contains a unique solution that might meet the stated goals. Some question sets might have more than one correct solution, while others might not have a correct solution.

After you answer a question in this section, you will NOT be able to return to it. As a result, these questions will not appear in the review screen.

Your company has a Microsoft Office 365 tenant.

You suspect that several Office 365 features were recently updated.

You need to view a list of the features that were recently updated in the tenant.

Solution: You use Message center in the Microsoft 365 admin center.

Does this meet the goal?

A. Yes

B. No

Section: (none)
Explanation

Explanation/Reference:
Explanation:
The **Message center** in the Microsoft 365 admin center is where you would go to view a list of the features that were recently updated in the tenant. This is where Microsoft posts official messages with information including new and changed features, planned maintenance, or other important announcements.

Reference:
https://docs.microsoft.com/en-us/office365/admin/manage/message-center?view=o365-worldwide

QUESTION 4
Note: This question is part of a series of questions that present the same scenario. Each question in the series contains a unique solution that might meet the stated goals. Some question sets might have more than one correct solution, while others might not have a correct solution.

After you answer a question in this section, you will NOT be able to return to it. As a result, these questions will not appear in the review screen.

Your company has a Microsoft Office 365 tenant.

You suspect that several Office 365 features were recently updated.

You need to view a list of the features that were recently updated in the tenant.

Solution: You review the Security & Compliance report in the Microsoft 365 admin center.

Does this meet the goal?

A. Yes

B. No

Section: (none)
Explanation

Explanation/Reference:
Explanation:
The **Security & Compliance reports** in the Microsoft 365 admin center are reports regarding security and compliance for your Office 365 Services. For example, email usage reports, Data Loss Prevention reports etc. They do not display a list of the features that were recently updated in the tenant so this solution does not meet the goal.

To meet the goal, you need to use **Message center** in the Microsoft 365 admin center.

Reference:
https://docs.microsoft.com/en-us/microsoft-365/security/office-365-security/download-existing-reports

QUESTION 5

You recently migrated your on-premises email solution to Microsoft Exchange Online and are evaluating which licenses to purchase.

You want the members of two groups named IT and Managers to be able to use the features shown in the following table.

Feature	Available to
Microsoft Azure Active Directory (Azure AD) conditional access	IT group, Managers group
Microsoft Azure Active Directory (Azure AD) Privileged Identity Management	IT group

The IT group contains 50 users. The Managers group contains 200 users.

You need to recommend which licenses must be purchased for the planned solution. The solution must minimize licensing costs.

Which licenses should you recommend?

A. 250 Microsoft 365 E3 only
B. 50 Microsoft 365 E3 and 200 Microsoft 365 E5
C. 250 Microsoft 365 E5 only
D. 200 Microsoft 365 E3 and 50 Microsoft 365 E5

Section: (none)
Explanation

Explanation/Reference:
Explanation:
Microsoft Azure Active Directory Privileged Identity Management requires an Azure AD Premium P2 license. This license comes as part of the Microsoft 365 E5 license. Therefore, we need 50 Microsoft 365 E5 licenses for the IT group.
Conditional Access requires the Azure AD Premium P1 license. This comes as part of the Microsoft E3 license. Therefore, we need 200 Microsoft 365 E3 licenses for the Managers group.

Reference:
https://docs.microsoft.com/en-us/azure/active-directory/privileged-identity-management/subscription-requirements

QUESTION 6
You have a Microsoft 365 tenant that contains Microsoft Exchange Online.

You plan to enable calendar sharing with a partner organization named adatum.com. The partner organization also has a Microsoft 365 tenant.

You need to ensure that the calendar of every user is available to the users in adatum.com immediately.

What should you do?

A. From the Exchange admin center, create a sharing policy.
B. From the Exchange admin center, create a new organization relationship.
C. From the Microsoft 365 admin center, modify the Organization profile settings.
D. From the Microsoft 365 admin center, configure external site sharing.

Section: (none)
Explanation

Explanation/Reference:
Explanation:
You need to set up an organization relationship to share calendar information with an external business partner. Office 365 admins can set up an organization relationship with another Office 365 organization or with an Exchange on-premises organization.

Reference:
https://docs.microsoft.com/en-us/exchange/sharing/organization-relationships/create-an-organization-relationship

QUESTION 7
Your company has an on-premises Microsoft Exchange Server 2016 organization and a Microsoft 365 Enterprise subscription.

You plan to migrate mailboxes and groups to Exchange Online. You

start a new migration batch.

Users report slow performance when they use the on-premises Exchange Server organization.

You discover that the migration is causing the slow performance.

You need to reduce the impact of the mailbox migration on the end-users.

What should you do?

A. Create a mail flow rule.
B. Configure back pressure.
C. Modify the migration endpoint settings.

D. Create a throttling policy.

Section: (none)
Explanation

Explanation/Reference:
Explanation:
The migration is causing the slow performance. This suggests that the on-premise Exchange server is struggling under the load of copying the mailboxes to Exchange Online. You can reduce the load on the on-premise server by reducing the maximum number of concurrent mailbox migrations. Migrating just a few mailboxes at a time will have less of a performance impact than migrating many mailboxes concurrently.

Reference:
https://support.microsoft.com/en-gb/help/2797784/how-to-manage-the-maximum-concurrent-migration-batches-in-exchange-onl

QUESTION 8
You have a Microsoft 365 subscription.

You need to prevent phishing email messages from being delivered to your organization.

What should you do?

A. From the Exchange admin center, create an anti-malware policy.
B. From Security & Compliance, create a DLP policy.
C. From Security & Compliance, create a new threat management policy.
D. From the Exchange admin center, create a spam filter policy.

Section: (none)
Explanation

Explanation/Reference:
Explanation:
Anti-phishing protection is part of Office 365 Advanced Threat Protection (ATP). To prevent phishing email messages from being delivered to your organization, you need to configure a threat management policy.

ATP anti-phishing is only available in Advanced Threat Protection (ATP). ATP is included in subscriptions, such as Microsoft 365 Enterprise, Microsoft 365 Business, Office 365 Enterprise E5, Office 365 Education A5, etc.

Reference:
https://docs.microsoft.com/en-us/office365/securitycompliance/set-up-anti-phishing-policies

QUESTION 9
Your company has a Microsoft 365 subscription. All identities are managed in the cloud.

The company purchases a new domain name.

You need to ensure that all new mailboxes use the new domain as their primary email address.

What are two possible ways to achieve the goal? Each correct answer presents a complete solution.

NOTE: Each correct selection is worth one point.

A. Run the `Update-EmailAddressPolicy` Windows PowerShell command
B. From the Exchange admin center, select **mail flow**, and then configure the email address policies.
C. From the Microsoft 365 admin center, select **Setup**, and then configure the domains.
D. Run the `Set-EmailAddressPolicy` Windows PowerShell command.
E. From the Azure Active Directory admin center, configure the custom domain names.

Section: (none)
Explanation

Explanation/Reference:
Explanation:
Email address policies define the rules that create email addresses for recipients in your Exchange organization whether this is Exchange on-premise or Exchange online.

You can configure email address policies using the graphical interface of the Exchange Admin Center or by using PowerShell with the `Set-EmailAddressPolicy` cmdlet.

The `Set-EmailAddressPolicy` cmdlet is used to modify an email address policy. The `Update-EmailAddressPolicy` cmdlet is used to apply an email address policy to users.

Reference:
https://docs.microsoft.com/en-us/exchange/email-addresses-and-address-books/email-address-policies/email-address-policies?view=exchserver-2019

QUESTION 10
Your company has a Microsoft Azure Active Directory (Azure AD) tenant named contoso.com that includes the users shown in the following table.

Name	Usage location	Membership
User1	United States	Group1, Group2
User2	*Not set*	Group2
User3	*Not set*	Group1
User4	Canada	Group1

Group2 is a member of Group1.

You assign a Microsoft Office 365 Enterprise E3 license to Group1.

How many Office 365 E3 licenses are assigned?

A. 1
B. 2
C. 3
D. 4

Section: (none)
Explanation

Explanation/Reference:
Explanation:
Group-based licensing currently does not support groups that contain other groups (nested groups). If you apply a license to a nested group, only the immediate first-level user members of the group have the licenses applied. Therefore, User2 will not be assigned a license.

When Azure AD assigns group licenses, any users without a specified usage location inherit the location of the directory. Therefore, User3 will be assigned a license and his usage location will be set to the location of the directory.

Reference:
https://docs.microsoft.com/en-us/azure/active-directory/users-groups-roles/licensing-groups-assign

https://docs.microsoft.com/en-us/azure/active-directory/users-groups-roles/licensing-group-advanced

QUESTION 11
You have a Microsoft 365 subscription.

A new corporate security policy states that you must automatically send DLP incident reports to the users in the legal department.

You need to schedule the email delivery of the reports. The solution must ensure that the reports are sent as frequently as possible.

How frequently can you schedule the delivery of the reports?

A. hourly
B. monthly
C. weekly
D. daily

Section: (none)
Explanation

Explanation/Reference:
Explanation:

From the Dashboard in the Security and Compliance center, you can view various reports including the DLP Incidents report. From there you can configure a schedule to email the reports. In the schedule configuration, there are two choices for the frequency: Weekly or Monthly. Therefore, to ensure that the reports are sent as frequently as possible, you need to select Weekly.

Reference:
https://docs.microsoft.com/en-us/microsoft-365/security/office-365-security/create-a-schedule- for-a-report

QUESTION 12
Your company has a Microsoft 365 subscription.

You need to identify all the users in the subscription who are licensed for Microsoft Office 365 through a group membership. The solution must include the name of the group used to assign the license.

What should you use?

A. the Licenses blade in the Azure portal
B. Reports in the Microsoft 365 admin center
C. Active users in the Microsoft 365 admin center
D. Reports in Security & Compliance

Section: (none)
Explanation

Explanation/Reference:
Explanation:
In the Azure AD Admin Center, select Azure Active Directory then select Licenses to open the Licenses blade. From there you need to click on the 'Managed your purchased licenses link'. Select a license you want to view, for example Office 365 E3. This will then display a list of all users with that license. In the 'Assignment Paths' column, it will say 'Direct' for a license that has been assigned directly to a user or 'Inherited (Group Name)' for a license that has been assigned through a group.

Reference:
https://docs.microsoft.com/en-us/azure/active-directory/users-groups-roles/licensing-groups-assign

QUESTION 13
Your company has a Microsoft 365 subscription.

You upload several archive PST files to Microsoft 365 by using the Security & Compliance admin center.

A month later, you attempt to run an import job for the PST files.

You discover that the PST files were deleted from Microsoft 365.

What is the most likely cause of the files being deleted? More than one answer choice may achieve the goal. Select the **BEST** answer.

A. The PST files were corrupted and deleted by Microsoft 365 security features.
B. PST files are deleted automatically from Microsoft 365 after 30 days.
C. The size of the PST files exceeded a storage quota and caused the files to be deleted.
D. Another administrator deleted the PST files.

Section: (none)
Explanation

Explanation/Reference:
Explanation:
You can use the Office 365 Import Service to bulk-import PST files to Office 365 mailboxes.

When you use the network upload method to import PST files, you upload them to an Azure blob container named ingestiondata. If there are no import jobs in progress on the Import page in the Security & Compliance Center), then all PST files in the ingestiondata container in Azure are deleted 30 days after the most recent import job was created in the Security & Compliance Center.

Reference:
https://docs.microsoft.com/en-us/office365/securitycompliance/faqimporting-pst-files-to-office-365

QUESTION 14
Your company has a main office and 20 branch offices in North America and Europe. Each branch connects to the main office by using a WAN link. All the offices connect to the Internet and resolve external host names by using the main office connections.

You plan to deploy Microsoft 365 and to implement a direct Internet connection in each office.

You need to recommend a change to the infrastructure to provide the quickest possible access to Microsoft 365 services.

What is the best recommendation to achieve the goal? More than one answer choice may achieve the goal. Select the **BEST** answer.

A. For all the client computers in the branch offices, modify the MTU setting by using a Group Policy object (GPO).
B. In each branch office, deploy a proxy server that has user authentication enabled.
C. In each branch office, deploy a firewall that has packet inspection enabled.
D. In the branch offices, configure name resolution so that all external hosts are redirected to public DNS servers directly.

Section: (none)
Explanation

Explanation/Reference:
Explanation:

Being a cloud service, Office 365 would be classed as an external host to the office computers.

All the offices connect to the Internet and resolve external host names by using the main office connections. This means that all branch office computers perform DNS lookups and connect to the Internet over the WAN link.

Each branch office will have a direct connection to the Internet so the quickest possible access to Microsoft 365 services would be by using the direct Internet connections. However, the DNS lookups would still go over the WAN links to main office. The solution to provide the quickest possible access to Microsoft 365 services is to configure DNS name resolution so that the computers use public DNS servers for external hosts. That way DNS lookups for Office 365 and the connections to Office 365 will use the direct Internet connections.

QUESTION 15
Your network contains an Active Directory forest named adatum.local. The forest contains 500 users and uses adatum.com as a UPN suffix.

You deploy a Microsoft 365 tenant.

You implement directory synchronization and sync only 50 support users.

You discover that five of the synchronized users have usernames that use a UPN suffix of onmicrosoft.com.

You need to ensure that all synchronized identities retain the UPN set in their on-premises user account.

What should you do?

A. From the Microsoft 365 admin center, add adatum.com as a custom domain name.
B. From Windows PowerShell, run the `Set-ADDomain -AllowedDNSSuffixes adatum.com` command.
C. From Active Directory Users and Computers, modify the UPN suffix of the five user accounts.
D. From the Microsoft 365 admin center, add adatum.local as a custom domain name.

Section: (none)
Explanation

Explanation/Reference:
Explanation:
The question states that only five of the synchronized users have usernames that use a UPN suffix of onmicrosoft.com. Therefore the other 45 users have the correct UPN suffix. This tells us that the adatum.com domain has already been added to Office 365 as a custom domain.
The forest is named adatum.local and uses adatum.com as a UPN suffix. User accounts in the domain will have adatum.local as their default UPN suffix. To use adatum.com as the UPN suffix, each user account will need to be configured to use adatum.com as the UPN suffix.
Any synchronized user account that has adatum.local as a UPN suffix will be configured to use a UPN suffix of onmicrosoft.com because adatum.local cannot be added to Office 365 as a custom domain.
Therefore, the reason that the five synchronized users have usernames with a UPN suffix of

onmicrosoft.com is because their accounts were not configured to use the UPN suffix of contoso.com.

Reference:
https://docs.microsoft.com/en-us/office365/enterprise/prepare-a-non-routable-domain-for-directory-synchronization

QUESTION 16
Your company has on-premises servers and a Microsoft Azure Active Directory (Azure AD) tenant.

Several months ago, the Azure AD Connect Health agent was installed on all the servers.

You review the health status of all the servers regularly.

Recently, you attempted to view the health status of a server named Server1 and discovered that the server is **NOT** listed on the Azure Active Directory Connect Servers list.

You suspect that another administrator removed Server1 from the list.

You need to ensure that you can view the health status of Server1.

What are two possible ways to achieve the goal? Each correct answer presents a complete solution.

NOTE: Each correct selection is worth one point.

A. From Windows PowerShell, run the `Register-AzureADConnectHealthSyncAgent` cmdlet.
B. From Azure Cloud shell, run the `Connect-AzureAD` cmdlet.
C. From Server1, change the Azure AD Connect Health services Startup type to **Automatic (Delayed Start)**.
D. From Server1, change the Azure AD Connect Health services Startup type to **Automatic**.
E. From Server1, reinstall the Azure AD Connect Health agent.

Section: (none)
Explanation

Explanation/Reference:
Explanation:
question states that another administrator removed Server1 from the list. To view the health status of Server1, you need to re-register the AD Connect Health Sync Agent. You can do this manually by running the `Register-AzureADConnectHealthSyncAgent` cmdlet. Alternatively, you can reinstall the Azure AD Connect Health agent. The Azure AD Connect Health agent is registered as part of the installation.

Reference:
https://docs.microsoft.com/en-us/azure/active-directory/hybrid/how-to-connect-health-agent-install

QUESTION 17
You have a Microsoft 365 subscription.

You suspect that several Microsoft Office 365 applications or services were recently updated.

You need to identify which applications or services were recently updated.

What are two possible ways to achieve the goal? Each correct answer presents a complete solution.

NOTE: Each correct selection is worth one point.

A. From the Microsoft 365 admin center, review the Message center blade.
B. From the Office 365 Admin mobile app, review the messages.
C. From the Microsoft 365 admin center, review the Products blade.
D. From the Microsoft 365 admin center, review the Service health blade.

Section: (none)
Explanation

Explanation/Reference:
Explanation:
The Message center in the Microsoft 365 admin center is where you would go to view a list of the features that were recently updated in the tenant. This is where Microsoft posts official messages with information including new and changed features, planned maintenance, or other important announcements.
The messages displayed in the Message center can also be viewed by using the Office 365 Admin mobile app.

Reference:
https://docs.microsoft.com/en-us/office365/admin/manage/message-center?view=o365-worldwide

https://docs.microsoft.com/en-us/office365/admin/admin-overview/admin-mobile-app?view=o365-worldwide

QUESTION 18
Note: This question is part of a series of questions that present the same scenario. Each question in the series contains a unique solution that might meet the stated goals. Some question sets might have more than one correct solution, while others might not have a correct solution.

After you answer a question in this section, you will NOT be able to return to it. As a result, these questions will not appear in the review screen.

Your company has a Microsoft Office 365 tenant.

You suspect that several Office 365 features were recently updated.

You need to view a list of the features that were recently updated in the tenant.

Solution: You use **Monitoring and reports** from the Compliance admin center.

Does this meet the goal?

A. Yes
B. No

Section: (none)
Explanation

Explanation/Reference:
Explanation:
Depending on what your organization's Office 365 subscription includes, the **Dashboard** in Security & Compliance includes several widgets, such as Threat Management Summary, Threat Protection Status, Global Weekly Threat Detections, Malware, etc. The Compliance admin center in Microsoft 365 contains much of the same information but also includes additional entries focusing on alerts, data insights.

The **Monitoring and reports** section from the Compliance admin center does not display a list of the features that were recently updated in the tenant so this solution does not meet the goal.

To meet the goal, you need to use **Message center** in the Microsoft 365 admin center.

Reference:
https://docs.microsoft.com/en-us/office365/admin/manage/message-center?view=o365-worldwide

QUESTION 19
Note: This question is part of a series of questions that present the same scenario. Each question in the series contains a unique solution that might meet the stated goals. Some question sets might have more than one correct solution, while others might not have a correct solution.

After you answer a question in this section, you will NOT be able to return to it. As a result, these questions will not appear in the review screen.

Your network contains an Active Directory domain named contoso.com that is synced to Microsoft Azure Active Directory (Azure AD).

You manage Windows 10 devices by using Microsoft System Center Configuration Manager (Current Branch).

You configure a pilot for co-management.

You add a new device named Device1 to the domain. You install the Configuration Manager client on Device1.

You need to ensure that you can manage Device1 by using Microsoft Intune and Configuration Manager.

Solution: You add Device1 to an Active Directory group.

Does this meet the goal?

A. Yes
B. No

Section: (none)
Explanation

Explanation/Reference:
Explanation:
Device1 has the Configuration Manager client installed so you can manage Device1 by using Configuration Manager.
To manage Device1 by using Microsoft Intune, the device has to be enrolled in Microsoft Intune. In the Co-management Pilot configuration, you configure a Configuration Manager Device Collection that determines which devices are auto-enrolled in Microsoft Intune. You need to add Device1 to the Device Collection, not an Active Directory Group. Therefore, this solution does not meet the requirements.

Reference:
https://docs.microsoft.com/en-us/configmgr/comanage/how-to-enable

QUESTION 20
Note: This question is part of a series of questions that present the same scenario. Each question in the series contains a unique solution that might meet the stated goals. Some question sets might have more than one correct solution, while others might not have a correct solution.

After you answer a question in this section, you will NOT be able to return to it. As a result, these questions will not appear in the review screen.

Your network contains an Active Directory domain named contoso.com that is synced to Microsoft Azure Active Directory (Azure AD).

You manage Windows 10 devices by using Microsoft System Center Configuration Manager (Current Branch).

You configure a pilot for co-management.

You add a new device named Device1 to the domain. You install the Configuration Manager client on Device1.

You need to ensure that you can manage Device1 by using Microsoft Intune and Configuration Manager.

Solution: Define a Configuration Manager device collection as the pilot collection. Add Device1 to the collection.

Does this meet the goal?

A. Yes
B. No

QUESTION 21
Note: This question is part of a series of questions that present the same scenario. Each question in the series contains a unique solution that might meet the stated goals. Some question sets might have more than one correct solution, while others might not have a correct solution.

After you answer a question in this section, you will NOT be able to return to it. As a result, these questions will not appear in the review screen.

Your network contains an Active Directory domain named contoso.com that is synced to Microsoft Azure Active Directory (Azure AD).

You manage Windows 10 devices by using Microsoft System Center Configuration Manager (Current Branch).

You configure a pilot for co-management.

You add a new device named Device1 to the domain. You install the Configuration Manager client on Device1.

You need to ensure that you can manage Device1 by using Microsoft Intune and Configuration Manager.

Solution: You create a device configuration profile from the Intune admin center.

Does this meet the goal?

A. Yes
B. No

Explanation

Explanation:
Device1 has the Configuration Manager client installed so you can manage Device1 by using Configuration Manager.
To manage Device1 by using Microsoft Intune, the device has to be enrolled in Microsoft Intune. In the Co-management Pilot configuration, you configure a Configuration Manager Device Collection that determines which devices are auto-enrolled in Microsoft Intune. You need to add Device1 to the Device Collection. You do not need to create a device configuration profile from the Intune admin center. Therefore, this solution does not meet the requirements.

Reference:
https://docs.microsoft.com/en-us/configmgr/comanage/how-to-enable

QUESTION 22
You have a Microsoft 365 subscription.

You configure a data loss prevention (DLP) policy.

You discover that users are incorrectly marking content as false positive and bypassing the DLP policy.

You need to prevent the users from bypassing the DLP policy. What

should you configure?

A. actions
B. exceptions
C. incident reports
D. user overrides

Section: (none)
Explanation

Explanation:
A DLP policy can be configured to allow users to override a policy tip and report a false positive.

You can educate your users about DLP policies and help them remain compliant without blocking their work. For example, if a user tries to share a document containing sensitive information, a DLP policy can both send them an email notification and show them a policy tip in the context of the document library that allows them to override the policy if they have a business justification. The same policy tips also appear in Outlook on the web, Outlook, Excel, PowerPoint, and Word. If you find that users are incorrectly marking content as false positive and bypassing the DLP policy, you can configure the policy to not allow user overrides.

Reference:
https://docs.microsoft.com/en-us/office365/securitycompliance/data-loss-prevention-policies

QUESTION 23

In Microsoft 365, you configure a data loss prevention (DLP) policy named Policy1. Policy1 detects the sharing of United States (US) bank account numbers in email messages and attachments.

Policy1 is configured as shown in the exhibit. (Click the **Exhibit** tab.)

Use actions to protect content when the conditions are met.

Restrict access or encrypt the content

◉ Block people from sharing and resrtrict access to shared content

By default, users are blocked from sending email messages to people. You can choose who has access to shared SharePoint and OneDrive content.

Block these people from accessing SharePoint and OneDrive content

○ Everyone. Only the content owner, the lastmodifier, and the site admin will continue to have access.

◉ Only people ourtside your organization. People inside your organization will contibue to have access

○ Encrypt email messages (applies only to content to Exchange)

You need to ensure that internal users can email documents that contain US bank account numbers to external users who have an email suffix of contoso.com.

What should you configure?

A. an action
B. a group
C. a condition
D. an exception

Section: (none)
Explanation

Explanation/Reference:
Explanation:
You need to add an exception. In the Advanced Settings of the DLP policy, you can add a rule to configure the Conditions and Actions. There is also an 'Add Exception' button. This gives you several options that you can select as the exception. One of the options is 'except when recipient domain is'. You need to select that option and enter the domain name contoso.com.

Reference:
https://docs.microsoft.com/en-us/office365/securitycompliance/data-loss-prevention-policies#how-dlp-policies-work

QUESTION 24

Your company uses on-premises Windows Server File Classification Infrastructure 9FCl). Some documents on the on-premises file servers are classifies as Confidential.

You migrate the files from the on-premises file servers to Microsoft SharePoint Online.

You need to ensure that you can implement data loss prevention (DLP) policies for the uploaded files based on the Confidential classification.

What should you do first?

A. From the SharePoint admin center, create a managed property.
B. From the SharePoint admin center, configure hybrid search.
C. From the Security & Compliance Center PowerShell, run the `New-DlpComplianceRule` cmdlet.
D. From the Security & Compliance Center PowerShell, run the `New-DataClassification` cmdlet.

Section: (none)
Explanation

Explanation/Reference:
Explanation:
Your organization might use Windows Server FCI to identify documents with personally identifiable information (PII) such as social security numbers, and then classify the document by setting the Personally Identifiable Information property to High, Moderate, Low, Public, or Not PII based on the type and number of occurrences of PII found in the document. In Office 365, you can create a DLP policy that identifies documents that have that property set to specific values, such as High and Medium, and then takes an action such as blocking access to those files.

Before you can use a Windows Server FCI property or other property in a DLP policy, you need to create a managed property in the SharePoint admin center.

Reference:
https://docs.microsoft.com/en-us/microsoft-365/compliance/protect-documents-that-have-fci-or-other-properties

QUESTION 25
Your company has 10 offices.

The network contains an Active Directory domain named contoso.com. The domain contains 500 client computers. Each office is configured as a separate subnet.

You discover that one of the offices has the following:

- Computers that have several preinstalled applications
- Computers that use nonstandard computer names
- Computers that have Windows 10 preinstalled
- Computers that are in a workgroup

You must configure the computers to meet the following corporate requirements:

- All the computers must be joined to the domain.
- All the computers must have computer names that use a prefix of CONTOSO.
- All the computers must only have approved corporate applications installed.

You need to recommend a solution to redeploy the computers. The solution must minimize the deployment time.

A. a provisioning package
B. wipe and load refresh
C. Windows Autopilot
D. an in-place upgrade

Section: (none)
Explanation

Explanation/Reference:
Explanation:
By using a provisioning package, IT administrators can create a self-contained package that contains all of the configuration, settings, and apps that need to be applied to a device.

Incorrect Answers:
C: With Windows Autopilot the user can set up pre-configured devices without the need consult their IT administrator.
D: Use the In-Place Upgrade option when you want to keep all (or at least most) existing applications.

Reference:
https://docs.microsoft.com/en-us/windows/deployment/windows-10-deployment-scenarios

https://docs.microsoft.com/en-us/windows/deployment/windows-autopilot/windows-autopilot

QUESTION 26
You have a Microsoft 365 subscription.

You recently configured a Microsoft SharePoint Online tenant in the subscription.

You plan to create an alert policy.

You need to ensure that an alert is generated only when malware is detected in more than five documents stored in SharePoint Online during a period of 10 minutes.

What should you do first?

A. Enable Microsoft Office 365 Cloud App Security.
B. Deploy Windows Defender Advanced Threat Protection (Windows Defender ATP).
C. Enable Microsoft Office 365 Analytics.

Section: (none)
Explanation

Explanation/Reference:

Explanation:

An alert policy consists of a set of rules and conditions that define the user or admin activity that generates an alert, a list of users who trigger the alert if they perform the activity, and a threshold that defines how many times the activity has to occur before an alert is triggered.

In this question, we would use the "Malware detected in file" activity in the alert settings then configure the threshold (5 detections) and the time window (10 minutes).

The ability to configure alert policies based on a threshold or based on unusual activity requires Advanced Threat Protection (ATP).

Reference:
https://docs.microsoft.com/en-us/microsoft-365/compliance/alert-policies

QUESTION 27

From the Microsoft Azure Active Directory (Azure AD) Identity Protection dashboard, you view the risk events shown in the exhibit. (Click the **Exhibit** tab.)

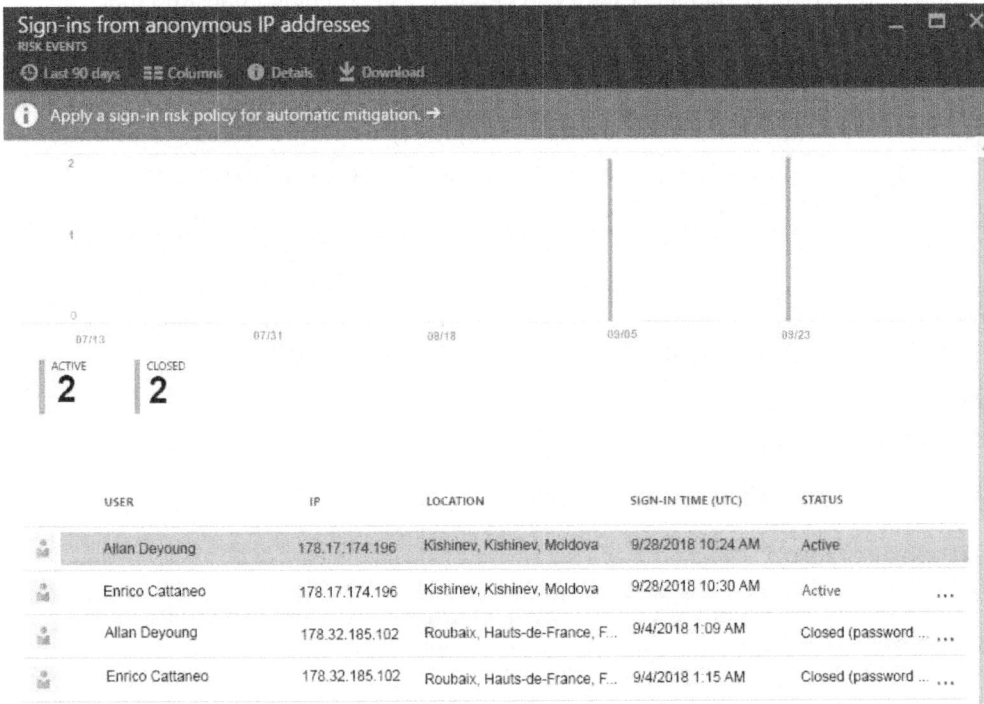

	USER	IP	LOCATION	SIGN-IN TIME (UTC)	STATUS	
	Allan Deyoung	178.17.174.196	Kishinev, Kishinev, Moldova	9/28/2018 10:24 AM	Active	
	Enrico Cattaneo	178.17.174.196	Kishinev, Kishinev, Moldova	9/28/2018 10:30 AM	Active	...
	Allan Deyoung	178.32.185.102	Roubaix, Hauts-de-France, F...	9/4/2018 1:09 AM	Closed (password ...	...
	Enrico Cattaneo	178.32.185.102	Roubaix, Hauts-de-France, F...	9/4/2018 1:15 AM	Closed (password ...	...

You need to reduce the likelihood that the sign-ins are identified as risky.

What should you do?

A. From the Security & Compliance admin center, add the users to the Security Readers role group.
B. From the Conditional access blade in the Azure Active Directory admin center, create named locations.
C. From the Azure Active Directory admin center, configure the trusted IPs for multi-factor authentication.
D. From the Security & Compliance admin center, create a classification label.

Section: (none)
Explanation

Explanation/Reference:
Explanation:
A named location can be configured as a trusted location. Typically, trusted locations are network areas that are controlled by your IT department. In addition to Conditional Access, trusted named locations are also used by Azure Identity Protection and Azure AD security reports to reduce false positives for risky sign-ins.

Reference:
https://docs.microsoft.com/en-us/azure/active-directory/conditional-access/location-condition

QUESTION 28
You have a Microsoft 365 tenant.

You have a line-of-business application named App1 that users access by using the My Apps portal.

After some recent security breaches, you implement a conditional access policy for App1 that uses Conditional Access App Control.

You need to be alerted by email if impossible travel is detected for a user of App1. The solution must ensure that alerts are generated for App1 only.

What should you do?

A. From Microsoft Cloud App Security, modify the impossible travel alert policy.
B. From Microsoft Cloud App Security, create a Cloud Discovery anomaly detection policy.
C. From the Azure Active Directory admin center, modify the conditional access policy.
D. From Microsoft Cloud App Security, create an app discovery policy.

Section: (none)
Explanation

Explanation/Reference:
Explanation:
Impossible travel detection identifies two user activities (is a single or multiple sessions) originating from geographically distant locations within a time period shorter than the time it would have taken the user to travel from the first location to the second.
We need to modify the policy so that it applies to App1 only.

Reference:
https://docs.microsoft.com/en-us/cloud-app-security/anomaly-detection-policy

QUESTION 29
Your network contains an on-premises Active Directory domain.

Your company has a security policy that prevents additional software from being installed on domain controllers.

You need to monitor a domain controller by using Microsoft Azure Advanced Threat Protection (ATP).

What should you do? More than once choice may achieve the goal. Select the **BEST** answer.

A. Deploy an Azure ATP standalone sensor, and then configure port mirroring.
B. Deploy an Azure ATP standalone sensor, and then configure detections.
C. Deploy an Azure ATP sensor, and then configure detections.
D. Deploy an Azure ATP sensor, and then configure port mirroring.

Section: (none)
Explanation

Explanation/Reference:
Explanation:
If you're installing on a domain controller, you don't need a standalone ATP sensor. You need to configure the detections to detect application installations. With an ATP sensor (non-standalone), you don't need to configure port mirroring.

Reference:
https://docs.microsoft.com/en-us/azure-advanced-threat-protection/install-atp-step5

https://docs.microsoft.com/en-us/azure-advanced-threat-protection/atp-capacity-planning#choosing-the-right-sensor-type-for-your-deployment

QUESTION 30
Your network contains an on-premises Active Directory domain named contoso.com. The domain contains 1,000 Windows 10 devices.

You perform a proof of concept (PoC) deployment of Windows Defender Advanced Threat Protection (ATP) for 10 test devices. During the onboarding process, you configure Windows Defender ATP-related data to be stored in the United States.

You plan to onboard all the devices to Windows Defender ATP data in Europe.

What should you do first?

A. Create a workspace
B. Offboard the test devices
C. Delete the workspace

D. Onboard a new device

Section: (none)
Explanation

Explanation/Reference:
Explanation:
When onboarding Windows Defender ATP for the first time, you can choose to store your data in Microsoft Azure datacenters in the European Union, the United Kingdom, or the United States. Once configured, you cannot change the location where your data is stored.
The only way to change the location is to offboard the test devices then onboard them again with the new location.

Reference:
https://docs.microsoft.com/en-us/windows/security/threat-protection/microsoft-defender-atp/data-storage-privacy#do-i-have-the-flexibility-to-select-where-to-store-my-data

QUESTION 31
You implement Microsoft Azure Advanced Threat Protection (Azure ATP).

You have an Azure ATP sensor configured as shown in the following exhibit.

Updates

Updates

Domain controller restart during updates (?)   [OFF]

NAME	TYPE	VERSION	AUTOM...	DELAYE...	STATUS
LON-DC1	Sensor	2.48.5521	on	on	Up to date

Save

How long after the Azure ATP cloud service is updated will the sensor update?

A. 1 hour
B. 7 days
C. 48 hours

D. 12 hours

E. 72 hours

Section: (none)
Explanation

Explanation/Reference:
Explanation:
The exhibit shows that the sensor is configure for **Delayed update.**
Given the rapid speed of ongoing Azure ATP development and release updates, you may decide to define a subset group of your sensors as a delayed update ring, allowing for a gradual sensor update process. Azure ATP enables you to choose how your sensors are updated and set each sensor as a **Delayed update** candidate.
Sensors not selected for delayed update are updated automatically, each time the Azure ATP service is updated. Sensors set to **Delayed update** are updated on a delay of 72 hours, following the official release of each service update.

Reference:
https://docs.microsoft.com/en-us/azure-advanced-threat-protection/sensor-update

QUESTION 32
Your company has a Microsoft 365 E3 subscription.

All devices run Windows 10 Pro and are joined to Microsoft Azure Active Directory (Azure AD).

You need to change the edition of Windows 10 to Enterprise the next time users sign in to their computer. The solution must minimize downtime for the users.

What should you use?

A. Subscription Activation

B. Windows Update

C. Windows Autopilot

D. an in-place upgrade

Section: (none)
Explanation

Explanation/Reference:
Explanation:
When initially deploying new Windows devices, Windows Autopilot leverages the OEM-optimized version of Windows 10 that is preinstalled on the device, saving organizations the effort of having to maintain custom images and drivers for every model of device being used. Instead of re-imaging the device, your existing Windows 10 installation can be transformed into a "business-ready" state, applying settings and policies, installing apps, and even changing the edition of Windows 10 being used (e.g. from Windows 10 Pro to Windows 10 Enterprise) to support advanced features.

Reference:
https://docs.microsoft.com/en-us/windows/deployment/windows-autopilot/windows-autopilot

QUESTION 33
Your network contains an Active Directory domain named contoso.com. The domain contains 1000 Windows 8.1 devices.

You plan to deploy a custom Windows 10 Enterprise image to the Windows 8.1 devices.

You need to recommend a Windows 10 deployment method.

What should you recommend?

A. Wipe and load refresh
B. Windows Autopilot
C. a provisioning package
D. an in-place upgrade

Section: (none)
Explanation

Explanation/Reference:
Explanation:
To deploy a custom image, you must use the wipe and load refresh method. You cannot deploy a custom image by using an in-place upgrade, Windows Autopilot or a provisioning package.

Reference:
https://docs.microsoft.com/en-us/windows/deployment/windows-10-deployment-scenarios

QUESTION 34
You use Microsoft System Center Configuration manager (Current Branch) to manage devices.

Your company uses the following types of devices:

- Windows 10
- Windows 8.1
- Android
- iOS

Which devices can be managed by using co-management?

A. Windows 10 and Windows 8.1 only
B. Windows 10, Android, and iOS only
C. Windows 10 only
D. Windows 10, Windows 8.1, Android, and iOS

Section: (none)
Explanation

Explanation/Reference:
Explanation:

You can manage only Windows 10 devices by using co-management.

When you concurrently manage Windows 10 devices with both Configuration Manager and Microsoft Intune, this configuration is called co-management. When you manage devices with Configuration Manager and enroll to a third-party MDM service, this configuration is called coexistence.

Reference:
https://docs.microsoft.com/en-us/configmgr/comanage/overview

QUESTION 35
Your company has 20 employees. Each employee has a mailbox hosted in Outlook.com.

The company purchases a Microsoft 365 subscription.

You plan to migrate all the mailboxes to Microsoft 365.

You need to recommend which type of migration to use for the mailboxes.

What should you recommend?

A. staged migration
B. cutover migration
C. minimal hybrid migration
D. IMAP migration

Section: (none)
Explanation

Explanation/Reference:
Explanation:
To migrate mailboxes from Outlook.com to Office 365, you need to use the IMAP migration method.

After you've added your users to Office 365, you can use Internet Message Access Protocol (IMAP) to migrate email for those users from their IMAP-enabled email servers.
In the Microsoft 365 admin center, go to **Setup** > **Data migration** to start migrating IMAP enabled emails. The email migrations page is pre-configured for migrations from Gmail, Outlook, Hotmail and Yahoo. You can also enter your own IMAP server name and connection parameters to migrate from an email service that is not listed.

References:
https://docs.microsoft.com/en-us/exchange/mailbox-migration/migrating-imap-mailboxes/imap-migration-in-the-admin-center

QUESTION 36
Your network contains an on-premises Active Directory domain named contoso.com that is synced to a Microsoft Azure Active Directory (Azure AD) tenant.

The on-premises network contains a file server named Server1. Server1 has a share named Share1 that contains company documents.

Your company purchases a Microsoft 365 subscription.

You plan to migrate data from Share1 to Microsoft 365. Only data that was created or modified during the last three months will be migrated.

You need to identify all the files in Share1 that were modified or created during the last 90 days.

What should you use?

A. Server Manager
B. Microsoft SharePoint Migration Tool
C. Resource Monitor
D. Usage reports from the Microsoft 365 admin center

Section: (none)
Explanation

Explanation/Reference:
Explanation:
You can use the Microsoft SharePoint Migration Tool to migrate files from a file server to SharePoint Online.
The Microsoft SharePoint Migration Tool has a number of filters you can use to define which files will be migrated. One filter setting is "Migrate files modified after". This setting will only migrate files modified after the selected date.
The first phase of a migration is to perform a scan of the source files to create a manifest of the files that will be migrated. You can use this manifest to identify all the files in Share1 that were modified or created during the last 90 days.

References:
https://docs.microsoft.com/en-us/sharepointmigration/spmt-settings

QUESTION 37
Your company has two offices. The offices are located in Seattle and New York.

The company uses a third-party email system.

You implement Microsoft 365.

You move all the users in the Seattle office to Exchange Online. You configure Microsoft 365 to successfully receive all the email messages sent to the Seattle office users.

All the users in the New York office continue to use the third-party email system.

The users use the email domains shown in the following table.

Users in	Email domain
Seattle	Contoso.com
New York	Adatum.com

You need to ensure that all the email messages sent to the New York office users are delivered successfully. The solution must ensure that all the email messages for the users in both offices are routed through Microsoft 365.

You create the required DNS records and Send connectors.

What should you do next from Microsoft 365?

A. From Microsoft 365 admin center, set the default domain. From the Exchange admin center, create a transport rule for all the email messages sent to adatum.com.
B. From Microsoft 365 admin center, add the adatum.com domain. From the Exchange admin center, configure adatum.com as an internal relay domain.
C. From Microsoft 365 admin center, add the adatum.com domain. From the Exchange admin center, configure adatum.com as an authoritative domain.
D. From Microsoft 365 admin center, set the default domain. From the Exchange admin center, configure adatum.com as a remote domain.

Section: (none)
Explanation

Explanation/Reference:
Explanation:
The first step is to configure Exchange Online to accept emails for the adatum.com domain. To do this, we add the domain in Microsoft 365. When you add your domain to Microsoft 365, it's called an accepted domain.

The next step is to tell Exchange Online what to do with those emails. You need to configure the adatum.com domain as either an authoritative domain or an internal relay domain.

Authoritative domain means that the mailboxes for that domain are hosted in Office 365. In this question, the mailboxes for the adatum.com domain are hosted on the third-party email system. Therefore, we need to configure the adatum.com domain as an internal relay domain. For an internal relay domain, Exchange Online will receive the email for the adatum.com domain and then 'relay' (forward) the email on to the third-party email server.

References:
https://docs.microsoft.com/en-us/exchange/mail-flow-best-practices/manage-accepted-domains/manage-accepted-domains

QUESTION 38
You have a Microsoft 365 subscription.

You add a domain named contoso.com.

When you attempt to verify the domain, you are prompted to send a verification email to admin@contoso.com.

You need to change the email address used to verify the domain.

What should you do?

A. From the domain registrar, modify the contact information of the domain
B. Add a TXT record to the DNS zone of the domain
C. Modify the NS records for the domain
D. From the Microsoft 365 admin center, change the global administrator of the Microsoft 365 subscription

Section: (none)
Explanation

Explanation/Reference:
Explanation:
The email address that is used to verify that you own the domain is the email address listed with the domain registrar for the registered contact for the domain.

Reference:
https://docs.microsoft.com/en-us/microsoft-365/admin/setup/add-domain?view=o365-worldwide

QUESTION 39
Your company uses email, calendar, contact, and task services in Microsoft Outlook.com.

You purchase a Microsoft 365 subscription and plan to migrate all users from Outlook.com to Microsoft 365.

You need to identify which user data can be migrated to Microsoft 365. Which

type of data should you identify?

A. task
B. email
C. calendar
D. contacts

Section: (none)
Explanation

Explanation/Reference:
Explanation:
You can use the Internet Message Access Protocol (IMAP) to migrate user email from Gmail, Exchange, Outlook.com, and other email systems that support IMAP migration. When you migrate the user's email by using IMAP migration, only the items in the users' inbox or other mail folders are migrated. Contacts, calendar items, and tasks can't be migrated with IMAP, but they can be by a user.

Reference:

https://docs.microsoft.com/en-us/exchange/mailbox-migration/mailbox-migration#migrate-email- from-another-imap-enabled-email-system

Design and Implement Microsoft 365 Services

Testlet 2

This is a case study. **Case studies are not timed separately. You can use as much exam time as you would like to complete each case**. However, there may be additional case studies and sections on this exam. You must manage your time to ensure that you are able to complete all questions included on this exam in the time provided.

To answer the questions included in a case study, you will need to reference information that is provided in the case study. Case studies might contain exhibits and other resources that provide more information about the scenario that is described in the case study. Each question is independent of the other questions in this case study.

At the end of this case study, a review screen will appear. This screen allows you to review your answer and to make changes before you move to the next section of the exam. After you begin a new section, you cannot return to this section.

To start the case study
To display the first question in this case study, click the **Next** button. Use the buttons in the left pane to explore the content of the case study before you answer the questions. Clicking these buttons displays information such as business requirements, existing environment, and problem statements. When you are ready to answer a question, click the **Question** button to return to the question.

Overview
Contoso, Ltd. is a consulting company that has a main office in Montreal and two branch offices in Seattle and New York.

The offices have the users and devices shown in the following table.

Office	Users	Laptops	Desktops	Mobile devices
Montreal	2,500	2,800	300	3,100
Seattle	1,000	1,100	200	1,500
New York	300	320	30	400

Contoso recently purchased a Microsoft 365 E5 subscription.

Existing Environment
The network contains an Active directory forest named contoso.com and a Microsoft Azure Active Directory (Azure AD) tenant named contoso.onmicrosoft.com.

You recently configured the forest to sync to the Azure AD tenant. You

add and then verify adatum.com as an additional domain name. All

servers run Windows Server 2016.

All desktop computers and laptops run Windows 10 Enterprise and are joined to contoso.com.

All the mobile devices in the Montreal and Seattle offices run Android. All the mobile devices in the New York office run iOS.

Contoso has the users shown in the following table.

Name	Role
User1	*None*
User2	*None*
User3	Customer Lockbox access approver
User4	*None*

Contoso has the groups shown in the following table.

Name	Type	Membership rule
Group1	Assigned	*Not applicable*
Group 2	Dynamic	(user.department –eq "Finance")

Microsoft Office 365 licenses are assigned only to Group2.

The network also contains external users from a vendor company who have Microsoft accounts that use a suffix of @outlook.com.

Requirements

Planned Changes
Contoso plans to provide email addresses for all the users in the following domains:

- East.adatum.com
- Contoso.adatum.com
- Humongousinsurance.com

Technical Requirements
Contoso identifies the following technical requirements:

- All new users must be assigned Office 365 licenses automatically.
- The principle of least privilege must be used whenever possible.

Security Requirements
Contoso identifies the following security requirements:

- Vendors must be able to authenticate by using their Microsoft account when accessing Contoso resources.
- User2 must be able to view reports and schedule the email delivery of security and compliance reports.

- The members of Group1 must be required to answer a security question before changing their password.
- User3 must be able to manage Office 365 connectors.
- User4 must be able to reset User3 password.

QUESTION 1
You need to add the custom domain names to Office 365 to support the planned changes as quickly as possible.

What should you create to verify the domain names successfully?

A. three alias (CNAME) records
B. one text (TXT) record
C. one alias (CNAME) record
D. three text (TXT) records

Section: (none)
Explanation

Explanation/Reference:
Explanation:
Contoso plans to provide email addresses for all the users in the following domains:
- East.adatum.com
- Contoso.adatum.com
- Humongousinsurance.com

To verify three domain names, you need to add three TXT records.

Reference:
https://docs.microsoft.com/en-us/office365/admin/setup/add-domain?view=o365-worldwide

Design and Implement Microsoft 365 Services

Testlet 3

This is a case study. **Case studies are not timed separately. You can use as much exam time as you would like to complete each case**. However, there may be additional case studies and sections on this exam. You must manage your time to ensure that you are able to complete all questions included on this exam in the time provided.

To answer the questions included in a case study, you will need to reference information that is provided in the case study. Case studies might contain exhibits and other resources that provide more information about the scenario that is described in the case study. Each question is independent of the other questions in this case study.

At the end of this case study, a review screen will appear. This screen allows you to review your answer and to make changes before you move to the next section of the exam. After you begin a new section, you cannot return to this section.

To start the case study
To display the first question in this case study, click the **Next** button. Use the buttons in the left pane to explore the content of the case study before you answer the questions. Clicking these buttons displays information such as business requirements, existing environment, and problem statements. When you are ready to answer a question, click the **Question** button to return to the question.

Overview
Fabrikam, Inc. is an electronics company that produces consumer products. Fabrikam has 10,000 employees worldwide.

Fabrikam has a main office in London and branch offices in major cities in Europe, Asia, and the United States.

Existing Environment
Active Directory Environment
The network contains an Active Directory forest named fabrikam.com. The forest contains all the identities used for user and computer authentication.

Each department is represented by a top-level organizational unit (OU) that contains several child OUs for user accounts and computer accounts.

All users authenticate to on-premises applications by signing in to their device by using a UPN format of *username@fabrikam.com.*

Fabrikam does **NOT** plan to implement identity federation.

Network Infrastructure

Each office has a high-speed connection to the Internet.

Each office contains two domain controllers. All domain controllers are configured as a DNS server.

The public zone for fabrikam.com is managed by an external DNS server.

All users connect to an on-premises Microsoft Exchange Server 2016 organization. The users access their email by using Outlook Anywhere, Outlook on the web, or the Microsoft Outlook app for iOS. All the Exchange servers have the latest cumulative updates installed.

All shared company documents are stored on a Microsoft SharePoint Server farm.

Requirements
Planned Changes
Fabrikam plans to implement a Microsoft 365 Enterprise subscription and move all email and shared documents to the subscription.

Fabrikam plans to implement two pilot projects:

- Project1: During Project1, the mailboxes of 100 users in the sales department will be moved to Microsoft 365.
- Project2: After the successful completion of Project1, Microsoft Teams & Skype for Business will be enabled in Microsoft 365 for the sales department users.

Fabrikam plans to create a group named UserLicenses that will manage the allocation of all Microsoft 365 bulk licenses.

Technical Requirements
Fabrikam identifies the following technical requirements:

- All users must be able to exchange email messages successfully during Project1 by using their current email address.
- Users must be able to authenticate to cloud services if Active Directory becomes unavailable.
- A user named User1 must be able to view all DLP reports from the Microsoft 365 admin center.
- Microsoft Office 365 ProPlus applications must be installed from a network share only.
- Disruptions to email access must be minimized.

Application Requirements
Fabrikam identifies the following application requirements:

- An on-premises web application named App1 must allow users to complete their expense reports online. App1 must be available to users from the My Apps portal.
- The installation of feature updates for Office 365 ProPlus must be minimized.

Security Requirements
Fabrikam identifies the following security requirements:

- After the planned migration to Microsoft 365, all users must continue to authenticate to their mailbox and to SharePoint sites by using their UPN.
- The memberships of UserLicenses must be validated monthly. Unused user accounts must be removed from the group automatically.
- After the planned migration to Microsoft 365, all users must be signed in to on-premises and cloud-based applications automatically.
- The principle of least privilege must be used.

QUESTION 1

You are evaluating the required processes for Project1.

You need to recommend which DNS record must be created before adding a domain name for the project.

Which DNS record should you recommend?

A. alias (CNAME)
B. host information (HINFO)
C. host (A)
D. mail exchanger (MX)

Section: (none)
Explanation

Explanation/Reference:
Explanation:
When you add a custom domain to Office 365, you need to verify that you own the domain. You can do this by adding either an MX record or a TXT record to the DNS for that domain.

Reference:
https://docs.microsoft.com/en-us/office365/admin/get-help-with-domains/create-dns-records-at- any-dns-hosting-provider?view=o365-worldwide

QUESTION 2

You are evaluating the required processes for Project1.

You need to recommend which DNS record must be created before adding a domain name for the project.

Which DNS record should you recommend?

A. alias (CNAME)
B. text (TXT)
C. host (AAAA)
D. pointer (PTR)

Section: (none)
Explanation

Explanation/Reference:

Explanation:

When you add a custom domain to Office 365, you need to verify that you own the domain. You can do this by adding either an MX record or a TXT record to the DNS for that domain.

Reference:

https://docs.microsoft.com/en-us/office365/admin/get-help-with-domains/create-dns-records-at- any-dns-hosting-provider?view=o365-worldwide

Manage User Identity and Roles

Question Set 1

QUESTION 1
You have a Microsoft 365 subscription that contains a Microsoft Azure Active Directory (Azure AD) tenant named contoso.com. The tenant includes a user named User1.

You enable Azure AD Identity Protection.

You need to ensure that User1 can review the list in Azure AD Identity Protection of users flagged for risk. The solution must use the principle of least privilege.

To which role should you add User1?

A. Security reader
B. User administrator
C. Owner
D. Global administrator

Section: (none)
Explanation

Explanation/Reference:
Explanation:
The risky sign-ins reports are available to users in the following roles:
- Security Administrator
- Global Administrator
- Security Reader

Of the three roles listed above, the Security Reader role has the least privilege.

Reference:
https://docs.microsoft.com/en-us/azure/active-directory/reports-monitoring/concept-risky-sign-ins

QUESTION 2
Your network contains three Active Directory forests.

You create a Microsoft Azure Active Directory (Azure AD) tenant.

You plan to sync the on-premises Active Directory to Azure AD.

You need to recommend a synchronization solution. The solution must ensure that the synchronization can complete successfully and as quickly as possible if a single server fails.

What should you include in the recommendation?

A. three Azure AD Connect sync servers and three Azure AD Connect sync servers in staging mode

B. one Azure AD Connect sync server and one Azure AD Connect sync server in staging mode
C. three Azure AD Connect sync servers and one Azure AD Connect sync server in staging mode
D. six Azure AD Connect sync servers and three Azure AD Connect sync servers in staging mode

Section: (none)
Explanation

Explanation/Reference:
Explanation:
Azure AD Connect can be active on only one server. You can install Azure AD Connect on another server for redundancy but the additional installation would need to be in Staging mode. An Azure AD connect installation in Staging mode is configured and ready to go but it needs to be manually switched to Active to perform directory synchronization.

Reference:
https://docs.microsoft.com/en-us/azure/active-directory/hybrid/how-to-connect-install-custom

QUESTION 3
Your company has 10,000 users who access all applications from an on-premises data center.

You plan to create a Microsoft 365 subscription and to migrate data to the cloud.

You plan to implement directory synchronization.

User accounts and group accounts must sync to Microsoft Azure Active Directory (Azure AD) successfully.

You discover that several user accounts fail to sync to Azure AD.

You need to resolve the issue as quickly as possible.

What should you do?

A. From Active Directory Administrative Center, search for all the users, and then modify the properties of the user accounts.
B. Run `idfix.exe`, and then click **Complete**.
C. From Windows PowerShell, run the `Start-AdSyncCycle -PolicyType Delta` command.
D. Run `idfix.exe`, and then click **Edit**.

Section: (none)
Explanation

Explanation/Reference:
Explanation:
IdFix is used to perform discovery and remediation of identity objects and their attributes in an on-premises Active Directory environment in preparation for migration to Azure Active Directory.

IdFix is intended for the Active Directory administrators responsible for directory synchronization with Azure Active Directory.

Reference:
https://docs.microsoft.com/en-us/office365/enterprise/prepare-directory-attributes-for-synch- with-idfix

https://www.microsoft.com/en-gb/download/details.aspx?id=36832

QUESTION 4

Your network contains an Active Directory forest. The forest contains two domains named contoso.com and adatum.com.

Your company recently purchased a Microsoft 365 subscription.

You deploy a federated identity solution to the environment.

You use the following command to configure contoso.com for federation.

```
Convert-MsolDomaintoFederated -DomainName contoso.com
```

In the Microsoft 365 tenant, an administrator adds and verifies the adatum.com domain name.

You need to configure the adatum.com Active Directory domain for federated authentication.

Which two actions should you perform before you run the Azure AD Connect wizard? Each correct answer presents part of the solution.

NOTE: Each correct selection is worth one point.

A. From Windows PowerShell, run the `Convert-MsolDomaintoFederated -DomainName contoso.com -SupportMultipleDomain` command.
B. From Windows PowerShell, run the `New-MsolFederatedDomain -SupportMultipleDomain -DomainName contoso.com` command.
C. From Windows PowerShell, run the `New-MsolFederatedDomain -DomainName adatum.com` command.
D. From Windows PowerShell, run the `Update-MSOLFederatedDomain -DomainName contoso.com -SupportMultipleDomain` command.
E. From the federation server, remove the Microsoft Office 365 relying party trust.

Section: (none)
Explanation

Explanation/Reference:
Explanation:
When the `Convert-MsolDomaintoFederated -DomainName contoso.com` command was run, a relying party trust was created.
Adding a second domain (adatum.com in this case) will only work if the `SupportMultipleDomain` switch was used when the initial federation was configured by running the `Convert-MsolDomaintoFederated -DomainName contoso.com` command.

Therefore, we need to start again by removing the relying party trust then running the `Convert-MsolDomaintoFederated` command again with the `SupportMultipleDomain` switch.

QUESTION 5

Your network contains a single Active Directory domain and two Microsoft Azure Active Directory (Azure AD) tenants.

You plan to implement directory synchronization for both Azure AD tenants. Each tenant will contain some of the Active Directory users.

You need to recommend a solution for the planned directory synchronization.

What should you include in the recommendation?

- A. Deploy two servers that run Azure AD Connect, and then filter the users for each tenant by using organizational unit (OU)-based filtering.
- B. Deploy two servers that run Azure AD Connect, and then filter the users for each tenant by using domain-based filtering
- C. Deploy one server that runs Azure AD Connect, and then filter the users for each tenant by using organizational unit (OU)-based filtering.
- D. Deploy one server that runs Azure AD Connect, and then filter the users for each tenant by using domain-based filtering.

Section: (none)
Explanation

Explanation/Reference:
Explanation:
There's a 1:1 relationship between an Azure AD Connect sync server and an Azure AD tenant. For each Azure AD tenant, you need one Azure AD Connect sync server installation. Therefore, we need to deploy two servers that run Azure AD Connect for the two Azure AD tenants.

Each user account can only be synchronized to one Azure AD tenant. Therefore, we need a way of splitting the users between the two Azure AD tenants. Azure AD Connect offers three ways to filter which users get synchronized to an Azure AD tenant. You can use domain-based filtering if you have multiple domains in a forest, attribute-based filtering or OU-based filtering.

Reference:
https://docs.microsoft.com/en-us/azure/active-directory/hybrid/plan-connect-topologies#multiple-azure-ad-tenants

https://docs.microsoft.com/en-us/azure/active-directory/hybrid/how-to-connect-sync-configure-filtering

QUESTION 6

Your company has a Microsoft Azure Active Directory (Azure AD) tenant named contoso.onmicrosoft.com that contains a user named User1.

You suspect that an imposter is signing in to Azure AD by using the credentials of User1.

You need to ensure that an administrator named Admin1 can view all the sign in details of User1 from the past 24 hours.

To which three roles should you add Admin1? Each correct answer presents a complete solution.

NOTE: Each correct selection is worth one point.

A. Security administrator
B. Password administrator
C. User administrator
D. Compliance administrator
E. Reports reader
F. Security reader

Section: (none)
Explanation

Explanation/Reference:
Explanation:
Users in the Security Administrator, Security Reader, Global Reader, and Report Reader roles can view the sign in details.

Reference:
https://docs.microsoft.com/en-us/azure/active-directory/reports-monitoring/concept-sign-ins

QUESTION 7
You have a Microsoft 365 subscription.

You plan to enable Microsoft Azure Information Protection.

You need to ensure that only the members of a group named PilotUsers can protect content.

What should you do?

A. Run the `Add-AadrmRoleBaseAdministrator` cmdlet.
B. Create an Azure Information Protection policy.
C. Configure the protection activation status for Azure Information Protection.
D. Run the `Set-AadrmOnboardingControlPolicy` cmdlet.

Section: (none)
Explanation

Explanation/Reference:
Explanation:
If you don't want all users to be able to protect documents and emails immediately by using

Azure Rights Management, you can configure user onboarding controls by using the
Set-AadrmOnboardingControlPolicy

Reference:
https://docs.microsoft.com/en-us/azure/information-protection/activate-service

QUESTION 8
Your company has a Microsoft 365 subscription.

You need to identify which users performed the following privileged administration tasks:

- Deleted a folder from the second-stage Recycle Bin if Microsoft SharePoint
- Opened a mailbox of which the user was not the owner
- Reset a user password

What should you use?

A. Microsoft Azure Active Directory (Azure AD) audit logs
B. Microsoft Azure Active Directory (Azure AD) sign-ins
C. Security & Compliance content search
D. Security & Compliance audit log search

Section: (none)
Explanation

Explanation/Reference:
Explanation:
You can view the required information in the audit logs. The Azure AD audit logs provide records
of system activities for compliance. To access the audit report, select Audit logs in the Activity
section of Azure Active Directory.

Reference:
https://docs.microsoft.com/en-us/azure/active-directory/reports-monitoring/concept-audit-logs

QUESTION 9
You have a Microsoft 365 subscription. You have a user named User1.

You need to ensure that User1 can place a hold on all mailbox content.

What permission should you assign to User1?

A. the User management administrator role from the Microsoft 365 admin center
B. the eDiscovery Manager role from the Security & Compliance admin center
C. the Information Protection administrator role from the Azure Active Directory admin center
D. the Compliance Management role from the Exchange admin center

Section: (none)
Explanation

Explanation:
To create a query-based In-Place Hold, a user requires both the Mailbox Search and Legal Hold roles to be assigned directly or via membership in a role group that has both roles assigned. To create an In-Place Hold without using a query, which places all mailbox items on hold, you must have the Legal Hold role assigned. The Discovery Management role group is assigned both roles.

Reference:
https://docs.microsoft.com/en-us/Exchange/permissions/feature-permissions/policy-and-compliance-permissions?view=exchserver-2019

QUESTION 10

Your company has a Microsoft Azure Active Directory (Azure AD) tenant named contoso.com.

You sign up for Microsoft Store for Business.

The tenant contains the users shown in the following table.

Name	Microsoft Store for Business role	Azure AD role
User1	Purchaser	None
User2	Basic Purchaser	None
User3	None	Application administrator
User4	None	Cloud application administrator
User5	None	None

Microsoft Store for Business has the following Shopping behavior settings:

- Allow users to shop is set to **On**.
- Make everyone a Basic Purchaser is set to **Off**.

You need to identify which users can install apps from the Microsoft for Business private store.

Which users should you identify?

A. A. user1, User2, User3, User4, and User5
B. User1 only
C. User1 and User2 only
D. User3 and User4 only
E. User1, User2, User3, and User4 only

Section: (none)
Explanation

Explanation:

Allow users to shop controls the shopping experience in Microsoft Store for Education. When this setting is on, Purchasers and Basic Purchasers can purchase products and services from Microsoft Store for Education.

Reference:
https://docs.microsoft.com/en-us/microsoft-store/acquire-apps-microsoft-store-for-business

QUESTION 11
You have a Microsoft 365 subscription that contains a Microsoft Azure Active Directory (Azure AD) tenant named contoso.com.

In the tenant, you create a user named User1.

You need to ensure that User1 can publish retention labels from the Security & Compliance admin center. The solution must use the principle of least privilege.

To which role group should you add User1?

A. Security Administrator
B. Records Management
C. Compliance Administrator
D. eDiscovery Manager

Section: (none)
Explanation

Explanation/Reference:
Explanation:
Members of your compliance team who will create retention labels need permissions to the Security & Compliance Center. By default, your tenant admin has access to this location and can give compliance officers and other people access to the Security & Compliance Center, without giving them all of the permissions of a tenant admin. To do this, we recommend that you go to the Permissions page of the Security & Compliance Center, edit the Compliance Administrator role group, and add members to that role group.

Reference:
https://docs.microsoft.com/en-us/microsoft-365/compliance/labels#permissions

QUESTION 12
Your company has a Microsoft 365 E5 subscription.

Users in the research department work with sensitive data.

You need to prevent the research department users from accessing potentially unsafe websites by using hyperlinks embedded in email messages and documents. Users in other departments must not be restricted.

What should you do from the Security & Compliance admin center?

A. Create a data loss prevention (DLP) policy that has a Content contains condition.

B. Create a data loss prevention (DLP) policy that has a Content is shared condition.
C. Modify the default safe links policy.
D. Create a new safe links policy.

Section: (none)
Explanation

Explanation/Reference:
Explanation:
ATP Safe Links, a feature of Office 365 Advanced Threat Protection (ATP), can help protect your organization from malicious links used in phishing and other attacks. If you have the necessary permissions for the Office 365 Security & Compliance Center, you can set up ATP Safe Links policies to help ensure that when people click web addresses (URLs), your organization is protected. Your ATP Safe Links policies can be configured to scan URLs in email and URLs in Office documents.

Reference:
https://docs.microsoft.com/en-us/office365/securitycompliance/set-up-atp-safe-links-policies#policies-that-apply-to-specific-email-recipients

QUESTION 13
A user receives the following message when attempting to sign in to https://myapps.microsoft.com:

```
"Your sign-in was blocked. We've detected something unusual about this
sign-in. For example, you might be signing in from a new location,
device, or app. Before you can continue, we need to verify your
identity. Please contact your admin."
```

Which configuration prevents the users from signing in?

A. Security & Compliance supervision policies
B. Security & Compliance data loss prevention (DLP) policies
C. Microsoft Azure Active Directory (Azure AD) conditional access policies
D. Microsoft Azure Active Directory (Azure AD) Identity Protection policies

Section: (none)
Explanation

Explanation/Reference:
Explanation:
The user is being blocked due to a 'risky sign-in'. This can be caused by the user logging in from a device that hasn't been used to sign in before or from an unknown location.
Integration with Azure AD Identity Protection allows Conditional Access policies to identify risky sign-in behavior. Policies can then force users to perform password changes or multi-factor authentication to reduce their risk level or be blocked from access until an administrator takes manual action.

Reference:
https://docs.microsoft.com/en-us/azure/active-directory/conditional-access/overview

QUESTION 14
Note: This question is part of a series of questions that present the same scenario. Each question in the series contains a unique solution that might meet the stated goals. Some question sets might have more than one correct solution, while others might not have a correct solution.

After you answer a question in this section, you will NOT be able to return to it. As a result, these questions will not appear in the review screen.

Your network contains an Active Directory domain.

You deploy a Microsoft Azure Active Directory (Azure AD) tenant. Another

administrator configures the domain to synchronize to Azure AD.

You discover that 10 user accounts in an organizational unit (OU) are NOT synchronized to Azure AD. All the other user accounts synchronized successfully.

You review Azure AD Connect Health and discover that all the user account synchronizations completed successfully.

You need to ensure that the 10 user accounts are synchronized to Azure AD.

Solution: From the Synchronization Rules Editor, you create a new outbound synchronization rule.

Does this meet the goal?

A. Yes
B. No

Section: (none)
Explanation

Explanation/Reference:
Explanation:
The question states that "all the user account synchronizations completed successfully". Therefore, the synchronization rule is configured correctly. It is likely that the 10 user accounts are being excluded from the synchronization cycle by a filtering rule.

Reference:
https://docs.microsoft.com/en-us/azure/active-directory/hybrid/how-to-connect-sync-configure-filtering

QUESTION 15
Note: This question is part of a series of questions that present the same scenario. Each question in the series contains a unique solution that might meet the stated goals. Some question sets might have more than one correct solution, while others might not have a correct solution.

After you answer a question in this section, you will NOT be able to return to it. As a result, these questions will not appear in the review screen.

Your network contains an Active Directory domain.

You deploy a Microsoft Azure Active Directory (Azure AD) tenant. Another

administrator configures the domain to synchronize to Azure AD.

You discover that 10 user accounts in an organizational unit (OU) are NOT synchronized to Azure AD. All the other user accounts synchronized successfully.

You review Azure AD Connect Health and discover that all the user account synchronizations completed successfully.

You need to ensure that the 10 user accounts are synchronized to Azure AD.

Solution: You run `idfix.exe` and export the 10 user accounts.

Does this meet the goal?

A. Yes
B. No

Section: (none)
Explanation

Explanation/Reference:
Explanation:
The question states that "all the user account synchronizations completed successfully". If there were problems with the 10 accounts that needed fixing with idfix.exe, there would have been synchronization errors in Azure AD Connect Health.
It is likely that the 10 user accounts are being excluded from the synchronization cycle by a filtering rule.

Reference:
https://docs.microsoft.com/en-us/azure/active-directory/hybrid/how-to-connect-sync-configure-filtering

QUESTION 16
Note: This question is part of a series of questions that present the same scenario. Each question in the series contains a unique solution that might meet the stated goals. Some question sets might have more than one correct solution, while others might not have a correct solution.

After you answer a question in this section, you will NOT be able to return to it. As a result, these questions will not appear in the review screen.

Your network contains an Active Directory domain.

You deploy a Microsoft Azure Active Directory (Azure AD) tenant.

Another administrator configures the domain to synchronize to Azure AD.

You discover that 10 user accounts in an organizational unit (OU) are NOT synchronized to Azure AD. All the other user accounts synchronized successfully.

You review Azure AD Connect Health and discover that all the user account synchronizations completed successfully.

You need to ensure that the 10 user accounts are synchronized to Azure AD.

Solution: From Azure AD Connect, you modify the Azure AD credentials.

Does this meet the goal?

A. Yes
B. No

Section: (none)
Explanation

Explanation/Reference:
Explanation:
The question states that "all the user account synchronizations completed successfully". Therefore, the Azure AD credentials are configured correctly in Azure AD Connect. It is likely that the 10 user accounts are being excluded from the synchronization cycle by a filtering rule.

Reference:
https://docs.microsoft.com/en-us/azure/active-directory/hybrid/how-to-connect-sync-configure-filtering

QUESTION 17
You have a Microsoft 365 subscription that uses an Azure Active Directory (Azure AD) tenant named contoso.com. The tenant contains the users shown in the following table.

Name	Role
User1	Exchange administrator
User2	User administrator
User3	Global administrator
User4	None

You add another user named User5 to the User administrator role. You

need to identify which two management tasks User5 can perform.

Which two tasks should you identify? Each correct answer presents a complete solution.

NOTE: Each correct selection is worth one point.

A. Delete User2 and User4 only.
B. Reset the password of User2 and User4 only.
C. Delete User1, User2, and User4 only.
D. Delete any user in Azure AD.
E. Reset the password of any user in Azure AD.
F. Reset the password of User4 only.

Section: (none)
Explanation

Explanation/Reference:
Explanation:
Users with the User Administrator role can create users and manage all aspects of users with some restrictions (see below).

Only on users who are non-admins or in any of the following limited admin roles:
- Directory Readers
- Guest Inviter
- Helpdesk Administrator
- Message Center Reader
- Reports Reader
- User Administrator

Reference:
https://docs.microsoft.com/en-us/azure/active-directory/users-groups-roles/directory-assign-admin-roles#available-roles

QUESTION 18
Note: This question is part of a series of questions that present the same scenario. Each question in the series contains a unique solution that might meet the stated goals. Some question sets might have more than one correct solution, while others might not have a correct solution.

After you answer a question in this section, you will NOT be able to return to it. As a result, these questions will not appear in the review screen.

Your network contains an Active Directory domain.

You deploy a Microsoft Azure Active Directory (Azure AD) tenant. Another

administrator configures the domain to synchronize to Azure AD.

You discover that 10 user accounts in an organizational unit (OU) are NOT synchronized to Azure AD. All the other user accounts synchronized successfully.

You review Azure AD Connect Health and discover that all the user account synchronizations completed successfully.

You need to ensure that the 10 user accounts are synchronized to Azure AD.

Solution: From Azure AD Connect, you modify the filtering settings.

Does this meet the goal?

A. Yes
B. No

Explanation/Reference:
Explanation:
The question states that "all the user account synchronizations completed successfully".
Therefore, we know that Azure AD Connect is working and configured correctly. The only thing
that would prevent the 10 user accounts from being synchronized is that they are being
excluded from the synchronization cycle by a filtering rule.

Reference:
https://docs.microsoft.com/en-us/azure/active-directory/hybrid/how-to-connect-sync-configure-filtering

QUESTION 19
**Note: This question is part of a series of questions that present the same scenario. Each
question in the series contains a unique solution that might meet the stated goals. Some
question sets might have more than one correct solution, while others might not have a
correct solution.**

**After you answer a question in this section, you will NOT be able to return to it. As a
result, these questions will not appear in the review screen.**

Your company has 3,000 users. All the users are assigned Microsoft 365 E3 licenses.

Some users are assigned licenses for all Microsoft 365 services. Other users are assigned
licenses for only certain Microsoft 365 services.

You need to determine whether a user named User1 is licensed for Exchange Online only.

Solution: You run the `Get-MsolUser` cmdlet.

Does this meet the goal?

A. Yes
B. No

Explanation/Reference:
Explanation:

The `Get-MsolUser` cmdlet will tell you if a user is licensed for Microsoft 365 but it does not tell you which licenses are assigned.

Reference:
https://docs.microsoft.com/en-us/powershell/module/msonline/get-msoluser?view=azureadps-1.0

QUESTION 20
Note: This question is part of a series of questions that present the same scenario. Each question in the series contains a unique solution that might meet the stated goals. Some question sets might have more than one correct solution, while others might not have a correct solution.

After you answer a question in this section, you will NOT be able to return to it. As a result, these questions will not appear in the review screen.

Your company has 3,000 users. All the users are assigned Microsoft 365 E3 licenses.

Some users are assigned licenses for all Microsoft 365 services. Other users are assigned licenses for only certain Microsoft 365 services.

You need to determine whether a user named User1 is licensed for Exchange Online only.

Solution: You run the `Get-MsolAccountSku` cmdlet.

Does this meet the goal?

A. Yes
B. No

Section: (none)
Explanation

Explanation/Reference:
Explanation:
The Get-MsolAccountSku cmdlet returns all the SKUs that the company owns. It does not tell you which licenses are assigned to users.

Reference:
https://docs.microsoft.com/en-us/powershell/module/msonline/get-msolaccountsku?view=azureadps-1.0

QUESTION 21
Note: This question is part of a series of questions that present the same scenario. Each question in the series contains a unique solution that might meet the stated goals. Some question sets might have more than one correct solution, while others might not have a correct solution.

After you answer a question in this section, you will NOT be able to return to it. As a result, these questions will not appear in the review screen.

Your company has 3,000 users. All the users are assigned Microsoft 365 E3 licenses.

Some users are assigned licenses for all Microsoft 365 services. Other users are assigned licenses for only certain Microsoft 365 services.

You need to determine whether a user named User1 is licensed for Exchange Online only.

Solution: You launch the Azure portal, and then review the Licenses blade.

Does this meet the goal?

A. Yes
B. No

Section: (none)
Explanation

Explanation/Reference:
Explanation:
In the Licenses blade, click All Products then select the E3 License. This will display a list of all users assigned an E3 license. Select User1. You'll see how many services are assigned in the Enabled Services column. Click on the number in the Enabled Services column for User1 and you'll be taken to the licenses page for that user. Click on the number in the Enabled Services column for User1 again and a page will open which shows you exactly which services are enabled or disabled.
Alternatively, you can go into the user account properties directly then select Licenses. This will display the licenses blade for that user. You can then click on the number in the Enabled Services column for the user and a page will open which shows you exactly which services are enabled or disabled.

QUESTION 22
You have a Microsoft 365 subscription.

You view the service advisories shown in the following exhibit.

Some services have posted advisories

2018-10-05 08:43(UTC)   View history

All services	(i) Office 365 Portal	1 advisory
Incidents	(i) SharePoint Online	1 advisory
	(✓) Office Subscription	Service is healthy
Advisories	(✓) Microsoft Intune	Service is healthy
	(✓) Microsoft StaffHub	Service is healthy
	(✓) Microsoft Teams	Service is healthy
	(✓) Mobile Device Management for Office 365	Service is healthy
	(✓) Azure Information Protection	Service is healthy
	(✓) Exchange Online	Service is healthy

You need to ensure that users who administer Microsoft SharePoint Online can view the advisories to investigate health issues.

Which role should you assign to the users?

A. SharePoint administrator
B. Message Center reader
C. Reports reader
D. Service administrator

Section: (none)
Explanation

Explanation/Reference:
Explanation:
People who are assigned the global admin or service administrator role can view service health. To allow Exchange, SharePoint, and Skype for Business admins to view service health, they must also be assigned the Service admin role. For more information about roles that can view service health.

Reference:
https://docs.microsoft.com/en-us/office365/enterprise/view-service-health

QUESTION 23
You have a Microsoft 365 subscription that contains a Microsoft Azure Active Directory (Azure AD) tenant named contoso.com. The tenant includes a user named User1.

You enable Azure AD Identity Protection.

You need to ensure that User1 can review the list in Azure AD Identity Protection of users flagged for risk. The solution must use the principle of least privilege.

To which role should you add User1?

A. Reports reader
B. Security administrator
C. Owner
D. Compliance administrator

Section: (none)
Explanation

Explanation/Reference:
Explanation:
Either one of the following three roles can review the list in Azure AD Identity Protection of users flagged for risk:

- Security Administrator
- Global Administrator
- Security Reader

Reference:
https://docs.microsoft.com/en-us/azure/active-directory/reports-monitoring/concept-risky-sign-ins

QUESTION 24
You have a Microsoft 365 subscription that contains a Microsoft Azure Active Directory (Azure AD) tenant named contoso.com. The tenant includes a user named User1.

You enable Azure AD Identity Protection.

You need to ensure that User1 can review the list in Azure AD Identity Protection of users flagged for risk. The solution must use the principle of least privilege.

To which role should you add User1?

A. Security reader
B. User administrator
C. Owner
D. Service administrator

Section: (none)
Explanation

Explanation/Reference:
Explanation:
Either one of the following three roles can review the list in Azure AD Identity Protection of users flagged for risk:

- Security Administrator
- Global Administrator
- Security Reader

Reference:
https://docs.microsoft.com/en-us/azure/active-directory/reports-monitoring/concept-risky-sign-ins

QUESTION 25
You have a Microsoft 365 subscription that contains a Microsoft Azure Active Directory (Azure AD) tenant named contoso.com. The tenant includes a user named User1.

You enable Azure AD Identity Protection.

You need to ensure that User1 can review the list in Azure AD Identity Protection of users flagged for risk. The solution must use the principle of least privilege.

To which role should you add User1?

A. Reports reader
B. Security reader
C. Owner
D. Compliance administrator

Section: (none)
Explanation

Explanation/Reference:
Explanation:
Either one of the following three roles can review the list in Azure AD Identity Protection of users flagged for risk:

- Security Administrator
- Global Administrator
- Security Reader

Reference:
https://docs.microsoft.com/en-us/azure/active-directory/reports-monitoring/concept-risky-sign-ins

QUESTION 26
Your network contains an Active Directory domain named adatum.com that is synced to Microsoft Azure Active Directory (Azure AD).

The domain contains 100 user accounts.

The city attribute for all the users is set to the city where the user resides.

You need to modify the value of the city attribute to the three-letter airport code of each city.

What should you do?

A. From Azure Cloud Shell, run the `Get-AzureADUser` and `Set-AzureADUser` cmdlets.
B. From Azure Cloud Shell, run the `Get-ADUser` and `Set-ADUser` cmdlets.
C. From Windows PowerShell on a domain controller, run the `Get-ADUser` and `Set-ADUser` cmdlets.
D. From Azure Cloud Shell, run the `Get-MsolDUser` and `Set-MSOluser` cmdlets.

Section: (none)
Explanation

Explanation/Reference:
Explanation:
The user accounts are synced from the on-premise Active Directory to the Microsoft Azure Active Directory (Azure AD). Therefore, the city attribute must be changed in the on-premise Active Directory.

You can use Windows PowerShell on a domain controller and run the `Get-ADUser` cmdlet to get the required users and pipe the results into `Set-ADUser` cmdlet to modify the city attribute.

Incorrect Answers:
A, D: These answers suggest modifying the city attribute of the users in the Azure Active Directory which is incorrect.
B: This answer has the correct cmdlets but they need to be run on a domain controller, not in the Azure cloud shell.

Reference:
https://docs.microsoft.com/en-us/powershell/module/addsadministration/set-aduser?view=win10-ps

QUESTION 27
Your network contains a single Active Directory domain and two Microsoft Azure Active Directory (Azure AD) tenants.

You plan to implement directory synchronization for both Azure AD tenants. Each tenant will contain some of the Active Directory users.

You need to recommend a solution for the planned directory synchronization.

What should you include in the recommendation?

A. Deploy two servers that run Azure AD Connect, and then filter the users for each tenant by using organizational unit (OU)-based filtering.
B. Deploy one server that runs Azure AD Connect, and then filter the users for each tenant by using attribute-based filtering.
C. Deploy one server that runs Azure AD Connect, and then filter the users for each tenant by using organizational unit (OU)-based filtering.
D. Deploy one server that runs Azure AD Connect, and then filter the users for each tenant by using domain-based filtering.

Section: (none)
Explanation

Explanation/Reference:
Explanation:
There's a 1:1 relationship between an Azure AD Connect sync server and an Azure AD tenant. For each Azure AD tenant, you need one Azure AD Connect sync server installation. Therefore, we need to deploy two servers that run Azure AD Connect for the two Azure AD tenants.

Each user account can only be synchronized to one Azure AD tenant. Therefore, we need a way of splitting the users between the two Azure AD tenants. Azure AD Connect offers three ways to filter which users get synchronized to an Azure AD tenant. You can use domain-based filtering if you have multiple domains in a forest, attribute-based filtering or OU-based filtering.

Reference:
https://docs.microsoft.com/en-us/azure/active-directory/hybrid/plan-connect-topologies#multiple-azure-ad-tenants

https://docs.microsoft.com/en-us/azure/active-directory/hybrid/how-to-connect-sync-configure-filtering

QUESTION 28
You network contains an on-premises Active Directory domain named contoso.com. The domain contains a Microsoft Exchange Server 2019 organization.

You plan to sync the domain to Azure Active Directory (Azure AD) and to enable device writeback and group writeback.

You need to identify which group types will sync from Azure AD.

Which two group types should you identify? Each correct answer presents part of the solution.

NOTE: Each correct selection is worth one point.

A. an Office 365 group that uses the Assigned membership type
B. a security group that uses the Dynamic Device membership type
C. an Office 365 group that uses the Dynamic User membership type
D. a security group that uses the Assigned membership type
E. a security group that uses the Dynamic User membership type

Section: (none)
Explanation

Explanation/Reference:
Explanation:
Group writeback in Azure AD Connect synchronizes Office 365 groups only from Azure Active Directory back to the on-premise Active Directory.

Reference:
https://docs.microsoft.com/en-us/azure/active-directory/hybrid/how-to-connect-preview

QUESTION 29
You have a Microsoft 365 subscription.

You view the service advisories shown in the following exhibit.

Home > Service health

Some services have posted advisories   2018-10-05 06:4(UTC) View history

All services	ⓘ Office 365 Portal	1 advisory
Incidents	ⓘ SharePoint Online	1 advisory
	✓ Office Subscription	Service is healthy
Advisories	✓ Microsoft Intune	Service is healthy
	✓ Microsoft StaffHub	Service is healthy
	✓ Microsoft Teams	Service is healthy
	✓ Mobile Device Management for Office 365	Service is healthy
	✓ Azure Information Protection	Service is healthy
	✓ Exchange Online	Service is healthy

You need to ensure that a user named User1 can view the advisories to investigate service health issues.

Which role should you assign to User1?

A. Compliance administrator
B. Message Center reader
C. Reports reader
D. Service administrator

Section: (none)
Explanation

Explanation/Reference:
Explanation:
People who are assigned the global admin or service administrator role can view service health.
To allow Exchange, SharePoint, and Skype for Business admins to view service health, they must also be assigned the Service admin role.

Reference:
https://docs.microsoft.com/en-us/office365/enterprise/view-service-health

QUESTION 30
Your network contains an on-premises Active Directory domain that syncs to Azure Active Directory (Azure AD).

The on-premises network contains a Microsoft SharePoint Server 2019 farm.

The company purchases a Microsoft 365 subscription.

You have the users shown in the following table

Name	Source
User1	Windows Active Directory
User2	Azure Active Directory

You plan to assign User1 and User2 the required roles to run the SharePoint Hybrid Configuration Wizard.

User1 will be used for on-premises credentials and User2 will be used for cloud credentials.

You need to assign the correct role to User2. The solution must use the principle of least privilege.

Which role should you assign to User2?

A. Application administrator
B. SharePoint farm administrator
C. Global administrator
D. SharePoint administrator

Section: (none)
Explanation

Explanation/Reference:
Explanation:
To run the SharePoint Hybrid Configuration Wizard, you need to provide credentials of a user (in this case User2) of a Global Administrator account in Azure Active Directory.

Reference:
https://www.c-sharpcorner.com/article/sharepoint-2019-enable-hybrid-experience/

QUESTION 31
Your network contains an Active Directory forest named contoso.local.

You have a Microsoft 365 subscription.

You plan to implement a directory synchronization solution that will use password hash synchronization.

From the Microsoft 365 admin center, you verify the contoso.com domain name.

You need to prepare the environment for the planned directory synchronization solution.

What should you do first?

A. From the public DNS zone of contoso.com, add a new mail exchanger (MX) record.
B. From Active Directory Domains and Trusts, add contoso.com as a UPN suffix.
C. From the Microsoft 365 admin center, verify the contoso.local domain name.
D. From Active Directory Users and Computers, modify the UPN suffix for all users.

Section: (none)
Explanation

Explanation/Reference:
Explanation:
The on-premise Active Directory domain is named contoso.local. Therefore, all the domain users accounts will have a UPN suffix of contoso.local by default.
To enable directory synchronization that will use password hash synchronization, you need to configure the domain user accounts to have the same UPN suffix as the verified domain (contoso.com in this case). Before you can change the UPN suffix of the domain user accounts to contoso.com, you need to add contoso.com as a UPN suffix in the domain.

Reference:
https://docs.microsoft.com/en-us/azure/active-directory/hybrid/plan-connect-userprincipalname

QUESTION 32
Your company has a Microsoft 365 subscription.

Your plan to add 100 newly hired temporary users to the subscription next week.

You create the user accounts for the new users.

You need to assign licenses to the new users. Which

command should you run?

A.
```
$NewStaff = Get-AzureADUser -All -Department "Temp" -UsageLc
$NewStaff | foreach {Set-AzureADUser -LicenseOptions "contos
```

B.
```
$NewStaff = Get-AzureADUser -All -Department "Temp" -UsageLocat
$NewStaff | foreach {Set-AzureADUserLicense -AddLicenses "contc
```

C.
```
$NewStaff = Get-AzureADUser -All -Department "Temp" -UsageLocatic
$NewStaff | foreach {Set-AzureADUserLicense -LicenseOptions "cont
```

D. ```
    $NewStaff = Get-AzureADUser -All -Department "Temp" -UsageLocati
    $NewStaff | foreach {Set-AzureADUser -AddLicenses "contoso:ENTER
    ```

**Section: (none)**
**Explanation**

**Explanation/Reference:**
Explanation:
The first line gets all users from the Temp department that have a UsageLocation assigned and stores them in the $NewStaff variable. You cannot use PowerShell to assign a license to a user that does not have a UsageLocation configured.
The second line adds the licenses to each user in the $NewStaff variable.

Reference:
https://docs.microsoft.com/en-us/office365/enterprise/powershell/assign-licenses-to-user-accounts-with-office-365-powershell

**QUESTION 33**
Your network contains an Active Directory domain and a Microsoft Azure Active Directory (Azure AD) tenant.

The network uses a firewall that contains a list of allowed outbound domains.

You begin to implement directory synchronization.

You discover that the firewall configuration contains only the following domain names in the list of allowed domains:

- *.microsoft.com
- *.office.com

Directory synchronization fails.

You need to ensure that directory synchronization completes successfully.

What is the best approach to achieve the goal? More than one answer choice may achieve the goal. Select the **BEST** answer.

A. From the firewall, allow the IP address range of the Azure data center for outbound communication.
B. From Azure AD Connect, modify the Customize synchronization options task.
C. Deploy an Azure AD Connect sync server in staging mode.
D. From the firewall, create a list of allowed inbound domains.
E. From the firewall, modify the list of allowed outbound domains.

**Section: (none)**
**Explanation**
    ```

Explanation/Reference:
Explanation:
Azure AD Connect needs to be able to connect to various Microsoft domains such as login.microsoftonline.com. Therefore, you need to modify the list of allowed outbound domains on the firewall.

Reference:
https://docs.microsoft.com/en-us/azure/active-directory/hybrid/reference-connect-ports

QUESTION 34
Your network contains an on-premises Active Directory forest.

You are evaluating the implementation of Microsoft 365 and the deployment of an authentication strategy.

You need to recommend an authentication strategy that meets the following requirements:

- Allows users to sign in by using smart card-based certificates
- Allows users to connect to on-premises and Microsoft 365 services by using SSO

Which authentication strategy should you recommend?

A. password hash synchronization and seamless SSO
B. federation with Active Directory Federation Services (AD FS)
C. pass-through authentication and seamless SSO

Section: (none)
Explanation

Explanation/Reference:
Explanation:
Federation with Active Directory Federation Services (AD FS) is required to allow users to sign in by using smart card-based certificates.

Federated authentication
When you choose this authentication method, Azure AD hands off the authentication process to a separate trusted authentication system, such as on-premises Active Directory Federation Services (AD FS), to validate the user's password.
The authentication system can provide additional advanced authentication requirements. Examples are smartcard-based authentication or third-party multifactor authentication.

Reference:
https://docs.microsoft.com/en-us/azure/security/azure-ad-choose-authn

QUESTION 35
Your network contains two on-premises Active Directory forests named contoso.com and fabrikam.com. Fabrikam.com contains one domain and five domain controllers. Contoso.com contains the domains shown in the following table.

Name	Number of domain controllers
Contoso.com	2
East.contoso.com	3
West.contoso.com	3

You need to sync all the users from both the forests to a single Azure Active Directory (Azure AD) tenant by using Azure AD Connect.

What is the minimum number of Azure AD Connect sync servers required?

A. 1
B. 2
C. 3
D. 4

Section: (none)
Explanation

Explanation/Reference:
You can have only one active Azure AD Connect server synchronizing accounts to a single Azure Active Directory (Azure AD) tenant. You can have 'backup' Azure AD Connect servers, but these must be running in 'staging' mode. Staging mode means the Azure AD Connect instance is not actively synchronizing users but is ready to be bought online if the active Azure AD Connect instance goes offline.

When you have multiple forests, all forests must be reachable by a single Azure AD Connect sync server. The server must be joined to a domain. If necessary, to reach all forests, you can place the server in a perimeter network (also known as DMZ, demilitarized zone, and screened subnet).

References:
https://docs.microsoft.com/en-us/azure/active-directory/hybrid/plan-connect-topologies#multiple-forests-single-azure-ad-tenant

QUESTION 36
Your network contains an Active Directory domain named adatum.com that is synced to Microsoft Azure Active Directory (Azure AD).

The domain contains 100 user accounts.

The city attribute for all the users is set to the city where the user resides.

You need to modify the value of the city attribute to the three-letter airport code of each city.

What should you do?

A. From Active Directory Administrative Center, select the Active Directory users, and then modify the Properties settings.

B. From the Microsoft 365 admin center, select the users, and then use the Bulk actions option.
C. From Azure Cloud Shell, run the `Get-MsolUser` and `Set-MSOluser` cmdlets.
D. From Windows PowerShell on a domain controller, run the `Get-AzureADUser` and `Set-AzureADUser` cmdlets.

Section: (none)
Explanation

Explanation/Reference:
Explanation:
The user accounts are synced from the on-premise Active Directory to the Microsoft Azure Active Directory (Azure AD). Therefore, the city attribute must be changed in the on-premise Active Directory.
You can modify certain attributes of multiple user accounts simultaneously by selecting them in Active Directory Administrative Center or Active Directory Users and Computers, right clicking then selecting Properties.
The other three options all suggest modifying the city attribute of the users in the Azure Active Directory which is incorrect.

Reference:
https://blogs.technet.microsoft.com/canitpro/2015/11/25/step-by-step-managing-multiple-user-accounts-via-active-directory-admin-center/

QUESTION 37
Your network contains an Active Directory domain named adatum.com that is synced to Microsoft Azure Active Directory (Azure AD).

The domain contains 100 user accounts.

The city attribute for all the users is set to the city where the user resides.

You need to modify the value of the city attribute to the three-letter airport code of each city.

What should you do?

A. From Active Directory Administrative Center, select the Active Directory users, and then modify the Properties settings.
B. From Azure Cloud Shell, run the `Get-AzureADUser` and `Set-AzureADUser` cmdlets.
C. From Azure Cloud Shell, run the `Get-ADUser` and `Set-ADUser` cmdlets.
D. From Windows PowerShell on a domain controller, run the `Get-AzureADUser` and `Set-AzureADUser` cmdlets.

Section: (none)
Explanation

Explanation/Reference:
Explanation:
The user accounts are synced from the on-premise Active Directory to the Microsoft Azure

Active Directory (Azure AD). Therefore, the city attribute must be changed in the on-premise Active Directory.
You can modify certain attributes of multiple user accounts simultaneously by selecting them in Active Directory Administrative Center or Active Directory Users and Computers, right clicking then selecting Properties.
The other three options all suggest modifying the city attribute of the users in the Azure Active Directory which is incorrect.

Reference:
https://blogs.technet.microsoft.com/canitpro/2015/11/25/step-by-step-managing-multiple-user-accounts-via-active-directory-admin-center/

QUESTION 38
You have a Microsoft 365 subscription that contains a Microsoft Azure Active Directory (Azure AD) tenant named contoso.com. The tenant includes a user named User1.

You enable Azure AD Identity Protection.

You need to ensure that User1 can review the list in Azure AD Identity Protection of users flagged for risk. The solution must use the principle of least privilege.

To which role should you add User1?

A. Security reader
B. User administrator
C. Service administrator
D. Reports reader

Section: (none)
Explanation

Explanation/Reference:
Explanation:
Either one of the following three roles can review the list in Azure AD Identity Protection of users flagged for risk:

- Security Administrator
- Global Administrator
- Security Reader

Reference:
https://docs.microsoft.com/en-us/azure/active-directory/reports-monitoring/concept-risky-sign-ins

QUESTION 39
You have a Microsoft 365 subscription that contains a Microsoft Azure Active Directory (Azure AD) tenant named contoso.com. The tenant includes a user named User1.

You enable Azure AD Identity Protection.

You need to ensure that User1 can review the list in Azure AD Identity Protection of users flagged for risk. The solution must use the principle of least privilege.

To which role should you add User1?

A. Compliance administrator
B. Global administrator
C. Owner
D. Security administrator

Section: (none)
Explanation

Explanation/Reference:
Explanation:
Either one of the following three roles can review the list in Azure AD Identity Protection of users flagged for risk:

- Security Administrator
- Global Administrator
- Security Reader

Using the principle of least privilege, we should add User1 to the Security Administrator role.

Reference:
https://docs.microsoft.com/en-us/azure/active-directory/reports-monitoring/concept-risky-sign-ins

QUESTION 40
Your network contains an Active Directory domain named adatum.com that is synced to Microsoft Azure Active Directory (Azure AD).

The domain contains 100 user accounts.

The city attribute for all the users is set to the city where the user resides.

You need to modify the value of the city attribute to the three-letter airport code of each city.

What should you do?

A. From Active Directory Administrative Center, select the Active Directory users, and then modify the Properties settings.
B. From the Microsoft 365 admin center, select the users, and then use the Bulk actions option.
C. From Azure Cloud Shell, run the `Get-AzureADUser` and `Set-AzureADUser` cmdlets.
D. From Azure portal, select all the Azure AD users, and then use the User settings blade.

Section: (none)
Explanation

Explanation/Reference:

Explanation:
The user accounts are synced from the on-premise Active Directory to the Microsoft Azure Active Directory (Azure AD). Therefore, the city attribute must be changed in the on-premise Active Directory.
You can modify certain attributes of multiple user accounts simultaneously by selecting them in Active Directory Administrative Center or Active Directory Users and Computers, right clicking then selecting Properties.
The other three options all suggest modifying the city attribute of the users in the Azure Active Directory which is incorrect.

Reference:
https://blogs.technet.microsoft.com/canitpro/2015/11/25/step-by-step-managing-multiple-user-accounts-via-active-directory-admin-center/

QUESTION 41
You have a Microsoft 365 subscription that contains an Azure Active Directory (Azure AD) tenant named contoso.com.

Corporate policy states that user passwords must not include the word Contoso.

What should you do to implement the corporate policy?

A. From the Azure Active Directory admin center, configure the Password protection settings.
B. From the Microsoft 365 admin center, configure the Password policy settings.
C. From Azure AD Identity Protection, configure a sign-in risk policy.
D. From the Azure Active Directory admin center, create a conditional access policy.

Section: (none)
Explanation

Explanation/Reference:
Explanation:
The Password protection settings allows you to specify a banned password list of phrases that users cannot use as part of their passwords.

References:
https://docs.microsoft.com/en-us/azure/active-directory/authentication/howto-password-ban-bad-on-premises-operations

https://docs.microsoft.com/en-us/azure/active-directory/authentication/howto-password-ban-bad-configure

https://docs.microsoft.com/en-us/azure/active-directory/authentication/concept-password-ban-bad#custom-banned-password-list

Manage User Identity and Roles

Testlet 2

This is a case study. **Case studies are not timed separately. You can use as much exam time as you would like to complete each case**. However, there may be additional case studies and sections on this exam. You must manage your time to ensure that you are able to complete all questions included on this exam in the time provided.

To answer the questions included in a case study, you will need to reference information that is provided in the case study. Case studies might contain exhibits and other resources that provide more information about the scenario that is described in the case study. Each question is independent of the other questions in this case study.

At the end of this case study, a review screen will appear. This screen allows you to review your answer and to make changes before you move to the next section of the exam. After you begin a new section, you cannot return to this section.

To start the case study
To display the first question in this case study, click the **Next** button. Use the buttons in the left pane to explore the content of the case study before you answer the questions. Clicking these buttons displays information such as business requirements, existing environment, and problem statements. When you are ready to answer a question, click the **Question** button to return to the question.

Overview
Contoso, Ltd. is a consulting company that has a main office in Montreal and two branch offices in Seattle and New York.

The offices have the users and devices shown in the following table.

Office	Users	Laptops	Desktops	Mobile devices
Montreal	2,500	2,800	300	3,100
Seattle	1,000	1,100	200	1,500
New York	300	320	30	400

Contoso recently purchased a Microsoft 365 E5 subscription.

Existing Environment
The network contains an Active directory forest named contoso.com and a Microsoft Azure Active Directory (Azure AD) tenant named contoso.onmicrosoft.com.

You recently configured the forest to sync to the Azure AD tenant. You

add and then verify adatum.com as an additional domain name. All

servers run Windows Server 2016.

All desktop computers and laptops run Windows 10 Enterprise and are joined to contoso.com.

All the mobile devices in the Montreal and Seattle offices run Android. All the mobile devices in the New York office run iOS.

Contoso has the users shown in the following table.

Name	Role
User1	*None*
User2	*None*
User3	Customer Lockbox access approver
User4	*None*

Contoso has the groups shown in the following table.

Name	Type	Membership rule
Group1	Assigned	*Not applicable*
Group 2	Dynamic	(user.department –eq "Finance")

Microsoft Office 365 licenses are assigned only to Group2.

The network also contains external users from a vendor company who have Microsoft accounts that use a suffix of @outlook.com.

Requirements

Planned Changes
Contoso plans to provide email addresses for all the users in the following domains:

- East.adatum.com
- Contoso.adatum.com
- Humongousinsurance.com

Technical Requirements
Contoso identifies the following technical requirements:

- All new users must be assigned Office 365 licenses automatically.
- The principle of least privilege must be used whenever possible.

Security Requirements
Contoso identifies the following security requirements:

- Vendors must be able to authenticate by using their Microsoft account when accessing Contoso resources.
- User2 must be able to view reports and schedule the email delivery of security and compliance reports.

- The members of Group1 must be required to answer a security question before changing their password.
- User3 must be able to manage Office 365 connectors.
- User4 must be able to reset User3 password.

QUESTION 1
Note: This question is part of a series of questions that present the same scenario. Each question in the series contains a unique solution that might meet the stated goals. Some question sets might have more than one correct solution, while others might not have a correct solution.

After you answer a question in this section, you will NOT be able to return to it. As a result, these questions will not appear in the review screen.

You need to assign User2 the required roles to meet the security requirements.

Solution: From the Office 365 admin center, you assign User2 the Security Reader role. From the Exchange admin center, you assign User2 the Compliance Management role.

Does this meet the goal?

A. Yes
B. No

Section: (none)
Explanation

Explanation/Reference:
Explanation:
- User2 must be able to view reports and schedule the email delivery of security and compliance reports.

The Security Reader role can view reports.
The Compliance Management role can schedule the email delivery of security and compliance reports.

Reference:
https://docs.microsoft.com/en-us/exchange/permissions-exo/permissions-exo

QUESTION 2
Note: This question is part of a series of questions that present the same scenario. Each question in the series contains a unique solution that might meet the stated goals. Some question sets might have more than one correct solution, while others might not have a correct solution.

After you answer a question in this section, you will NOT be able to return to it. As a result, these questions will not appear in the review screen.

You need to assign User2 the required roles to meet the security requirements.

Solution: From the Office 365 admin center, you assign User2 the Security Administrator role.

From the Exchange admin center, you add User2 to the View-Only Organization Management role.

Does this meet the goal?

A. Yes
B. No

Section: (none)
Explanation

Explanation/Reference:
Explanation:
- User2 must be able to view reports and schedule the email delivery of security and compliance reports.

The Security Administrator role can view reports but not schedule the email delivery of security and compliance reports.
The View-Only Organization Management role cannot schedule the email delivery of security and compliance reports.

Reference:
https://docs.microsoft.com/en-us/exchange/permissions-exo/permissions-exo

QUESTION 3
Note: This question is part of a series of questions that present the same scenario. Each question in the series contains a unique solution that might meet the stated goals. Some question sets might have more than one correct solution, while others might not have a correct solution.

After you answer a question in this section, you will NOT be able to return to it. As a result, these questions will not appear in the review screen.

You need to assign User2 the required roles to meet the security requirements.

Solution: From the Office 365 admin center, you assign User2 the Security Reader role. From the Exchange admin center, you assign User2 the Help Desk role.

Does this meet the goal?

A. Yes
B. No

Section: (none)
Explanation

Explanation/Reference:
Explanation:
- User2 must be able to view reports and schedule the email delivery of security and compliance reports.

The Security Reader role can view reports but not schedule the email delivery of security and compliance reports.
The Help Desk role cannot schedule the email delivery of security and compliance reports.

Reference:
https://docs.microsoft.com/en-us/exchange/permissions-exo/permissions-exo

QUESTION 4
Note: This question is part of a series of questions that present the same scenario. Each question in the series contains a unique solution that might meet the stated goals. Some question sets might have more than one correct solution, while others might not have a correct solution.

After you answer a question in this section, you will NOT be able to return to it. As a result, these questions will not appear in the review screen.

You need to assign User2 the required roles to meet the security requirements.

Solution: From the Office 365 admin center, you assign User2 the Records Management role. From the Exchange admin center, you assign User2 the Help Desk role.

Does this meet the goal?

A. Yes
B. No

Section: (none)
Explanation

Explanation/Reference:
Explanation:
- User2 must be able to view reports and schedule the email delivery of security and compliance reports.

The Records Management role cannot view reports or schedule the email delivery of security and compliance reports.
The Help Desk role cannot schedule the email delivery of security and compliance reports.

Reference:
https://docs.microsoft.com/en-us/exchange/permissions-exo/permissions-exo

QUESTION 5
To which Azure AD role should you add User4 to meet the security requirement?

A. Password administrator
B. Global administrator
C. Security administrator

D. Privileged role administrator

Explanation/Reference:
Explanation:
- User4 must be able to reset User3 password.

User3 is assigned the Customer Lockbox Access Approver role. Only global admins can reset the passwords of people assigned to this role as it's considered a privileged role.

Reference:
https://techcommunity.microsoft.com/t5/Security-Privacy-and-Compliance/Customer-Lockbox-Approver-Role-Now-Available/ba-p/223393

QUESTION 6
You need to assign User2 the required roles to meet the security requirements and the technical requirements.

To which two roles should you assign User2? Each correct answer presents part of the solution.

NOTE: Each correct selection is worth one point.

A. the Exchange View-only Organization Management role
B. the Microsoft 365 Records Management role
C. the Exchange Online Help Desk role
D. the Microsoft 365 Security Reader role
E. the Exchange Online Compliance Management role

Explanation/Reference:
Explanation:
- User2 must be able to view reports and schedule the email delivery of security and compliance reports.

The Security Reader role can view reports but not schedule the email delivery of security and compliance reports.
The Exchange Online Compliance Management role can schedule the email delivery of security and compliance reports.

Reference:
https://docs.microsoft.com/en-us/exchange/permissions-exo/permissions-exo

Testlet 3

This is a case study. **Case studies are not timed separately. You can use as much exam time as you would like to complete each case**. However, there may be additional case studies and sections on this exam. You must manage your time to ensure that you are able to complete all questions included on this exam in the time provided.

To answer the questions included in a case study, you will need to reference information that is provided in the case study. Case studies might contain exhibits and other resources that provide more information about the scenario that is described in the case study. Each question is independent of the other questions in this case study.

At the end of this case study, a review screen will appear. This screen allows you to review your answer and to make changes before you move to the next section of the exam. After you begin a new section, you cannot return to this section.

To start the case study
To display the first question in this case study, click the **Next** button. Use the buttons in the left pane to explore the content of the case study before you answer the questions. Clicking these buttons displays information such as business requirements, existing environment, and problem statements. When you are ready to answer a question, click the **Question** button to return to the question.

Overview
Fabrikam, Inc. is an electronics company that produces consumer products. Fabrikam has 10,000 employees worldwide.

Fabrikam has a main office in London and branch offices in major cities in Europe, Asia, and the United States.

Existing Environment
Active Directory Environment
The network contains an Active Directory forest named fabrikam.com. The forest contains all the identities used for user and computer authentication.

Each department is represented by a top-level organizational unit (OU) that contains several child OUs for user accounts and computer accounts.

All users authenticate to on-premises applications by signing in to their device by using a UPN format of *username@fabrikam.com*.

Fabrikam does **NOT** plan to implement identity federation.

Network Infrastructure

Each office has a high-speed connection to the Internet.

Each office contains two domain controllers. All domain controllers are configured as a DNS server.

The public zone for fabrikam.com is managed by an external DNS server.

All users connect to an on-premises Microsoft Exchange Server 2016 organization. The users access their email by using Outlook Anywhere, Outlook on the web, or the Microsoft Outlook app for iOS. All the Exchange servers have the latest cumulative updates installed.

All shared company documents are stored on a Microsoft SharePoint Server farm.

Requirements
Planned Changes
Fabrikam plans to implement a Microsoft 365 Enterprise subscription and move all email and shared documents to the subscription.

Fabrikam plans to implement two pilot projects:

- Project1: During Project1, the mailboxes of 100 users in the sales department will be moved to Microsoft 365.
- Project2: After the successful completion of Project1, Microsoft Teams & Skype for Business will be enabled in Microsoft 365 for the sales department users.

Fabrikam plans to create a group named UserLicenses that will manage the allocation of all Microsoft 365 bulk licenses.

Technical Requirements
Fabrikam identifies the following technical requirements:

- All users must be able to exchange email messages successfully during Project1 by using their current email address.
- Users must be able to authenticate to cloud services if Active Directory becomes unavailable.
- A user named User1 must be able to view all DLP reports from the Microsoft 365 admin center.
- Microsoft Office 365 ProPlus applications must be installed from a network share only.
- Disruptions to email access must be minimized.

Application Requirements
Fabrikam identifies the following application requirements:

- An on-premises web application named App1 must allow users to complete their expense reports online. App1 must be available to users from the My Apps portal.
- The installation of feature updates for Office 365 ProPlus must be minimized.

Security Requirements
Fabrikam identifies the following security requirements:

- After the planned migration to Microsoft 365, all users must continue to authenticate to their mailbox and to SharePoint sites by using their UPN.
- The memberships of UserLicenses must be validated monthly. Unused user accounts must be removed from the group automatically.
- After the planned migration to Microsoft 365, all users must be signed in to on-premises and cloud-based applications automatically.
- The principle of least privilege must be used.

QUESTION 1

Which role should you assign to User1?

A. Security Administrator
B. Records Management
C. Security Reader
D. Hygiene Management

Section: (none)
Explanation

Explanation/Reference:
Explanation:
- A user named User1 must be able to view all DLP reports from the Microsoft 365 admin center.

Users with the Security Reader role have global read-only access on security-related features, including all information in Microsoft 365 security center, Azure Active Directory, Identity Protection, Privileged Identity Management, as well as the ability to read Azure Active Directory sign-in reports and audit logs, and in Office 365 Security & Compliance Center.

Reference:
https://docs.microsoft.com/en-us/azure/active-directory/users-groups-roles/directory-assign-admin-roles

Manage Access and Authentication

Question Set 1

QUESTION 1
Your company has a Microsoft 365 subscription that has multi-factor authentication configured for all users.

Users that connect to Microsoft 365 services report that they are prompted for multi-factor authentication multiple times a day.

You need to reduce the number of times the users are prompted for multi-factor authentication on their company-owned devices. Your solution must ensure that users are still prompted for MFA.

What should you do?

A. Enable the multi-factor authentication trusted IPs setting, and then verify each device as a trusted device.
B. Enable the remember multi-factor authentication setting, and then verify each device as a trusted device.
C. Enable the multi-factor authentication trusted IPs setting, and then join all client computers to Microsoft Azure Active Directory (Azure AD).
D. Enable the remember multi-factor authentication setting, and then join all client computers to Microsoft Azure Active Directory (Azure AD).

Section: (none)
Explanation

Explanation/Reference:
Explanation:
The remember Multi-Factor Authentication feature for devices and browsers that are trusted by the user is a free feature for all Multi-Factor Authentication users. Users can bypass subsequent verifications for a specified number of days, after they've successfully signed-in to a device by using Multi-Factor Authentication. The feature enhances usability by minimizing the number of times a user has to perform two-step verification on the same device.

Reference:
https://docs.microsoft.com/en-us/azure/active-directory/authentication/howto-mfa-mfasettings

QUESTION 2
Your company has a Microsoft 365 subscription and a Microsoft Azure Active Directory (Azure AD) tenant named contoso.onmicrosoft.com.

An external vendor has a Microsoft account that has a username of user1@outlook.com. You

plan to provide user1@outlook.com with access to several resources in the subscription.

You need to add the external user account to contoso.onmicrosoft.com. The solution must ensure that the external vendor can authenticate by using user1@outlook.com.

What should you do?

A. From Azure Cloud Shell, run the `New-AzureADUser` cmdlet and specify `-UserPrincipalName user1@outlook.com`.

B. From the Microsoft 365 admin center, add a contact, and then specify user1@outlook.com as the email address.

C. From the Azure portal, add a new guest user, and then specify user1@outlook.com as the email address.

D. From the Azure portal, add a custom domain name, and then create a new Azure AD user and use user1@outlook.com as the username.

Section: (none)
Explanation

Explanation/Reference:
Explanation:
You can invite guest users to the directory, to a group, or to an application. After you invite a user through any of these methods, the invited user's account is added to Azure Active Directory (Azure AD), with a user type of Guest. The guest user must then redeem their invitation to access resources. An invitation of a user does not expire.
The invitation will include a link to create a Microsoft account. The user can then authenticate using their Microsoft account. In this question, the external vendor already has a Microsoft account (user1@outlook.com) so he can authenticate using that.

Reference:
https://docs.microsoft.com/en-us/azure/active-directory/b2b/add-users-administrator

QUESTION 3
You have a Microsoft 365 subscription that contains several Microsoft SharePoint Online sites.

You discover that users from your company can invite external users to access files on the SharePoint sites.

You need to ensure that the company users can invite only authenticated guest users to the sites.

What should you do?

A. From the Microsoft 365 admin center, configure a partner relationship.
B. From SharePoint Online Management Shell, run the `Set-SPOSite` cmdlet.
C. From the Azure Active Directory admin center, configure a conditional access policy.
D. From the SharePoint admin center, configure the sharing settings.

Section: (none)
Explanation

Explanation/Reference:
Explanation:

You need to set the Sharing settings to 'Existing Guests'. This setting allows sharing only with guests who are already in your directory. These guests may exist in your directory because they previously accepted sharing invitations or because they were manually added.

Reference:
https://docs.microsoft.com/en-us/sharepoint/turn-external-sharing-on-or-off

QUESTION 4
Your company has a hybrid deployment of Microsoft 365.

Users authenticate by using pass-through authentication. Several Microsoft Azure AD Connect Authentication Agents are deployed.

You need to verify whether all the Authentication Agents are used for authentication.

What should you do?

A. From the Azure portal, use the Troubleshoot option on the Pass-through authentication page.
B. From Performance Monitor, use the #PTA authentications counter.
C. From the Azure portal, use the Diagnostics settings on the Monitor blade.
D. From Performance Monitor, use the Kerberos authentications counter.

Section: (none)
Explanation

Explanation/Reference:
Explanation:
On the Troubleshoot page, you can view how many agents are configured. If you click on the agents link, you can view the status of each agent. Each agent will have a status of Active or Inactive.

Reference:
https://docs.microsoft.com/en-us/azure/active-directory/hybrid/tshoot-connect-pass-through-authentication

QUESTION 5
Note: This question is part of a series of questions that present the same scenario. Each question in the series contains a unique solution that might meet the stated goals. Some question sets might have more than one correct solution, while others might not have a correct solution.

After you answer a question in this section, you will NOT be able to return to it. As a result, these questions will not appear in the review screen.

You have a Microsoft 365 subscription.

You discover that some external users accessed content on a Microsoft SharePoint site. You modify the SharePoint sharing policy to prevent sharing outside your organization.

You need to be notified if the SharePoint policy is modified in the future.

Solution: From the SharePoint site, you create an alert.

Does this meet the goal?

A. Yes
B. No

Section: (none)
Explanation

Explanation/Reference:
Explanation:
You need to create a threat management policy in the Security & Compliance admin center.

QUESTION 6
Note: This question is part of a series of questions that present the same scenario. Each question in the series contains a unique solution that might meet the stated goals. Some question sets might have more than one correct solution, while others might not have a correct solution.

After you answer a question in this section, you will NOT be able to return to it. As a result, these questions will not appear in the review screen.

You have a Microsoft 365 subscription.

You discover that some external users accessed content on a Microsoft SharePoint site. You modify the SharePoint sharing policy to prevent sharing outside your organization.

You need to be notified if the SharePoint policy is modified in the future.

Solution: From the SharePoint admin center, you modify the sharing settings.

Does this meet the goal?

A. Yes
B. No

Section: (none)
Explanation

Explanation/Reference:
Explanation:
You need to create a threat management policy in the Security & Compliance admin center.

QUESTION 7
Note: This question is part of a series of questions that present the same scenario. Each question in the series contains a unique solution that might meet the stated goals. Some question sets might have more than one correct solution, while others might not have a

correct solution.

After you answer a question in this section, you will NOT be able to return to it. As a result, these questions will not appear in the review screen.

You have a Microsoft 365 subscription.

You discover that some external users accessed content on a Microsoft SharePoint site. You modify the SharePoint sharing policy to prevent sharing outside your organization.

You need to be notified if the SharePoint policy is modified in the future.

Solution: From the Security & Compliance admin center, you create a threat management policy.

Does this meet the goal?

A. Yes
B. No

Section: (none)
Explanation

Explanation/Reference:
Explanation:
We can create a threat management policy to alert us when the sharing policy is changed. Create a new Alert policy > under Category select Threat Management > under 'Activity is' scroll down to the 'Site administration activities' and select 'Changed a sharing policy'.

QUESTION 8
Note: This question is part of a series of questions that present the same scenario. Each question in the series contains a unique solution that might meet the stated goals. Some question sets might have more than one correct solution, while others might not have a correct solution.

After you answer a question in this section, you will NOT be able to return to it. As a result, these questions will not appear in the review screen.

You have a Microsoft 365 subscription.

You need to prevent users from accessing your Microsoft SharePoint Online sites unless the users are connected to your on-premises network.

Solution: From the Device Management admin center, you a trusted location and compliance policy.

Does this meet the goal?

A. Yes
B. No

Section: (none)
Explanation

Explanation/Reference:
Explanation:
You need to configure a conditional access policy, not a compliance policy.
Conditional Access in SharePoint Online can be configured to use an IP Address white list to allow access.

Reference:
https://techcommunity.microsoft.com/t5/Microsoft-SharePoint-Blog/Conditional-Access-in-SharePoint-Online-and-OneDrive-for/ba-p/46678

QUESTION 9
Note: This question is part of a series of questions that present the same scenario. Each question in the series contains a unique solution that might meet the stated goals. Some question sets might have more than one correct solution, while others might not have a correct solution.

After you answer a question in this section, you will NOT be able to return to it. As a result, these questions will not appear in the review screen.

You have a Microsoft 365 subscription.

You need to prevent users from accessing your Microsoft SharePoint Online sites unless the users are connected to your on-premises network.

Solution: From the Microsoft 365 admin center, you configure the Organization profile settings.

Does this meet the goal?

A. Yes
B. No

Section: (none)
Explanation

Explanation/Reference:
Explanation:
You need to configure a trusted location and a conditional access policy.
Conditional Access in SharePoint Online can be configured to use an IP Address white list to allow access.

Reference:
https://techcommunity.microsoft.com/t5/Microsoft-SharePoint-Blog/Conditional-Access-in-SharePoint-Online-and-OneDrive-for/ba-p/46678

QUESTION 10
Note: This question is part of a series of questions that present the same scenario. Each question in the series contains a unique solution that might meet the stated goals. Some

question sets might have more than one correct solution, while others might not have a correct solution.

After you answer a question in this section, you will NOT be able to return to it. As a result, these questions will not appear in the review screen.

You have a Microsoft 365 subscription.

You need to prevent users from accessing your Microsoft SharePoint Online sites unless the users are connected to your on-premises network.

Solution: From the Azure Active Directory admin center, you create a trusted location and a conditional access policy.

Does this meet the goal?

A. Yes
B. No

Section: (none)
Explanation

Explanation/Reference:
Explanation:
Conditional Access in SharePoint Online can be configured to use an IP Address white list to allow access.
With named locations, you can create logical groupings of IP address ranges, for example your office IP range. You can then mark the named location as a trusted location.
Mark as trusted location - A flag you can set for a named location to indicate a trusted location. Typically, trusted locations are network areas that are controlled by your IT department. You would then configure the conditional access policy to allow access only from the trusted location.

Reference:
https://docs.microsoft.com/en-us/azure/active-directory/conditional-access/location-condition

https://techcommunity.microsoft.com/t5/Microsoft-SharePoint-Blog/Conditional-Access-in-SharePoint-Online-and-OneDrive-for/ba-p/46678

QUESTION 11
You have a Microsoft 365 subscription and a Microsoft Azure Active Directory (Azure AD) tenant named contoso.com.

Contoso.com is configured as shown in the following exhibit.

External collaboration settings

⊟ Save   ✕ Discard

Guest users permissions are limited ⓘ

Yes	**No**

Admins and users in the guest inviter role can invite ⓘ

Yes	**No**

Members can invite ⓘ

Yes	No

Guests can invite ⓘ

Yes	No

Collaboration restrictions

◉ Allow invitations to be sent to any domain (most inclusive)
◯ Deny invitations to the specified domains
◯ Allow invitations only to the specified domains (most restrictive)

You need to ensure that guest users can be created in the tenant.

Which setting should you modify?

A. Guests can invite.
B. Guest users permissions are limited.
C. Members can invite.
D. Admins and users in the guest inviter role can invite.
E. Deny invitations to the specified domains.

Section: (none)
Explanation

Explanation/Reference:
Explanation:
The setting "Admins and users in the guest inviter role can invite" is set to No. This means that no one can create guest accounts because they cannot 'invite' guests. This setting needs to be changed to Yes to ensure that guest users can be created in the tenant.

Reference:
https://docs.microsoft.com/en-us/azure/active-directory/b2b/delegate-invitations

https://docs.microsoft.com/en-us/azure/active-directory/fundamentals/users-default-permissions

QUESTION 12
Your company recently purchased a Microsoft 365 subscription.

You enable Microsoft Azure Multi-Factor Authentication (MFA) for all 500 users in the Azure Active Directory (Azure AD) tenant.

You need to generate a report that lists all the users who completed the Azure MFA registration process.

What is the best approach to achieve the goal? More than one answer choice may achieve the goal. Select the **BEST** answer.

A. From Azure Cloud Shell, run the `Get-AzureADUser` cmdlet.
B. From Azure Cloud Shell, run the `Get-MsolUser` cmdlet.
C. From the Azure Active Directory admin center, use the Usage & insights blade.
D. From the Azure Active Directory admin center, use the Risky sign-ins blade.

Section: (none)
Explanation

Explanation/Reference:
Explanation:
You can use the `Get-MsolUser` cmdlet to generate a report that lists all the users who completed the Azure MFA registration process. The full command would look like this:

```
Get-MsolUser -All | Where-Object {$_.StrongAuthenticationMethods.Count
-eq 0} | Select-Object -Property UserPrincipalName
```

Reference:
https://docs.microsoft.com/en-us/azure/active-directory/authentication/howto-mfa-reporting

QUESTION 13
You have a Microsoft 365 Enterprise subscription.

You have a conditional access policy to force multi-factor authentication when accessing Microsoft SharePoint from a mobile device.

You need to view which users authenticated by using multi-factor authentication.

What should you do?

A. From the Microsoft 365 admin center, view the Security & Compliance reports.
B. From the Azure Active Directory admin center, view the user sign-ins.
C. From the Microsoft 365 admin center, view the Usage reports.
D. From the Azure Active Directory admin center, view the audit logs.

Section: (none)
Explanation

Explanation/Reference:
Explanation:
With the **sign-ins activity report** in the Azure portal, you can get the information you need to determine how your environment is doing.
The sign-ins report can provide you with information about the usage of managed applications and user sign-in activities, which includes information about multi-factor authentication (MFA) usage. The MFA data gives you insights into how MFA is working in your organization. It enables you to answer questions like:
- Was the sign-in challenged with MFA?
- How did the user complete MFA?
- Why was the user unable to complete MFA?
- How many users are challenged for MFA?
- How many users are unable to complete the MFA challenge?
- What are the common MFA issues end users are running into?

Reference:
https://docs.microsoft.com/en-us/azure/active-directory/authentication/howto-mfa-reporting

QUESTION 14
You have a Microsoft 365 Enterprise E5 subscription.

You need to enforce multi-factor authentication on all cloud-based applications for the users in the finance department.

What should you do?

A. Create a sign-in risk policy.
B. Create a new app registration.
C. Assign an Enterprise Mobility + Security E5 license to the finance department users.
D. Configure the sign-in status for the user accounts of the finance department users.

Section: (none)
Explanation

Explanation/Reference:
Explanation:
You can configure a sign-in risk policy that applies to the Finance department users. The policy can be configured to 'Allow access' but with multi-factor authentication as a requirement.

Reference:
https://docs.microsoft.com/en-us/azure/active-directory/identity-protection/howto-sign-in-risk-policy

QUESTION 15
Your network contains an on-premises Active Directory domain named contoso.local. The domain contains five domain controllers.

Your company purchases Microsoft 365 and creates a Microsoft Azure Active Directory (Azure AD) tenant named contoso.onmicrosoft.com.

You plan to implement pass-through authentication.

You need to prepare the environment for the planned implementation of pass-through authentication.

Which three actions should you perform? Each correct answer presents part of the solution.

NOTE: Each correct selection is worth one point.

- A. Modify the email address attribute for each user account.
- B. From the Azure portal, add a custom domain name.
- C. From Active Directory Domains and Trusts, add a UPN suffix.
- D. Modify the User logon name for each user account.
- E. From the Azure portal, configure an authentication method.
- F. From a domain controller, install an Authentication Agent.

Section: (none)
Explanation

Explanation/Reference:
Explanation:
To implement pass-through authentication, you need to install and configure Azure AD Connect.

The on-premise Active Directory domain is named contoso.local. Before you can configure Azure AD Connect, you need to purchase a routable domain, for example, contoso.com. You then need to add the domain contoso.com to Microsoft as a custom domain name.

The user accounts in the Active Directory domain need to be configured to use the domain name contoso.com as a UPN suffix. You need to add contoso.com to the Active Directory first by using Active Directory Domains and Trusts to add contoso.com add a UPN suffix. You can then configure each account to use the new UPN suffix.

An Authentication Agent is required on a domain controller to perform the authentication when pass-through authentication is used. When the custom domain and user accounts are configured, you can install and configure Azure AD Connect. An Authentication Agent is installed when you select the pass-through authentication option in the Azure AD Connect configuration or you can install the Authentication Agent manually.

Reference:
https://docs.microsoft.com/en-us/azure/active-directory/hybrid/how-to-connect-pta-quick-start

QUESTION 16
Note: This question is part of a series of questions that present the same scenario. Each question in the series contains a unique solution that might meet the stated goals. Some question sets might have more than one correct solution, while others might not have a correct solution.

After you answer a question in this section, you will NOT be able to return to it. As a result, these questions will not appear in the review screen.

Your company plans to deploy several Microsoft Office 365 services.

You need to design an authentication strategy for the planned deployment. The solution must meet the following requirements:

- Users must be able to authenticate during business hours only.
- Authentication requests must be processed successfully if a single server fails.
- When the password for an on-premises user account expires, the new password must be enforced the next time the user signs in.
- Users who connect to Office 365 services from domain-joined devices that are connected to the internal network must be signed in automatically.

Solution: You design an authentication strategy that contains a pass-through authentication model. The solution contains two servers that have an Authentication Agent installed and password hash synchronization configured.

Does this meet the goal?

A. Yes
B. No

Section: (none)
Explanation

Explanation/Reference:
Explanation:
This solution meets the following goals:
- Users must be able to authenticate during business hours only.
- Authentication requests must be processed successfully if a single server fails.
- When the password for an on-premises user account expires, the new password must be enforced the next time the user signs in.

However, the following goal is not met:
- Users who connect to Office 365 services from domain-joined devices that are connected to the internal network must be signed in automatically.

You would need to configure Single-sign on (SSO) to meet the last requirement.

Reference:

https://docs.microsoft.com/en-us/azure/security/azure-ad-choose-authn

QUESTION 17
Note: This question is part of a series of questions that present the same scenario. Each question in the series contains a unique solution that might meet the stated goals. Some question sets might have more than one correct solution, while others might not have a correct solution.

After you answer a question in this section, you will NOT be able to return to it. As a result, these questions will not appear in the review screen.

Your company plans to deploy several Microsoft Office 365 services.

You need to design an authentication strategy for the planned deployment. The solution must meet the following requirements:

- Users must be able to authenticate during business hours only.
- Authentication requests must be processed successfully if a single server fails.
- When the password for an on-premises user account expires, the new password must be enforced the next time the user signs in.
- Users who connect to Office 365 services from domain-joined devices that are connected to the internal network must be signed in automatically.

Solution: You design an authentication strategy that contains a pass-through authentication model. You install an Authentication Agent on three servers and configure seamless SSO.

Does this meet the goal?

A. Yes
B. No

Section: (none)
Explanation

Explanation/Reference:
Explanation:
This solution meets all the requirements:
- Users must be able to authenticate during business hours only. (This can be configured by using Logon Hours in Active Directory. Pass-through authentication passes authentication to the on-premise Active Directory)
- Authentication requests must be processed successfully if a single server fails. (We have Authentication Agents running on three servers)
- When the password for an on-premises user account expires, the new password must be enforced the next time the user signs in. (This can be configured in Active Directory. Pass-through authentication passes authentication to the on-premise Active Directory)
- Users who connect to Office 365 services from domain-joined devices that are connected to the internal network must be signed in automatically. (This goal is met by seamless SSO)

Reference:
https://docs.microsoft.com/en-us/azure/security/azure-ad-choose-authn

QUESTION 18
Note: This question is part of a series of questions that present the same scenario. Each question in the series contains a unique solution that might meet the stated goals. Some question sets might have more than one correct solution, while others might not have a correct solution.

After you answer a question in this section, you will NOT be able to return to it. As a result, these questions will not appear in the review screen.

Your company plans to deploy several Microsoft Office 365 services.

You need to design an authentication strategy for the planned deployment. The solution must meet the following requirements:

- Users must be able to authenticate during business hours only.
- Authentication requests must be processed successfully if a single server fails.
- When the password for an on-premises user account expires, the new password must be enforced the next time the user signs in.
- Users who connect to Office 365 services from domain-joined devices that are connected to the internal network must be signed in automatically.

Solution: You design an authentication strategy that uses password hash synchronization and seamless SSO. The solution contains two servers that have an Authentication Agent installed.

Does this meet the goal?

A. Yes
B. No

Section: (none)
Explanation

Explanation/Reference:
Explanation:
This solution meets the following requirements:
- Users who connect to Office 365 services from domain-joined devices that are connected to the internal network must be signed in automatically.
- Authentication requests must be processed successfully if a single server fails.

The following requirements are not met:
- Users must be able to authenticate during business hours only.
- When the password for an on-premises user account expires, the new password must be enforced the next time the user signs in.

To meet these two requirements, you would have to configure pass-through authentication.

Reference:
https://docs.microsoft.com/en-us/azure/security/azure-ad-choose-authn

QUESTION 19
You have a Microsoft 365 Enterprise E5 subscription.

You need to enforce multi-factor authentication on all cloud-based applications for the users in the finance department.

What should you do?

A. Create an activity policy.
B. Create a new app registration.
C. Create a conditional access policy.
D. Create a session policy.

Section: (none)
Explanation

Explanation/Reference:
Explanation:
You can configure a conditional access policy that applies to the Finance department users. The policy can be configured to 'Allow access' but with multi-factor authentication as a requirement.

The reference below explains how to create a conditional access policy that requires MFA for all users. To apply the policy to finance users only, you would select Users and Group in the Include section instead of All Users and then specify the finance department group.

Reference:
https://docs.microsoft.com/en-us/azure/active-directory/conditional-access/howto-conditional-access-policy-all-users-mfa

QUESTION 20
You have a Microsoft 365 subscription.

Your company deploys an Active Directory Federation Services (AD FS) solution.

You need to configure the environment to audit AD FS user authentication.

Which two actions should you perform? Each correct answer presents part of the solution.

NOTE: Each correct selection is worth one point.

A. From all the AD FS servers, run `auditpol.exe`.
B. From all the domain controllers, run the `Set-AdminAuditLogConfig` cmdlet and specify the `-LogLevel` parameter.
C. On a domain controller, install Azure AD Connect Health for AD DS.
D. From the Azure AD Connect server, run the `Register-AzureADConnectHealthSyncAgent` cmdlet.
E. On an AD FS server, install Azure AD Connect Health for AD FS.

Section: (none)
Explanation

Explanation/Reference:
Explanation:
To audit AD FS user authentication, you need to install Azure AD Connect Health for AD FS. The agent should be installed on an AD FS server. After the installation, you need to register the agent by running the `Register-AzureADConnectHealthSyncAgent` cmdlet.

Reference:
https://docs.microsoft.com/en-us/azure/active-directory/hybrid/how-to-connect-health-agent-install

https://docs.microsoft.com/en-us/azure/active-directory/hybrid/how-to-connect-health-adfs

QUESTION 21
Note: This question is part of a series of questions that present the same scenario. Each question in the series contains a unique solution that might meet the stated goals. Some question sets might have more than one correct solution, while others might not have a correct solution.

After you answer a question in this section, you will NOT be able to return to it. As a result, these questions will not appear in the review screen.

Your network contains an Active Directory forest.

You deploy Microsoft 365.

You plan to implement directory synchronization.

You need to recommend a security solution for the synchronized identities. The solution must meet the following requirements:

- Users must be able to authenticate successfully to Microsoft 365 services if Active Directory becomes unavailable.
- User passwords must be 10 characters or more.

Solution: Implement password hash synchronization and configure password protection in the Azure AD tenant.

Does this meet the goal?

A. Yes
B. No

Section: (none)
Explanation

Explanation/Reference:
Explanation:
This solution meets the following requirement:
- Users must be able to authenticate successfully to Microsoft 365 services if Active Directory becomes unavailable. (this is because the authentication is performed by Azure Active Directory).

This solution does not meet the following requirement:
- Users passwords must be 10 characters or more.

To meet this requirement, you would need to configure the Default Domain Policy in the on-premise Active Directory.

Azure Password Protection can prevent users from using passwords from a 'banned password' list but it cannot be configured to require that passwords must be 10 characters or more.

Reference:
https://docs.microsoft.com/en-us/azure/active-directory/hybrid/how-to-connect-password-hash-synchronization

QUESTION 22
Note: This question is part of a series of questions that present the same scenario. Each question in the series contains a unique solution that might meet the stated goals. Some question sets might have more than one correct solution, while others might not have a correct solution.

After you answer a question in this section, you will NOT be able to return to it. As a result, these questions will not appear in the review screen.

Your network contains an Active Directory forest.

You deploy Microsoft 365.

You plan to implement directory synchronization.

You need to recommend a security solution for the synchronized identities. The solution must meet the following requirements:

- Users must be able to authenticate successfully to Microsoft 365 services if Active Directory becomes unavailable.
- User passwords must be 10 characters or more.

Solution: Implement pass-through authentication and modify the password settings from the Default Domain Policy in Active Directory.

Does this meet the goal?

A. Yes
B. No

Section: (none)
Explanation

Explanation/Reference:
Explanation:

This solution does not meet the following requirement:

- Users must be able to authenticate successfully to Microsoft 365 services if Active Directory becomes unavailable.

This is because with pass-through authentication, the authentication is performed by the on-premise Active Directory.

This solution does meet the following requirement:
- User passwords must be 10 characters or more.

Configuring the Default Domain Policy in the on-premise Active Directory meets the requirement.

Reference:
https://docs.microsoft.com/en-us/azure/active-directory/hybrid/how-to-connect-password-hash-synchronization

QUESTION 23

You have a Microsoft 365 subscription that uses an Azure Active Directory (Azure AD) tenant named contoso.com.

A temporary employee at your company uses an email address of user1@outlook.com.

You need to ensure that the temporary employee can sign in to contoso.com by using the user1@outlook.com account.

What should you do?

A. From the Azure Active Directory admin center, create a new user.
B. From the Microsoft 365 admin center, create a new contact.
C. From the Azure Active Directory admin center, create a new guest user.
D. From the Microsoft 365 admin center, create a new user.

Section: (none)
Explanation

Explanation/Reference:
Explanation:
You can invite guest users to the directory, to a group, or to an application. After you invite a user through any of these methods, the invited user's account is added to Azure Active Directory (Azure AD), with a user type of Guest. The guest user must then redeem their invitation to access resources. An invitation of a user does not expire.
The invitation will include a link to create a Microsoft account. The user can then authenticate using their Microsoft account. In this question, the external vendor already has a Microsoft account (user1@outlook.com) so he can authenticate using that.

Reference:
https://docs.microsoft.com/en-us/azure/active-directory/b2b/add-users-administrator

QUESTION 24

Your company has an Azure Active Directory (Azure AD) tenant named contoso.com that contains 10,000 users.

The company has a Microsoft 365 subscription.

You enable Azure Multi-Factor Authentication (MFA) for all the users in contoso.com.

You run the following query.

```
search "SigninLogs" | where ResultDescription == "User did not pass
the MFA challenge."
```

The query returns blank results.

You need to ensure that the query returns the expected results.

What should you do?

A. From the Azure Active Directory admin center, configure the diagnostics settings to archive logs to an Azure Storage account.
B. From the Security & Compliance admin center, turn on auditing.
C. From the Security & Compliance admin center, enable Office 365 Analytics.
D. From the Azure Active Directory admin center, configure the diagnostics settings to send logs to an Azure Log Analytics workplace.

Section: (none)
Explanation

Explanation/Reference:
Explanation:
You can now send audit logs to Azure Log Analytics. This gives you much easier reporting on audit events and the ability to perform queries such as the one in this question.

References:
https://docs.microsoft.com/en-us/azure/active-directory/reports-monitoring/howto-integrate-activity-logs-with-log-analytics

QUESTION 25
You have a Microsoft 365 Enterprise E5 subscription.

You need to enforce multi-factor authentication on all cloud-based applications for the users in the finance department.

What should you do?

A. Create an activity policy.
B. Create a new app registration.
C. Create a sign-in risk policy.
D. Create a session policy.

Section: (none)
Explanation

Explanation:
You can configure a sign-in risk policy that applies to the Finance department users. The policy can be configured to 'Allow access' but with multi-factor authentication as a requirement.

Reference:
https://docs.microsoft.com/en-us/azure/active-directory/identity-protection/howto-sign-in-risk-policy

QUESTION 26
Note: This question is part of a series of questions that present the same scenario. Each question in the series contains a unique solution that might meet the stated goals. Some question sets might have more than one correct solution, while others might not have a correct solution.

After you answer a question in this section, you will NOT be able to return to it. As a result, these questions will not appear in the review screen.

Your network contains an Active Directory forest.

You deploy Microsoft 365.

You plan to implement directory synchronization.

You need to recommend a security solution for the synchronized identities. The solution must meet the following requirements:

- Users must be able to authenticate successfully to Microsoft 365 services if Active Directory becomes unavailable.
- User passwords must be 10 characters or more.

Solution: Implement pass-through authentication and configure password protection in the Azure AD tenant.

Does this meet the goal?

A. Yes
B. No

Section: (none)
Explanation

Explanation/Reference:
Explanation:
This solution does not meet the following requirement:
- Users must be able to authenticate successfully to Microsoft 365 services if Active Directory becomes unavailable.
This is because with pass-through authentication, the authentication is performed by the on-premise Active Directory.

This solution does not meet the following requirement:

- Users passwords must be 10 characters or more.

To meet this requirement, you would need to configure the Default Domain Policy in the on-premise Active Directory.

Azure Password Protection can prevent users from using passwords from a 'banned password' list but it cannot be configured to require that passwords must be 10 characters or more.

Reference:
https://docs.microsoft.com/en-us/azure/active-directory/hybrid/how-to-connect-password-hash-synchronization

QUESTION 27
Note: This question is part of a series of questions that present the same scenario. Each question in the series contains a unique solution that might meet the stated goals. Some question sets might have more than one correct solution, while others might not have a correct solution.

After you answer a question in this section, you will NOT be able to return to it. As a result, these questions will not appear in the review screen.

Your network contains an Active Directory forest.

You deploy Microsoft 365.

You plan to implement directory synchronization.

You need to recommend a security solution for the synchronized identities. The solution must meet the following requirements:

- Users must be able to authenticate successfully to Microsoft 365 services if Active Directory becomes unavailable.
- User passwords must be 10 characters or more.

Solution: Implement password hash synchronization and modify the password settings from the Default Domain Policy in Active Directory.

Does this meet the goal?

A. Yes
B. No

Section: (none)
Explanation

Explanation/Reference:
Explanation:
This solution meets the requirements:
- Users must be able to authenticate successfully to Microsoft 365 services if Active Directory becomes unavailable. (this is because the authentication is performed by Azure Active Directory).
- Users passwords must be 10 characters or more. (the Default Domain Policy in the on-

premise Active Directory can be configured to require the password length)

Reference:
https://docs.microsoft.com/en-us/azure/active-directory/hybrid/how-to-connect-password-hash-synchronization

QUESTION 28
Your company has three main offices and one branch office. The branch office is used for research.

The company plans to implement a Microsoft 365 tenant and to deploy multi-factor authentication.

You need to recommend a Microsoft 365 solution to ensure that multi-factor authentication is enforced only for users in the branch office.

What should you include in the recommendation?

A. Microsoft Azure Active Directory (Azure AD) conditional access.
B. Microsoft Azure Active Directory (Azure AD) password protection.
C. a Microsoft 365 Device Management device compliance policy.
D. a Microsoft 365 Device Management device configuration profile.

Section: (none)
Explanation

Explanation/Reference:
Explanation:
With Azure Active Directory (Azure AD) Conditional Access, you can control how authorized users can access your cloud apps. The location condition of a Conditional Access policy enables you to tie access controls settings to the network locations of your users.

For this question, we need to configure a location condition in a conditional access policy and apply the policy to users in that location (the branch office). The conditional access policy can be required to 'Allow Access' but 'Required MFA'.

Reference:
https://docs.microsoft.com/en-us/azure/active-directory/conditional-access/location-condition

QUESTION 29
Your network contains an Active Directory domain named contoso.com.

All users authenticate by using a third-party authentication solution.

You purchase Microsoft 365 and plan to implement several Microsoft 365 services.

You need to recommend an identity strategy that meets the following requirements:

- Provides seamless SSO
- Minimizes the number of additional servers required to support the solution
- Stores the passwords of all the users in Microsoft Azure Active Directory (Azure AD)

- Ensures that all the users authenticate to Microsoft 365 by using their on-premises user account

You are evaluating the implementation of federation.

Which two requirements are met by using federation? Each correct answer presents a complete solution.

NOTE: Each correct selection is worth one point.

A. minimizes the number of additional servers required to support the solution
B. provides seamless SSO
C. stores the passwords of all the users in Azure AD
D. ensures that all the users authenticate to Microsoft 365 by using their on-premises user account

Section: (none)
Explanation

Explanation/Reference:
Explanation:
When you choose this federation as the authentication method, Azure AD hands off the authentication process to a separate trusted authentication system, such as on-premises Active Directory Federation Services (AD FS), to validate the user's password. AD FS can use on-premise Active Directory as an authentication provider. AD FS can also provide SSO when using Active Directory as an authentication provider.

Incorrect Answers:
A: Additional servers are required to support the AD FS infrastructure.
C: The passwords are not synchronised to Azure AD.

Reference:
https://docs.microsoft.com/en-us/azure/security/azure-ad-choose-authn

QUESTION 30
Note: This question is part of a series of questions that present the same scenario. Each question in the series contains a unique solution that might meet the stated goals. Some question sets might have more than one correct solution, while others might not have a correct solution.

After you answer a question in this section, you will NOT be able to return to it. As a result, these questions will not appear in the review screen.

Your company plans to deploy several Microsoft Office 365 services.

You need to design an authentication strategy for the planned deployment. The solution must meet the following requirements:

- Users must be able to authenticate during business hours only.
- Authentication requests must be processed successfully if a single server fails.

- When the password for an on-premises user account expires, the new password must be enforced the next time the user signs in.
- Users who connect to Office 365 services from domain-joined devices that are connected to the internal network must be signed in automatically.

Solution: You design an authentication strategy that uses federation authentication by using Active Directory Federation Services (AD FS). The solution contains two AD FS servers and two Web Application Proxies.

Does this meet the goal?

A. Yes
B. No

Section: (none)
Explanation

Explanation/Reference:
Explanation:
This solution meets the following requirements:
- Users must be able to authenticate during business hours only.
- Authentication requests must be processed successfully if a single server fails.
- When the password for an on-premises user account expires, the new password must be enforced the next time the user signs in.

The following requirement is not met:
- Users who connect to Office 365 services from domain-joined devices that are connected to the internal network must be signed in automatically.

To meet this requirement, you would need to configure seamless Single Sign-on (SSO)

Reference:
https://docs.microsoft.com/en-us/azure/security/azure-ad-choose-authn

QUESTION 31
Your network contains an Active Directory domain named contoso.com. The domain contains five domain controllers.

You purchase Microsoft 365 and plan to implement several Microsoft 365 services.

You need to identify an authentication strategy for the planned Microsoft 365 deployment. The solution must meet the following requirements:

- Ensure that users can access Microsoft 365 by using their on-premises credentials.
- Use the existing server infrastructure only.
- Store all user passwords on-premises only.
- Be highly available.

Which authentication strategy should you identify?

A. pass-through authentication and seamless SSO

B. pass-through authentication and seamless SSO with password hash synchronization
C. password hash synchronization and seamless SSO
D. federation

Section: (none)
Explanation

Explanation/Reference:
Explanation:
Azure AD Pass-through Authentication. Provides a simple password validation for Azure AD authentication services by using a software agent that runs on one or more on-premises servers. The servers validate the users directly with your on-premises Active Directory, which ensures that the password validation doesn't happen in the cloud.

Incorrect Answers:
B: Password hash synchronization replicates passwords to Azure Active Directory. This does not meet the following requirement: Store all user passwords on-premises only
C: Password hash synchronization replicates passwords to Azure Active Directory. This does not meet the following requirement: Store all user passwords on-premises only
D: Federation requires additional servers running Active Directory Federation Services. This does not meet the following requirement: Use the existing server infrastructure only.

Reference:
https://docs.microsoft.com/en-us/azure/security/fundamentals/choose-ad-authn

QUESTION 32
Your network contains an on-premises Active Directory domain.

You have a Microsoft 365 subscription.

You implement a directory synchronization solution that uses pass-through authentication.

You configure Microsoft Azure Active Directory (Azure AD) smart lockout as shown in the following exhibit.

Custom smart lockout

Lockout threshold ❶   5   ✓

Lockout duration in seconds ❶   60   ✓

Custom banned passwords

Enforce custom list ❶ | **Yes** | No |

Custom banned password list ❶
```
password
Pa$$w0rd
Pa55w0rd
Contoso
```
                                                                                 ✓

Password protection for Windows Server Active Directory

Enable password protection on Windows Server Active Directory ❶ | **Yes** | No |

Mode ❶ | Enforced | **Audit** |

You discover that Active Directory users can use the passwords in the custom banned passwords list.

You need to ensure that banned passwords are effective for all users.

Which three actions should you perform? Each correct answer presents part of the solution.

NOTE: Each correct selection is worth one point.

A. From a domain controller, install the Azure AD Password Protection Proxy.
B. From a domain controller, install the Microsoft AAD Application Proxy connector.
C. From Custom banned passwords, modify the Enforce custom list setting.
D. From Password protection for Windows Server Active Directory, modify the Mode setting.
E. From all the domain controllers, install the Azure AD Password Protection DC Agent.
F. From Active Directory, modify the Default Domain Policy.

Section: (none)
Explanation

Explanation/Reference:
Explanation:
Azure AD password protection is a feature that enhances password policies in an organization. On-premises deployment of password protection uses both the global and custom banned-password lists that are stored in Azure AD. It does the same checks on-premises as Azure AD does for cloud-based changes. These checks are performed during password changes and password reset scenarios.

You need to install the Azure AD Password Protection Proxy on a domain controller and install the Azure AD Password Protection DC Agent on all domain controllers. When the proxy and agent are installed and configured, Azure AD password protection will work.

In the exhibit, the password protection is configured in Audit mode. This is used for testing. To enforce the configured policy, you need to set the password protection setting to Enforced.

Reference:
https://docs.microsoft.com/en-us/azure/active-directory/authentication/howto-password-ban-bad-on-premises-deploy

https://docs.microsoft.com/en-us/azure/active-directory/authentication/concept-password-ban-bad-on-premises

QUESTION 33
You have a Microsoft Azure Active Directory (Azure AD) tenant named contoso.onmicrosoft.com.

An external user has a Microsoft account that uses an email address of user1@outlook.com.

An administrator named Admin1 attempts to create a user account for the external user and receives the error message shown in the following exhibit.

> ! Unable to invite user User1@outlook.c... 6:12 PM
>
> You do not have permission to invite external users. Contact your administrator to get permission.

You need to ensure that Admin1 can add the user.

What should you do from the Azure Active Directory admin center?

A. Add a custom domain name named outlook.com.
B. Modify the Authentication methods.
C. Modify the External collaboration settings.
D. Assign Admin1 the Security administrator role.

Section: (none)
Explanation

Explanation/Reference:
Explanation:
In the External Collaboration settings, you can set the following invitation policies:
- Turn off invitations
- Only admins and users in the Guest Inviter role can invite
- Admins, the Guest Inviter role, and members can invite
- All users, including guests, can invite

In this question, an Admin user is unable to invite the guest user. This suggests that invitations are turned off altogether.

Reference:
https://docs.microsoft.com/en-us/azure/active-directory/b2b/delegate-invitations

Testlet 2

This is a case study. **Case studies are not timed separately. You can use as much exam time as you would like to complete each case**. However, there may be additional case studies and sections on this exam. You must manage your time to ensure that you are able to complete all questions included on this exam in the time provided.

To answer the questions included in a case study, you will need to reference information that is provided in the case study. Case studies might contain exhibits and other resources that provide more information about the scenario that is described in the case study. Each question is independent of the other questions in this case study.

At the end of this case study, a review screen will appear. This screen allows you to review your answer and to make changes before you move to the next section of the exam. After you begin a new section, you cannot return to this section.

To start the case study
To display the first question in this case study, click the **Next** button. Use the buttons in the left pane to explore the content of the case study before you answer the questions. Clicking these buttons displays information such as business requirements, existing environment, and problem statements. When you are ready to answer a question, click the **Question** button to return to the question.

Overview
Contoso, Ltd. is a consulting company that has a main office in Montreal and two branch offices in Seattle and New York.

The offices have the users and devices shown in the following table.

Office	Users	Laptops	Desktops	Mobile devices
Montreal	2,500	2,800	300	3,100
Seattle	1,000	1,100	200	1,500
New York	300	320	30	400

Contoso recently purchased a Microsoft 365 E5 subscription.

Existing Environment
The network contains an Active directory forest named contoso.com and a Microsoft Azure Active Directory (Azure AD) tenant named contoso.onmicrosoft.com.

You recently configured the forest to sync to the Azure AD tenant. You

add and then verify adatum.com as an additional domain name. All

servers run Windows Server 2016.

All desktop computers and laptops run Windows 10 Enterprise and are joined to contoso.com.

All the mobile devices in the Montreal and Seattle offices run Android. All the mobile devices in the New York office run iOS.

Contoso has the users shown in the following table.

Name	Role
User1	*None*
User2	*None*
User3	Customer Lockbox access approver
User4	*None*

Contoso has the groups shown in the following table.

Name	Type	Membership rule
Group1	Assigned	*Not applicable*
Group 2	Dynamic	(user.department –eq "Finance")

Microsoft Office 365 licenses are assigned only to Group2.

The network also contains external users from a vendor company who have Microsoft accounts that use a suffix of @outlook.com.

Requirements

Planned Changes
Contoso plans to provide email addresses for all the users in the following domains:

- East.adatum.com
- Contoso.adatum.com
- Humongousinsurance.com

Technical Requirements
Contoso identifies the following technical requirements:

- All new users must be assigned Office 365 licenses automatically.
- The principle of least privilege must be used whenever possible.

Security Requirements
Contoso identifies the following security requirements:

- Vendors must be able to authenticate by using their Microsoft account when accessing Contoso resources.
- User2 must be able to view reports and schedule the email delivery of security and compliance reports.

- The members of Group1 must be required to answer a security question before changing their password.
- User3 must be able to manage Office 365 connectors.
- User4 must be able to reset User3 password.

QUESTION 1
You need to meet the security requirement for Group1.

What should you do?

A. Configure all users to sign in by using multi-factor authentication.
B. Modify the properties of Group1.
C. Assign Group1 a management role.
D. Modify the Password reset properties of the Azure AD tenant.

Section: (none)
Explanation

Explanation/Reference:
Explanation:
- The members of Group1 must be required to answer a security question before changing their password.

If SSPR (Self Service Password Reset) is enabled, you must select at least one of the following options for the authentication methods. Sometimes you hear these options referred to as "gates."

Mobile app notification
Mobile app code Email
Mobile phone Office
phone Security
questions

You can specify the required authentication methods in the Password reset properties of the Azure AD tenant. In this case, you should set the required authentication method to be 'Security questions'.

Reference:
https://docs.microsoft.com/en-us/azure/active-directory/authentication/concept-sspr-howitworks

QUESTION 2
You need to meet the security requirement for the vendors.

What should you do?

A. From the Azure portal, add an identity provider.
B. From Azure Cloud Shell, run the `New-AzureADUser` cmdlet and specify the `–UserPrincipalName` parameter.

C. From Azure Cloud Shell, run the `Set-AzureADUserExtension` cmdlet.

D. From the Azure portal, create guest accounts.

Section: (none)
Explanation

Explanation/Reference:
Explanation:

- Vendors must be able to authenticate by using their Microsoft account when accessing Contoso resources.

You can invite guest users to the directory, to a group, or to an application. After you invite a user through any of these methods, the invited user's account is added to Azure Active Directory (Azure AD), with a user type of Guest. The guest user must then redeem their invitation to access resources. An invitation of a user does not expire.
The invitation will include a link to create a Microsoft account. The user can then authenticate using their Microsoft account. In this question, the vendors already have Microsoft accounts so they can authenticate using them.

Reference:
https://docs.microsoft.com/en-us/azure/active-directory/b2b/add-users-administrator

QUESTION 3
You need to meet the security requirement for the vendors.

What should you do?

A. From Azure Cloud Shell, run the `Set-MsolUserPrincipalName` and specify the – `tenantID` parameter.

B. From Azure Cloud Shell, run the `Set-AzureADUserExtension` cmdlet.

C. Azure Cloud Shell, run the `New-AzureADUser` cmdlet and specify the – `UserPrincipalName` parameter.

D. From Azure Cloud Shell, run the `New-AzureADMSInvitation` cmdlet and specify the – `InvitedUserEmailAddress` parameter.

Section: (none)
Explanation

Explanation/Reference:
Explanation:

- Vendors must be able to authenticate by using their Microsoft account when accessing Contoso resources.

You can invite guest users to the directory, to a group, or to an application. After you invite a user through any of these methods, the invited user's account is added to Azure Active Directory (Azure AD), with a user type of Guest. The guest user must then redeem their invitation to access resources. An invitation of a user does not expire.
The invitation will include a link to create a Microsoft account. The user can then authenticate using their Microsoft account. In this question, the vendors already have Microsoft accounts so

they can authenticate using them.

In this solution, we are creating guest account invitations by using the `New-AzureADMSInvitation` cmdlet and specifying the `-InvitedUserEmailAddress` parameter.

Reference:
https://docs.microsoft.com/en-us/azure/active-directory/b2b/add-users-administrator

https://docs.microsoft.com/en-us/powershell/module/azuread/new-azureadmsinvitation?view=azureadps-2.0

Manage Access and Authentication

Testlet 3

This is a case study. **Case studies are not timed separately. You can use as much exam time as you would like to complete each case**. However, there may be additional case studies and sections on this exam. You must manage your time to ensure that you are able to complete all questions included on this exam in the time provided.

To answer the questions included in a case study, you will need to reference information that is provided in the case study. Case studies might contain exhibits and other resources that provide more information about the scenario that is described in the case study. Each question is independent of the other questions in this case study.

At the end of this case study, a review screen will appear. This screen allows you to review your answer and to make changes before you move to the next section of the exam. After you begin a new section, you cannot return to this section.

To start the case study
To display the first question in this case study, click the **Next** button. Use the buttons in the left pane to explore the content of the case study before you answer the questions. Clicking these buttons displays information such as business requirements, existing environment, and problem statements. When you are ready to answer a question, click the **Question** button to return to the question.

Overview
Fabrikam, Inc. is an electronics company that produces consumer products. Fabrikam has 10,000 employees worldwide.

Fabrikam has a main office in London and branch offices in major cities in Europe, Asia, and the United States.

Existing Environment
Active Directory Environment
The network contains an Active Directory forest named fabrikam.com. The forest contains all the identities used for user and computer authentication.

Each department is represented by a top-level organizational unit (OU) that contains several child OUs for user accounts and computer accounts.

All users authenticate to on-premises applications by signing in to their device by using a UPN format of *username@fabrikam.com*.

Fabrikam does **NOT** plan to implement identity federation.

Network Infrastructure

Each office has a high-speed connection to the Internet.

Each office contains two domain controllers. All domain controllers are configured as a DNS server.

The public zone for fabrikam.com is managed by an external DNS server.

All users connect to an on-premises Microsoft Exchange Server 2016 organization. The users access their email by using Outlook Anywhere, Outlook on the web, or the Microsoft Outlook app for iOS. All the Exchange servers have the latest cumulative updates installed.

All shared company documents are stored on a Microsoft SharePoint Server farm.

Requirements
Planned Changes
Fabrikam plans to implement a Microsoft 365 Enterprise subscription and move all email and shared documents to the subscription.

Fabrikam plans to implement two pilot projects:

- Project1: During Project1, the mailboxes of 100 users in the sales department will be moved to Microsoft 365.
- Project2: After the successful completion of Project1, Microsoft Teams & Skype for Business will be enabled in Microsoft 365 for the sales department users.

Fabrikam plans to create a group named UserLicenses that will manage the allocation of all Microsoft 365 bulk licenses.

Technical Requirements
Fabrikam identifies the following technical requirements:

- All users must be able to exchange email messages successfully during Project1 by using their current email address.
- Users must be able to authenticate to cloud services if Active Directory becomes unavailable.
- A user named User1 must be able to view all DLP reports from the Microsoft 365 admin center.
- Microsoft Office 365 ProPlus applications must be installed from a network share only.
- Disruptions to email access must be minimized.

Application Requirements
Fabrikam identifies the following application requirements:

- An on-premises web application named App1 must allow users to complete their expense reports online. App1 must be available to users from the My Apps portal.
- The installation of feature updates for Office 365 ProPlus must be minimized.

Security Requirements
Fabrikam identifies the following security requirements:

- After the planned migration to Microsoft 365, all users must continue to authenticate to their mailbox and to SharePoint sites by using their UPN.
- The memberships of UserLicenses must be validated monthly. Unused user accounts must be removed from the group automatically.
- After the planned migration to Microsoft 365, all users must be signed in to on-premises and cloud-based applications automatically.
- The principle of least privilege must be used.

QUESTION 1

You need to meet the application requirement for App1.

Which three actions should you perform? Each correct answer presents part of the solution.

NOTE: Each correct selection is worth one point.

A. From the Azure Active Directory admin center, configure the application URL settings.
B. From the Azure Active Directory admin center, add an enterprise application.
C. On an on-premises server, download and install the Microsoft AAD Application Proxy connector.
D. On an on-premises server, install the Hybrid Configuration wizard.
E. From the Microsoft 365 admin center, configure the Software download settings.

Section: (none)
Explanation

Explanation/Reference:
Explanation:
- An on-premises web application named App1 must allow users to complete their expense reports online. App1 must be available to users from the My Apps portal.

Application Proxy is a feature of Azure AD that enables users to access on-premises web applications from a remote client. Application Proxy includes both the Application Proxy service which runs in the cloud, and the Application Proxy connector which runs on an on-premises server. Azure AD, the Application Proxy service, and the Application Proxy connector work together to securely pass the user sign-on token from Azure AD to the web application.

In this question, we need to add an enterprise application in Azure and configure a Microsoft AAD Application Proxy connector to connect to the on-premises web application (App1).

Reference:
https://docs.microsoft.com/en-us/azure/active-directory/manage-apps/application-proxy#how-application-proxy-works

QUESTION 2

You need to ensure that all the sales department users can authenticate successfully during Project1 and Project2.

Which authentication strategy should you implement for the pilot projects?

A. password hash synchronization and seamless SSO
B. pass-through authentication
C. password hash synchronization
D. pass-through authentication and seamless SSO

Section: (none)
Explanation

Explanation/Reference:
Explanation:
- Project1: During Project1, the mailboxes of 100 users in the sales department will be moved to Microsoft 365.
- Project2: After the successful completion of Project1, Microsoft Teams & Skype for Business will be enabled in Microsoft 365 for the sales department users.
- After the planned migration to Microsoft 365, all users must be signed in to on-premises and cloud-based applications automatically.
- Fabrikam does NOT plan to implement identity federation.
- After the planned migration to Microsoft 365, all users must continue to authenticate to their mailbox and to SharePoint sites by using their UPN.

You need to enable password hash synchronization to enable the users to continue to authenticate to their mailbox and to SharePoint sites by using their UPN.

You need to enable SSO to enable all users to be signed in to on-premises and cloud-based applications automatically.

Reference:
https://docs.microsoft.com/en-us/azure/security/azure-ad-choose-authn

Plan Office 365 Workloads and Applications

Question Set 1

QUESTION 1
You have a Microsoft Azure Active Directory (Azure AD) tenant named contoso.com.

You add an app named App1 to the enterprise applications in contoso.com.

You need to configure self-service app access for App1.

What should you do first?

A. Assign App1 to users and groups.
B. Add an owner to App1.
C. Configure the provisioning mode for App1.
D. Configure an SSO method for App1.

Section: (none)
Explanation

Explanation/Reference:
Explanation:
The provisioning mode (manual or automatic) needs to be configured for an app before you can enable self-service application access.

Incorrect Answers:
A: If you're assign App1 to users and groups, the users will not need to use self-service to request access to the App. They would already have access to the app.
B: The app does not need an owner. You would configure an owner to delegate control of the app. Without an owner, a Global Admin could configure self-service.
D: The SSO method depends on the provisioning mode.

Reference:
https://docs.microsoft.com/en-us/azure/active-directory/manage-apps/manage-self-service-access

https://techcommunity.microsoft.com/t5/Azure-Active-Directory-Identity/Employee-Self-Service-App-Access-for-Azure-AD-now-in-preview/ba-p/243966

QUESTION 2
Note: This question is part of a series of questions that present the same scenario. Each question in the series contains a unique solution that might meet the stated goals. Some question sets might have more than one correct solution, while others might not have a correct solution.

After you answer a question in this section, you will NOT be able to return to it. As a result, these questions will not appear in the review screen.

Your company has a main office and three branch offices. All the branch offices connect to the main office by using a WAN link. The main office has a high-speed Internet connection. All the branch offices connect to the Internet by using the main office connection.

Users use Microsoft Outlook 2016 to connect to a Microsoft Exchange Server mailbox hosted in the main office.

The users report that when the WAN link in their office becomes unavailable, they cannot access their mailbox.

You create a Microsoft 365 subscription, and then migrate all the user data to Microsoft 365.

You need to ensure that all the users can continue to use Outlook to receive email messages if a WAN link fails.

Solution: You deploy a site-to-site VPN from each branch office to Microsoft Azure.

Does this meet the goal?

A. Yes
B. No

Section: (none)
Explanation

Explanation/Reference:
Explanation:
The question states that the branch offices connect to the Internet by using the main office connections. Therefore, all Internet traffic goes over the WAN link between the branch office and main office.
After the migration, the users connect to their mailboxes hosted in Exchange Online over the Internet and therefore over the WAN link.

If the WAN link goes down, the branch office users will not be able to connect to the Internet and therefore will not be able to access their email using Outlook.

A site-to-site VPN from each branch office to Microsoft Azure would still use the WAN link so this answer does achieve the goal.

The solution is to add a direct connection to the Internet from the branch offices, so their Internet traffic does not go over the WAN link.

QUESTION 3
You have a Microsoft 365 subscription.

Your company purchases a new financial application named App1.

From Cloud Discovery in Microsoft Cloud App Security, you view the Discovered apps page and discover that many applications have a low score because they are missing information about domain registration and consumer popularity.

You need to prevent the missing information from affecting the score.

What should you configure from the Cloud Discover settings?

A. App tags
B. Score metrics
C. Organization details
D. Default behavior

Section: (none)
Explanation

Explanation/Reference:
Explanation:
An app's score in Cloud Discovery is based on categories such as General, Security, Compliance and Legal. Each category has several parameters. For example, the domain registration and consumer popularity parameters are part of the General category. These parameters are known as Score Metrics.

You can modify the default weights given to the Cloud Discovery score configuration. By default, all the various parameters evaluated are given an equal weight. If there are certain parameters that are more or less important to your organization, you can adjust the weight of each score metric.

In this case, we need to lower the weight of the domain registration and consumer popularity score metrics.

Reference:
https://docs.microsoft.com/en-us/cloud-app-security/risk-score

QUESTION 4
Your company has an on-premises Microsoft Exchange Server 2013 organization. The

company has 100 users.

The company purchases Microsoft 365 and plans to move its entire infrastructure to the cloud.

The company does **NOT** plan to sync the on-premises Active Directory domain to Microsoft Azure Active Directory (Azure AD).

You need to recommend which type of migration to use to move all email messages, contacts, and calendar items to Exchange Online.

What should you recommend?

A. cutover migration
B. IMAP migration
C. remote move migration
D. staged migration

Explanation:
A cutover migration and an IMAP migration do not require the company to sync the on-premises Active Directory domain to Microsoft Azure Active Directory (Azure AD). Only a cutover migration meets the requirements in this question.
With a cutover migration, user accounts will need to be created in Azure Active Directory for each user. The mailboxes are all migrated in one go and MX records configured to redirect email to Microsoft 365.

Incorrect Answers:
B: Contacts, calendar items and tasks cannot be migrated with an IMAP migration.
C: A remote move migration requires a hybrid exchange configuration which requires that the on-premises Active Directory domain is synced to Microsoft Azure Active Directory (Azure AD).
D: A staged migration is recommended when your source email system is Microsoft Exchange Server 2003 or Microsoft Exchange Server 2007. You can't use a staged migration to migrate Exchange 2013 or Exchange 2010 mailboxes to Office 365. A staged migration also requires that the on-premises Active Directory domain is synced to Microsoft Azure Active Directory (Azure AD).

Reference:
https://docs.microsoft.com/en-us/exchange/mailbox-migration/cutover-migration-to-office-365

https://docs.microsoft.com/en-us/exchange/mailbox-migration/what-to-know-about-a-staged-migration

QUESTION 5
Your on-premises network contains five file servers. The file servers host shares that contain user data.

You plan to migrate the user data to a Microsoft 365 subscription.

You need to recommend a solution to import the user data into Microsoft OneDrive.

What should you include in the recommendation?

A. Configure the settings of the OneDrive client on your Windows 10 device.
B. Configure the Sync settings in the OneDrive admin center.
C. Run the SharePoint Hybrid Configuration Wizard.
D. Run the SharePoint Migration Tool.

Explanation:
The SharePoint Migration Tool lets you migrate content to SharePoint Online and OneDrive from the following locations:

- SharePoint Server 2013
- SharePoint Server 2010
- Network and local file shares

Reference:
https://docs.microsoft.com/en-us/sharepointmigration/introducing-the-sharepoint-migration-tool

EXAM 2

Design and Implement Microsoft 365 Services

Question Set 1

QUESTION 1
Note: This question is part of a series of questions that present the same scenario. Each question in the series contains a unique solution that might meet the stated goals. Some question sets might have more than one correct solution, while others might not have a correct solution.

After you answer a question in this section, you will NOT be able to return to it. As a result, these questions will not appear in the review screen.

Your company has a Microsoft Office 365 tenant.

You suspect that several Office 365 features were recently updated.

You need to view a list of the features that were recently updated in the tenant.

Solution: You review the Security & Compliance report in the Microsoft 365 admin center.

Does this meet the goal?

A. Yes
B. No

Section: (none)
Explanation

Explanation/Reference:
Explanation:
The **Security & Compliance reports** in the Microsoft 365 admin center are reports regarding security and compliance for your Office 365 Services. For example, email usage reports, Data Loss Prevention reports etc. They do not display a list of the features that were recently updated in the tenant so this solution does not meet the goal.

To meet the goal, you need to use **Message center** in the Microsoft 365 admin center.

Reference:
https://docs.microsoft.com/en-us/microsoft-365/security/office-365-security/download-existing-reports

QUESTION 2
You recently migrated your on-premises email solution to Microsoft Exchange Online and are evaluating which licenses to purchase.

You want the members of two groups named IT and Managers to be able to use the features shown in the following table.

Feature	Available to
Microsoft Azure Active Directory (Azure AD) conditional access	IT group, Managers group
Microsoft Azure Active Directory (Azure AD) Privileged Identity Management	IT group

The IT group contains 50 users. The Managers group contains 200 users.

You need to recommend which licenses must be purchased for the planned solution. The solution must minimize licensing costs.

Which licenses should you recommend?

A. 250 Microsoft 365 E3 only
B. 50 Microsoft 365 E3 and 200 Microsoft 365 E5
C. 250 Microsoft 365 E5 only
D. 200 Microsoft 365 E3 and 50 Microsoft 365 E5

Section: (none)
Explanation

Explanation/Reference:
Explanation:
Microsoft Azure Active Directory Privileged Identity Management requires an Azure AD Premium P2 license. This license comes as part of the Microsoft 365 E5 license. Therefore, we need 50 Microsoft 365 E5 licenses for the IT group.
Conditional Access requires the Azure AD Premium P1 license. This comes as part of the Microsoft E3 license. Therefore, we need 200 Microsoft 365 E3 licenses for the Managers group.

Reference:
https://docs.microsoft.com/en-us/azure/active-directory/privileged-identity-management/subscription-requirements

QUESTION 3
You have a Microsoft 365 tenant that contains Microsoft Exchange Online.

You plan to enable calendar sharing with a partner organization named adatum.com. The partner organization also has a Microsoft 365 tenant.

You need to ensure that the calendar of every user is available to the users in adatum.com immediately.

What should you do?

A. From the Exchange admin center, create a sharing policy.

B. From the Exchange admin center, create a new organization relationship.
C. From the Microsoft 365 admin center, modify the Organization profile settings.
D. From the Microsoft 365 admin center, configure external site sharing.

Section: (none)
Explanation

Explanation/Reference:
Explanation:
You need to set up an organization relationship to share calendar information with an external business partner. Office 365 admins can set up an organization relationship with another Office 365 organization or with an Exchange on-premises organization.

Reference:
https://docs.microsoft.com/en-us/exchange/sharing/organization-relationships/create-an-organization-relationship

QUESTION 4
Your company has an on-premises Microsoft Exchange Server 2016 organization and a Microsoft 365 Enterprise subscription.

You plan to migrate mailboxes and groups to Exchange Online. You

start a new migration batch.

Users report slow performance when they use the on-premises Exchange Server organization.

You discover that the migration is causing the slow performance.

You need to reduce the impact of the mailbox migration on the end-users.

What should you do?

A. Create a mail flow rule.
B. Configure back pressure.
C. Modify the migration endpoint settings.
D. Create a throttling policy.

Section: (none)
Explanation

Explanation/Reference:
Explanation:
The migration is causing the slow performance. This suggests that the on-premise Exchange server is struggling under the load of copying the mailboxes to Exchange Online. You can reduce the load on the on-premise server by reducing the maximum number of concurrent mailbox migrations. Migrating just a few mailboxes at a time will have less of a performance impact than migrating many mailboxes concurrently.

Reference:

https://support.microsoft.com/en-gb/help/2797784/how-to-manage-the-maximum-concurrent-migration-batches-in-exchange-onl

QUESTION 5

You have a Microsoft 365 subscription.

You need to prevent phishing email messages from being delivered to your organization.

What should you do?

A. From the Exchange admin center, create an anti-malware policy.
B. From Security & Compliance, create a DLP policy.
C. From Security & Compliance, create a new threat management policy.
D. From the Exchange admin center, create a spam filter policy.

Section: (none)
Explanation

Explanation/Reference:
Explanation:
Anti-phishing protection is part of Office 365 Advanced Threat Protection (ATP). To prevent phishing email messages from being delivered to your organization, you need to configure a threat management policy.

ATP anti-phishing is only available in Advanced Threat Protection (ATP). ATP is included in subscriptions, such as Microsoft 365 Enterprise, Microsoft 365 Business, Office 365 Enterprise E5, Office 365 Education A5, etc.

Reference:
https://docs.microsoft.com/en-us/office365/securitycompliance/set-up-anti-phishing-policies

QUESTION 6

Your company has a Microsoft 365 subscription. All identities are managed in the cloud.

The company purchases a new domain name.

You need to ensure that all new mailboxes use the new domain as their primary email address.

What are two possible ways to achieve the goal? Each correct answer presents a complete solution.

NOTE: Each correct selection is worth one point.

A. Run the `Update-EmailAddressPolicy` Windows PowerShell command
B. From the Exchange admin center, click mail flow, and then configure the email address policies.
C. From the Microsoft 365 admin center, click Setup, and then configure the domains.
D. Run the `Set-EmailAddressPolicy` Windows PowerShell command.
E. From the Azure Active Directory admin center, configure the custom domain names.

Section: (none)
Explanation

Explanation/Reference:
Explanation:
Email address policies define the rules that create email addresses for recipients in your Exchange organization whether this is Exchange on-premise or Exchange online.

You can configure email address policies using the graphical interface of the Exchange Admin Center or by using PowerShell with the `Set-EmailAddressPolicy` cmdlet.

The `Set-EmailAddressPolicy` cmdlet is used to modify an email address policy. The `Update-EmailAddressPolicy` cmdlet is used to apply an email address policy to users.

Reference:
https://docs.microsoft.com/en-us/exchange/email-addresses-and-address-books/email-address-policies/email-address-policies?view=exchserver-2019

QUESTION 7
Your company has a Microsoft Azure Active Directory (Azure AD) tenant named contoso.com that includes the users shown in the following table.

Name	Usage location	Membership
User1	United States	Group1, Group2
User2	*Not set*	Group2
User3	*Not set*	Group1
User4	Canada	Group1

Group2 is a member of Group1.

You assign a Microsoft Office 365 Enterprise E3 license to Group1.

You need to identity how many Office 365 E3 licenses are assigned.

How many Office 365 E3 licenses are assigned?

A. 1
B. 2
C. 3
D. 4

Section: (none)
Explanation

Explanation/Reference:

Explanation:
Group-based licensing currently does not support groups that contain other groups (nested groups). If you apply a license to a nested group, only the immediate first-level user members of the group have the licenses applied. Therefore, User2 will not be assigned a license.

When Azure AD assigns group licenses, any users without a specified usage location inherit the location of the directory. Therefore, User3 will be assigned a license and his usage location will be set to the location of the directory.

Reference:
https://docs.microsoft.com/en-us/azure/active-directory/users-groups-roles/licensing-groups-assign

https://docs.microsoft.com/en-us/azure/active-directory/users-groups-roles/licensing-group-advanced

QUESTION 8
You have a Microsoft 365 subscription.

A new corporate security policy states that you must automatically send DLP incident reports to the users in the legal department.

You need to schedule the email delivery of the reports. The solution must ensure that the reports are sent as frequently as possible.

How frequently can you share the reports?

A. hourly
B. monthly
C. weekly
D. daily

Section: (none)
Explanation

Explanation/Reference:
Explanation:
From the Dashboard in the Security and Compliance center, you can view various reports including the DLP Incidents report. From there you can configure a schedule to email the reports. In the schedule configuration, there are two choices for the frequency: Weekly or Monthly. Therefore, to ensure that the reports are sent as frequently as possible, you need to select Weekly.

Reference:
https://docs.microsoft.com/en-us/microsoft-365/security/office-365-security/create-a-schedule- for-a-report

QUESTION 9
Your company has a Microsoft 365 subscription.

You upload several archive PST files to Microsoft 365 by using the Security & Compliance admin center.

A month later, you attempt to run an import job for the PST files.

You discover that the PST files were deleted from Microsoft 365.

What is the most likely cause of the files being deleted? More than one answer choice may achieve the goal. Select the **BEST** answer.

A. The PST files were corrupted and deleted by Microsoft 365 security features.
B. PST files are deleted automatically from Microsoft 365 after 30 days.
C. The size of the PST files exceeded a storage quota and caused the files to be deleted.
D. Another administrator deleted the PST files.

Section: (none)
Explanation

Explanation/Reference:
Explanation:
You can use the Office 365 Import Service to bulk-import PST files to Office 365 mailboxes.

When you use the network upload method to import PST files, you upload them to an Azure blob container named ingestiondata. If there are no import jobs in progress on the Import page in the Security & Compliance Center), then all PST files in the ingestiondata container in Azure are deleted 30 days after the most recent import job was created in the Security & Compliance Center.

Reference:
https://docs.microsoft.com/en-us/office365/securitycompliance/faqimporting-pst-files-to-office-365

QUESTION 10
Your company has a main office and 20 branch offices in North America and Europe. Each branch office connects to the main office by using a WAN link. All the offices connect to the Internet and resolve external host names by using the main office connections.

You plan to deploy Microsoft 365 and to implement a direct Internet connection in each office.

You need to recommend a change to the infrastructure to provide the quickest possible access to Microsoft 365 services.

What is the best recommendation to achieve the goal? More than one answer choice may achieve the goal. Select the **BEST** answer.

A. For all the client computers in the branch offices, modify the MTU setting by using a Group Policy object (GPO).
B. In each branch office, deploy a proxy server that has user authentication enabled.
C. In each branch office, deploy a firewall that has packet inspection enabled.
D. In each branch office, configure name resolution so that all external hosts are redirected to

public DNS servers directly.

Explanation/Reference:
Explanation:
Being a cloud service, Office 365 would be classed as an external host to the office computers.

All the offices connect to the Internet and resolve external host names by using the main office connections. This means that all branch office computers perform DNS lookups and connect to the Internet over the WAN link.

Each branch office will have a direct connection to the Internet so the quickest possible access to Microsoft 365 services would be by using the direct Internet connections. However, the DNS lookups would still go over the WAN links to main office. The solution to provide the quickest possible access to Microsoft 365 services is to configure DNS name resolution so that the computers use public DNS servers for external hosts. That way DNS lookups for Office 365 and the connections to Office 365 will use the direct Internet connections.

QUESTION 11
Your network contains an Active Directory forest named adatum.local. The forest contains 500 users and uses adatum.com as a UPN suffix.

You deploy a Microsoft 365 tenant.

You implement directory synchronization and sync only 50 support users.

You discover that five of the synchronized users have usernames that use a UPN suffix of onmicrosoft.com.

You need to ensure that all synchronized identities retain the UPN set in their on-premises user account.

What should you do?

A. From the Microsoft 365 admin center, add adatum.com as a custom domain name.
B. From Windows PowerShell, run the `Set-ADDomain -AllowedDNSSuffixes adatum.com` command.
C. From Active Directory Users and Computers, modify the UPN suffix of the five user accounts.
D. From the Microsoft 365 admin center, add adatum.local as a custom domain name.

Explanation/Reference:
Explanation:
The question states that only five of the synchronized users have usernames that use a UPN suffix of onmicrosoft.com. Therefore the other 45 users have the correct UPN suffix. This tells

us that the adatum.com domain has already been added to Office 365 as a custom domain. The forest is named adatum.local and uses adatum.com as a UPN suffix. User accounts in the domain will have adatum.local as their default UPN suffix. To use adatum.com as the UPN suffix, each user account will need to be configured to use adatum.com as the UPN suffix. Any synchronized user account that has adatum.local as a UPN suffix will be configured to use a UPN suffix of onmicrosoft.com because adatum.local cannot be added to Office 365 as a custom domain.

Therefore, the reason that the five synchronized users have usernames with a UPN suffix of onmicrosoft.com is because their accounts were not configured to use the UPN suffix of contoso.com.

Reference:
https://docs.microsoft.com/en-us/office365/enterprise/prepare-a-non-routable-domain-for-directory-synchronization

QUESTION 12

Your company has on-premises servers and a Microsoft Azure Active Directory (Azure AD) tenant.

Several months ago, the Azure AD Connect Health agent was installed on all the servers.

You review the health status of all the servers regularly.

Recently, you attempted to view the health status of a server named Server1 and discovered that the server is **NOT** listed on the Azure Active Directory Connect Servers list.

You suspect that another administrator removed Server1 from the list.

You need to ensure that you can view the health status of Server1.

What are two possible ways to achieve the goal? Each correct answer presents a complete solution.

NOTE: Each correct selection is worth one point.

A. From Windows PowerShell, run the
   `Register-AzureADConnectHealthSyncAgent` cmdlet.
B. From Azure Cloud shell, run the `Connect-AzureAD` cmdlet.
C. From Server1, change the Azure AD Connect Health services Startup type to **Automatic (Delayed Start)**.
D. From Server1, change the Azure AD Connect Health services Startup type to **Automatic**.
E. From Server1, reinstall the Azure AD Connect Health agent.

Section: (none)
Explanation

Explanation/Reference:
Explanation:
question states that another administrator removed Server1 from the list. To view the health status of Server1, you need to re-register the AD Connect Health Sync Agent. You can do this

manually by running the `Register-AzureADConnectHealthSyncAgent` cmdlet. Alternatively, you can reinstall the Azure AD Connect Health agent. The Azure AD Connect Health agent is registered as part of the installation.

Reference:
https://docs.microsoft.com/en-us/azure/active-directory/hybrid/how-to-connect-health-agent-install

QUESTION 13
You have a Microsoft 365 subscription.

You suspect that several Microsoft Office 365 applications or services were recently updated.

You need to identify which applications or services were recently updated.

What are two possible ways to achieve the goal? Each correct answer presents a complete solution.

NOTE: Each correct selection is worth one point.

    A. From the Microsoft 365 admin center, review the Message center blade.
    B. From the Office 365 Admin mobile app, review the messages.
    C. From the Microsoft 365 admin center, review the Products blade.
    D. From the Microsoft 365 admin center, review the Service health blade.

Section: (none)
Explanation

Explanation/Reference:
Explanation:
The Message center in the Microsoft 365 admin center is where you would go to view a list of the features that were recently updated in the tenant. This is where Microsoft posts official messages with information including new and changed features, planned maintenance, or other important announcements.
The messages displayed in the Message center can also be viewed by using the Office 365 Admin mobile app.

Reference:
https://docs.microsoft.com/en-us/office365/admin/manage/message-center?view=o365-worldwide

https://docs.microsoft.com/en-us/office365/admin/admin-overview/admin-mobile-app?view=o365-worldwide

QUESTION 14
Note: This question is part of a series of questions that present the same scenario. Each question in the series contains a unique solution that might meet the stated goals. Some question sets might have more than one correct solution, while others might not have a correct solution.

After you answer a question in this section, you will NOT be able to return to it. As a result, these questions will not appear in the review screen.

Your company has a Microsoft Office 365 tenant.

You suspect that several Office 365 features were recently updated.

You need to view a list of the features that were recently updated in the tenant.

Solution: You use **Monitoring and reports** from the Compliance admin center. Does

this meet the goal?

A. Yes
B. No

Section: (none)
Explanation

Explanation/Reference:
Explanation:
Depending on what your organization's Office 365 subscription includes, the **Dashboard** in Security & Compliance includes several widgets, such as Threat Management Summary, Threat Protection Status, Global Weekly Threat Detections, Malware, etc. The Compliance admin center in Microsoft 365 contains much of the same information but also includes additional entries focusing on alerts, data insights.

The **Monitoring and reports** section from the Compliance admin center does not display a list of the features that were recently updated in the tenant so this solution does not meet the goal.

To meet the goal, you need to use **Message center** in the Microsoft 365 admin center.

Reference:
https://docs.microsoft.com/en-us/office365/admin/manage/message-center?view=o365-worldwide

QUESTION 15
DRAG DROP

Your network contains an on-premises Active Directory domain named contoso.com that is synced to a Microsoft Azure Active Directory (Azure AD) tenant. The on-premises domain contains a server named Server1 that runs Windows Server 2016 and 200 client computers that run Windows 10.

Your company purchases a Microsoft 365 subscription.

On Server1, you create a file share named Share1. You extract the Microsoft Office Deployment Tool (ODT) to Share1.

You need to deploy Office 365 ProPlus, and the French language pack from Share1 to the Windows 10 computers.

Which three actions should you perform in sequence? To answer, move the appropriate actions from the list of actions to the answer area and arrange them in the correct order.

Select and Place:

Actions   Answer Area

| Create an XML configuration file. |
| On Server1, run `setup.exe` and specify the /configure parameter. |
| On every client computer, run `setup.exe` and specify the /configure parameter. |
| On Server1, run `setup.exe` and specify the /package parameter. |
| On every client computer, run `setup.exe` and specify the /download parameter. |
| On Server1, run `setup.exe` and specify the /download parameter. |

Section: (none)
Explanation

Explanation/Reference:
Explanation:

Note:
Step 1: Create an XML configuration file with the source path and download path for the installation files.
Step 2: On the deployment server, run the ODT executable in download mode and with a reference to the XML configuration file.
Step 3: Create another XML configuration file with the source path to the installation files.
Step 4: On the client computer, run the ODT executable in configure mode and with a reference to the XML configuration file.

Reference:
https://docs.microsoft.com/en-us/DeployOffice/overview-of-the-office-2016-deployment-tool

QUESTION 16
Note: This question is part of a series of questions that present the same scenario. Each question in the series contains a unique solution that might meet the stated goals. Some question sets might have more than one correct solution, while others might not have a correct solution.

After you answer a question in this section, you will **NOT** be able to return to it. As a result, these questions will not appear in the review screen.

Your network contains an Active Directory domain named contoso.com that is synced to Microsoft Azure Active Directory (Azure AD).

You manage Windows 10 devices by using Microsoft System Center Configuration Manager (Current Branch).

You configure a pilot for co-management.

You add a new device named Device1 to the domain. You install the Configuration Manager client on Device1.

You need to ensure that you can manage Device1 by using Microsoft Intune and Configuration Manager.

Solution: You add Device1 to an Active Directory group.

Does this meet the goal?

A. Yes
B. No

Section: (none)
Explanation

Explanation/Reference:
Explanation:
Device1 has the Configuration Manager client installed so you can manage Device1 by using Configuration Manager.
To manage Device1 by using Microsoft Intune, the device has to be enrolled in Microsoft Intune. In the Co-management Pilot configuration, you configure a Configuration Manager Device Collection that determines which devices are auto-enrolled in Microsoft Intune. You need to add Device1 to the Device Collection, not an Active Directory Group. Therefore, this solution does not meet the requirements.

Reference:
https://docs.microsoft.com/en-us/configmgr/comanage/how-to-enable

QUESTION 17
Note: This question is part of a series of questions that present the same scenario. Each question in the series contains a unique solution that might meet the stated goals. Some question sets might have more than one correct solution, while others might not have a correct solution.

After you answer a question in this section, you will **NOT** be able to return to it. As a result, these questions will not appear in the review screen.

Your network contains an Active Directory domain named contoso.com that is synced to Microsoft Azure Active Directory (Azure AD).

You manage Windows 10 devices by using Microsoft System Center Configuration Manager (Current Branch).

You configure a pilot for co-management.

You add a new device named Device1 to the domain. You install the Configuration Manager client on Device1.

You need to ensure that you can manage Device1 by using Microsoft Intune and Configuration Manager.

Solution: Define a Configuration Manager device collection as the pilot collection. Add Device1 to the collection.

Does this meet the goal?

A. Yes
B. No

Section: (none)
Explanation

Explanation/Reference:
Explanation:
Device1 has the Configuration Manager client installed so you can manage Device1 by using Configuration Manager.
To manage Device1 by using Microsoft Intune, the device has to be enrolled in Microsoft Intune. In the Co-management Pilot configuration, you configure a Configuration Manager Device Collection that determines which devices are auto-enrolled in Microsoft Intune. You need to add Device1 to the Device Collection so that it auto-enrols in Microsoft Intune. You will then be able to manage Device1 using Microsoft Intune.

Reference:
https://docs.microsoft.com/en-us/configmgr/comanage/how-to-enable

QUESTION 18
You have a Microsoft 365 subscription.

You configure a data loss prevention (DLP) policy.

You discover that users are incorrectly marking content as false positive and bypassing the DLP policy.

You need to prevent the users from bypassing the DLP policy. What

should you configure?

A. actions
B. exceptions

C. incident reports

D. user overrides

Section: (none)
Explanation

Explanation/Reference:
Explanation:
A DLP policy can be configured to allow users to override a policy tip and report a false positive.

You can educate your users about DLP policies and help them remain compliant without blocking their work. For example, if a user tries to share a document containing sensitive information, a DLP policy can both send them an email notification and show them a policy tip in the context of the document library that allows them to override the policy if they have a business justification. The same policy tips also appear in Outlook on the web, Outlook, Excel, PowerPoint, and Word. If you find that users are incorrectly marking content as false positive and bypassing the DLP policy, you can configure the policy to not allow user overrides.

Reference:
https://docs.microsoft.com/en-us/office365/securitycompliance/data-loss-prevention-policies

QUESTION 19
In Microsoft 365, you configure a data loss prevention (DLP) policy named Policy1. Policy1 detects the sharing of United States (US) bank account numbers in email messages and attachments.

Policy1 is configured as shown in the exhibit. (Click the **Exhibit** tab.)

Use actions to protect content when the conditions are met.

Restrict access or encrypt the content

◉ Block people from sharing and resrtrict access to shared content

By default, users are blocked from sending email messages to people. You can choose who has access to shared SharePoint and OneDrive content.

Block these people from accessing SharePoint and OneDrive content

    ○ Everyone. Only the content owner, the lastmodifier, and the site admin will continue to have access.

    ◉ Only people ourtside your organization. People inside your organization will contibue to have access.

○ Encrypt email messages (applies only to content to Exchange)

You need to ensure that internal users can email documents that contain US bank account numbers to external users who have an email suffix of contoso.com.

What should you configure?

A. an action
B. a group
C. a condition
D. an exception

Section: (none)
Explanation

Explanation/Reference:
Explanation:
You need to add an exception. In the Advanced Settings of the DLP policy, you can add a rule to configure the Conditions and Actions. There is also an 'Add Exception' button. This gives you several options that you can select as the exception. One of the options is 'except when recipient domain is'. You need to select that option and enter the domain name contoso.com.

Reference:
https://docs.microsoft.com/en-us/office365/securitycompliance/data-loss-prevention-policies#how-dlp-policies-work

QUESTION 20
Your company uses on-premises Windows Server File Classification Infrastructure 9FCI). Some documents on the on-premises file servers are classifies as Confidential.

You migrate the files from the on-premises file servers to Microsoft SharePoint Online.

You need to ensure that you can implement data loss prevention (DLP) policies for the uploaded files based on the Confidential classification.

What should you do first?

A. From the SharePoint admin center, create a managed property.
B. From the SharePoint admin center, configurehybrid search.
C. From the Security & Compliance Center PowerShell, run the
   `New-DlpComplianceRule` cmdlet.
D. From the Security & Compliance Center PowerShell, run the
   `New-DataClassification` cmdlet.

Section: (none)
Explanation

Explanation/Reference:
Explanation:
Your organization might use Windows Server FCI to identify documents with personally identifiable information (PII) such as social security numbers, and then classify the document by setting the Personally Identifiable Information property to High, Moderate, Low, Public, or Not PII based on the type and number of occurrences of PII found in the document. In Office 365, you can create a DLP policy that identifies documents that have that property set to specific values, such as High and Medium, and then takes an action such as blocking access to those files.

Before you can use a Windows Server FCI property or other property in a DLP policy, you need to create a managed property in the SharePoint admin center.

Reference:
https://docs.microsoft.com/en-us/microsoft-365/compliance/protect-documents-that-have-fci-or-other-properties

QUESTION 21
HOTSPOT

You have a Microsoft Azure Active Directory (Azure AD) tenant named contoso.com.

You have three applications App1, App2, App3. The Apps use files that have the same file extensions.

Your company uses Windows Information Protection (WIP). WIP has the following configurations:

- Windows Information Protection mode: Silent
- Protected apps: App1
- Exempt apps: App2

From App1, you create a file named File1.

What is the effect of the configurations? To answer, select the appropriate options in the answer area.

Hot Area:

Answer Area

You can open File1 from:

App1 only
App1 and App2 only
App1 and App3 only
App1, App2, and App3

An action will be logged when you attempt to open File1 from:

App1 only
App3 only
App1 and App2 only
App2 and App3 only
App1, App2, and App3

Explanation/Reference:
Explanation:

Exempt apps: These apps are exempt from this policy and can access corporate data without restrictions.

Windows Information Protection mode: Silent: WIP runs silently, logging inappropriate data sharing, without stopping anything that would've been prompted for employee interaction while in Allow overrides mode. Unallowed actions, like apps inappropriately trying to access a network resource or WIP-protected data, are still stopped.

Reference:
https://docs.microsoft.com/en-us/intune/apps/windows-information-protection-policy-create

https://docs.microsoft.com/en-us/windows/security/information-protection/windows-information-protection/create-wip-policy-using-intune-azure

QUESTION 22
Your company has 10 offices.

The network contains an Active Directory domain named contoso.com. The domain contains 500 client computers. Each office is configured as a separate subnet.

You discover that one of the offices has the following:

- Computers that have several preinstalled applications
- Computers that use nonstandard computer names
- Computers that have Windows 10 preinstalled
- Computers that are in a workgroup

You must configure the computers to meet the following corporate requirements:

- All the computers must be joined to the domain.
- All the computers must have computer names that use a prefix of CONTOSO.
- All the computers must only have approved corporate applications installed.

You need to recommend a solution to redeploy the computers. The solution must minimize the deployment time.

A. a provisioning package
B. wipe and load refresh
C. Windows Autopilot
D. an in-place upgrade

Section: (none)
Explanation

Explanation/Reference:
Explanation:
By using a provisioning package, IT administrators can create a self-contained package that contains all of the configuration, settings, and apps that need to be applied to a device.

Incorrect Answers:
C: With Windows Autopilot the user can set up pre-configured devices without the need consult their IT administrator.
D: Use the In-Place Upgrade option when you want to keep all (or at least most) existing applications.

Reference:
https://docs.microsoft.com/en-us/windows/deployment/windows-10-deployment-scenarios

https://docs.microsoft.com/en-us/windows/deployment/windows-autopilot/windows-autopilot

QUESTION 23
You have a Microsoft 365 subscription.

You recently configured a Microsoft SharePoint Online tenant in the subscription.

You plan to create an alert policy.

You need to ensure that an alert is generated only when malware is detected in more than five documents stored in SharePoint Online during a period of 10 minutes.

What should you do first?

- A. Enable Microsoft Office 365 Cloud App Security.
- B. Deploy Windows Defender Advanced Threat Protection (Windows Defender ATP).
- C. Enable Microsoft Office 365 Analytics.

Section: (none)
Explanation

Explanation/Reference:
Explanation:
An alert policy consists of a set of rules and conditions that define the user or admin activity that generates an alert, a list of users who trigger the alert if they perform the activity, and a threshold that defines how many times the activity has to occur before an alert is triggered.

In this question, we would use the "Malware detected in file" activity in the alert settings then configure the threshold (5 detections) and the time window (10 minutes).

The ability to configure alert policies based on a threshold or based on unusual activity requires Advanced Threat Protection (ATP).

Reference:
https://docs.microsoft.com/en-us/microsoft-365/compliance/alert-policies

QUESTION 24

From the Microsoft Azure Active Directory (Azure AD) Identity Protection dashboard, you view the risk events shown in the exhibit. (Click the **Exhibit** tab.)

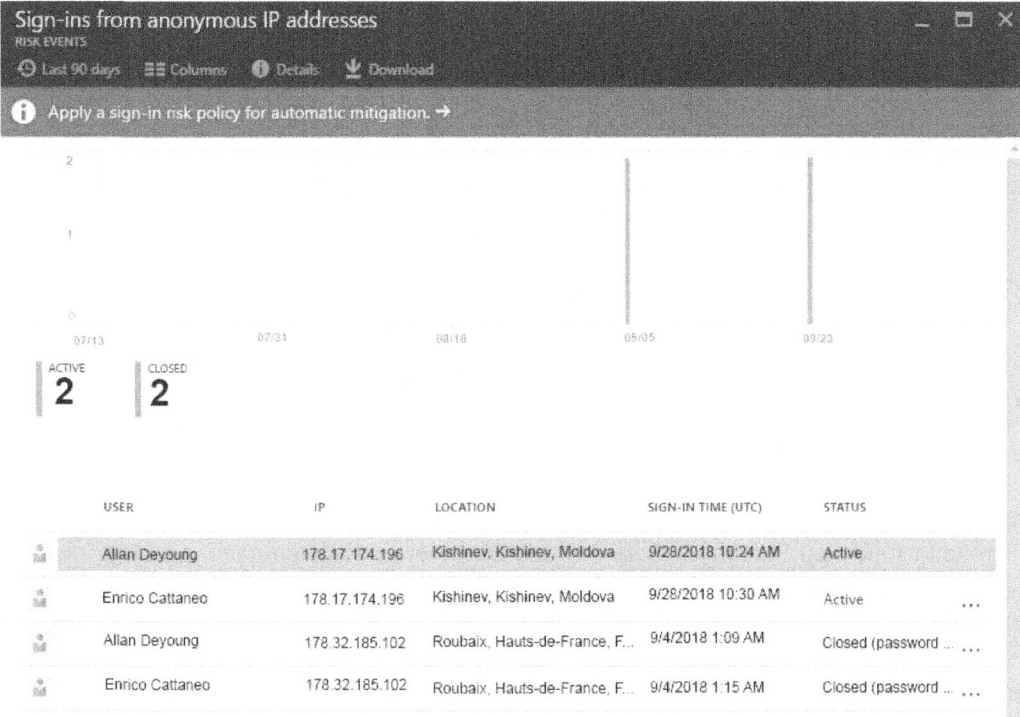

Sign-ins from anonymous IP addresses
RISK EVENTS

🕓 Last 90 days   ☶ Columns   ℹ Details   ⬇ Download

ℹ Apply a sign-in risk policy for automatic mitigation. →

2					
1					
0					
	07/13	07/31	08/18	09/05	09/23

ACTIVE   CLOSED
2   **2**

USER	IP	LOCATION	SIGN-IN TIME (UTC)	STATUS	
Allan Deyoung	178.17.174.196	Kishinev, Kishinev, Moldova	9/28/2018 10:24 AM	Active	
Enrico Cattaneo	178.17.174.196	Kishinev, Kishinev, Moldova	9/28/2018 10:30 AM	Active	...
Allan Deyoung	178.32.185.102	Roubaix, Hauts-de-France, F...	9/4/2018 1:09 AM	Closed (password ...	...
Enrico Cattaneo	178.32.185.102	Roubaix, Hauts-de-France, F...	9/4/2018 1:15 AM	Closed (password ...	...

You need to reduce the likelihood that the sign-ins are identified as risky.

What should you do?

A. From the Security & Compliance admin center, add the users to the Security Readers role group.
B. From the Conditional access blade in the Azure Active Directory admin center, create named locations.
C. From the Azure Active Directory admin center, configure the trusted IPs for multi-factor authentication.
D. From the Security & Compliance admin center, create a classification label.

Section: (none)
Explanation

Explanation/Reference:
Explanation:
A named location can be configured as a trusted location. Typically, trusted locations are network areas that are controlled by your IT department. In addition to Conditional Access,

trusted named locations are also used by Azure Identity Protection and Azure AD security reports to reduce false positives for risky sign-ins.

Reference:
https://docs.microsoft.com/en-us/azure/active-directory/conditional-access/location-condition

QUESTION 25
You have a Microsoft 365 tenant.

You have a line-of-business application named App1 that users access by using the My Apps portal.

After some recent security breaches, you implement a conditional access policy for App1 that uses Conditional Access App Control.

You need to be alerted by email if impossible travel is detected for a user of App1. The solution must ensure that alerts are generated for App1 only.

What should you do?

   A. From Microsoft Cloud App Security, modify the impossible travel alert policy.
   B. From Microsoft Cloud App Security, create a Cloud Discovery anomaly detection policy.
   C. From the Azure Active Directory admin center, modify the conditional access policy.
   D. From Microsoft Cloud App Security, create an app discovery policy.

Section: (none)
Explanation

Explanation/Reference:
Explanation:
Impossible travel detection identifies two user activities (is a single or multiple sessions) originating from geographically distant locations within a time period shorter than the time it would have taken the user to travel from the first location to the second.
We need to modify the policy so that it applies to App1 only.

Reference:
https://docs.microsoft.com/en-us/cloud-app-security/anomaly-detection-policy

QUESTION 26
Your network contains an on-premises Active Directory domain named contoso.com. The domain contains 1,000 Windows 10 devices.

You perform a proof of concept (PoC) deployment of Windows Defender Advanced Threat Protection (ATP) for 10 test devices. During the onboarding process, you configure Windows Defender ATP-related data to be stored in the United States.

You plan to onboard all the devices to Windows Defender ATP data in Europe.

What should you do first?

A. Create a workspace
B. Offboard the test devices
C. Delete the workspace
D. Onboard a new device

Section: (none)
Explanation

Explanation/Reference:
Explanation:
When onboarding Windows Defender ATP for the first time, you can choose to store your data in Microsoft Azure datacenters in the European Union, the United Kingdom, or the United States. Once configured, you cannot change the location where your data is stored.
The only way to change the location is to offboard the test devices then onboard them again with the new location.

Reference:
https://docs.microsoft.com/en-us/windows/security/threat-protection/microsoft-defender-atp/data-storage-privacy#do-i-have-the-flexibility-to-select-where-to-store-my-data

QUESTION 27
You implement Microsoft Azure Advanced Threat Protection (Azure ATP).

You have an Azure ATP sensor configured as shown in the following exhibit.

Updates

Updates

Domain controller restart
during updates
(?)
OFF

NAME	TYPE	VERSION	AUTOM...	DELAYE...	STATUS
LON-DC1	Sensor	2.48.5521	on	on	Up to date

Save

How long after the Azure ATP cloud service is updated will the sensor update?

A. 1 hour
B. 7 days
C. 48 hours
D. 12 hours
E. 72 hours

Section: (none)
Explanation

Explanation/Reference:
Explanation:
The exhibit shows that the sensor is configure for **Delayed update.**
Given the rapid speed of ongoing Azure ATP development and release updates, you may decide
to define a subset group of your sensors as a delayed update ring, allowing for a gradual sensor
update process. Azure ATP enables you to choose how your sensors are updated and set each
sensor as a **Delayed update** candidate.
Sensors not selected for delayed update are updated automatically, each time the Azure ATP
service is updated. Sensors set to **Delayed update** are updated on a delay of 72 hours,
following the official release of each service update.

Reference:
https://docs.microsoft.com/en-us/azure-advanced-threat-protection/sensor-update

QUESTION 28
Your company has a Microsoft 365 E3 subscription.

All devices run Windows 10 Pro and are joined to Microsoft Azure Active Directory (Azure AD).

You need to change the edition of Windows 10 to Enterprise the next time users sign in to their
computer. The solution must minimize downtime for the users.

What should you use?

A. Subscription Activation
B. Windows Update
C. Windows Autopilot
D. an in-place upgrade

Section: (none)
Explanation

Explanation/Reference:
Explanation:
When initially deploying new Windows devices, Windows Autopilot leverages the OEM-
optimized version of Windows 10 that is preinstalled on the device, saving organizations the
effort of having to maintain custom images and drivers for every model of device being used.
Instead of re-imaging the device, your existing Windows 10 installation can be transformed into
a "business-ready" state, applying settings and policies, installing apps, and even changing the
edition of Windows 10 being used (e.g. from Windows 10 Pro to Windows 10 Enterprise) to

support advanced features.

Reference:
https://docs.microsoft.com/en-us/windows/deployment/windows-autopilot/windows-autopilot

Design and Implement Microsoft 365 Services

Testlet 2

This is a case study. **Case studies are not timed separately. You can use as much exam time as you would like to complete each case**. However, there may be additional case studies and sections on this exam. You must manage your time to ensure that you are able to complete all questions included on this exam in the time provided.

To answer the questions included in a case study, you will need to reference information that is provided in the case study. Case studies might contain exhibits and other resources that provide more information about the scenario that is described in the case study. Each question is independent of the other questions in this case study.

At the end of this case study, a review screen will appear. This screen allows you to review your answer and to make changes before you move to the next section of the exam. After you begin a new section, you cannot return to this section.

To start the case study
To display the first question in this case study, click the **Next** button. Use the buttons in the left pane to explore the content of the case study before you answer the questions. Clicking these buttons displays information such as business requirements, existing environment, and problem statements. When you are ready to answer a question, click the **Question** button to return to the question.

Overview
Fabrikam, Inc. is an electronics company that produces consumer products. Fabrikam has 10,000 employees worldwide.

Fabrikam has a main office in London and branch offices in major cities in Europe, Asia, and the United States.

Existing Environment
Active Directory Environment
The network contains an Active Directory forest named fabrikam.com. The forest contains all the identities used for user and computer authentication.

Each department is represented by a top-level organizational unit (OU) that contains several child OUs for user accounts and computer accounts.

All users authenticate to on-premises applications by signing in to their device by using a UPN format of *username@fabrikam.com*.

Fabrikam does **NOT** plan to implement identity federation.

Network Infrastructure

Each office has a high-speed connection to the Internet.

Each office contains two domain controllers. All domain controllers are configured as a DNS server.

The public zone for fabrikam.com is managed by an external DNS server.

All users connect to an on-premises Microsoft Exchange Server 2016 organization. The users access their email by using Outlook Anywhere, Outlook on the web, or the Microsoft Outlook app for iOS. All the Exchange servers have the latest cumulative updates installed.

All shared company documents are stored on a Microsoft SharePoint Server farm.

Requirements
Planned Changes
Fabrikam plans to implement a Microsoft 365 Enterprise subscription and move all email and shared documents to the subscription.

Fabrikam plans to implement two pilot projects:

- Project1: During Project1, the mailboxes of 100 users in the sales department will be moved to Microsoft 365.
- Project2: After the successful completion of Project1, Microsoft Teams & Skype for Business will be enabled in Microsoft 365 for the sales department users.

Fabrikam plans to create a group named UserLicenses that will manage the allocation of all Microsoft 365 bulk licenses.

Technical Requirements
Fabrikam identifies the following technical requirements:

- All users must be able to exchange email messages successfully during Project1 by using their current email address.
- Users must be able to authenticate to cloud services if Active Directory becomes unavailable.
- A user named User1 must be able to view all DLP reports from the Microsoft 365 admin center.
- Microsoft Office 365 ProPlus applications must be installed from a network share only.
- Disruptions to email access must be minimized.

Application Requirements
Fabrikam identifies the following application requirements:

- An on-premises web application named App1 must allow users to complete their expense reports online.
- The installation of feature updates for Office 365 ProPlus must be minimized.

Security Requirements
Fabrikam identifies the following security requirements:

- After the planned migration to Microsoft 365, all users must continue to authenticate to their mailbox and to SharePoint sites by using their UPN.
- The memberships of UserLicenses must be validated monthly. Unused user accounts must be removed from the group automatically.
- After the planned migration to Microsoft 365, all users must be signed in to on-premises and cloud-based applications automatically.
- The principle of least privilege must be used.

QUESTION 1
You need to recommend which DNS record must be created before adding a domain name for the project.

You need to recommend which DNS record must be created before you begin the project.

Which DNS record should you recommend?

A. alias (CNAME)
B. host information (HINFO)
C. host (A)
D. mail exchanger (MX)

Section: (none)
Explanation

Explanation/Reference:
Explanation:
When you add a custom domain to Office 365, you need to verify that you own the domain. You can do this by adding either an MX record or a TXT record to the DNS for that domain.

Reference:
https://docs.microsoft.com/en-us/office365/admin/get-help-with-domains/create-dns-records-at- any-dns-hosting-provider?view=o365-worldwide

QUESTION 2
You need to recommend which DNS record must be created before adding a domain name for the project.

You need to recommend which DNS record must be created before you begin the project.

Which DNS record should you recommend?

A. alias (CNAME)
B. text (TXT)
C. host (AAAA)
D. pointer (PTR)

Section: (none)
Explanation

Explanation/Reference:
Explanation:
When you add a custom domain to Office 365, you need to verify that you own the domain. You can do this by adding either an MX record or a TXT record to the DNS for that domain.

Reference:
https://docs.microsoft.com/en-us/office365/admin/get-help-with-domains/create-dns-records-at- any-dns-hosting-provider?view=o365-worldwide

Manage User Identity and Roles

Question Set 1

QUESTION 1
Your network contains an Active Directory domain and a Microsoft Azure Active Directory (Azure AD) tenant.

The network uses a firewall that contains a list of allowed outbound domains.

You begin to implement directory synchronization.

You discover that the firewall configuration contains only the following domain names in the list of allowed domains:

- *.microsoft.com
- *.office.com

Directory synchronization fails.

You need to ensure that directory synchronization completes successfully.

What is the best approach to achieve the goal? More than one answer choice may achieve the goal. Select the **BEST** answer.

A. From the firewall, allow the IP address range of the Azure data center for outbound communication.
B. From Azure AD Connect, modify the Customize synchronization options task.
C. Deploy an Azure AD Connect sync server in staging mode.
D. From the firewall, create a list of allowed inbound domains.
E. From the firewall, modify the list of allowed outbound domains.

Section: (none)
Explanation

Explanation/Reference:
Explanation:
Azure AD Connect needs to be able to connect to various Microsoft domains such as login.microsoftonline.com. Therefore, you need to modify the list of allowed outbound domains on the firewall.

Reference:
https://docs.microsoft.com/en-us/azure/active-directory/hybrid/reference-connect-ports

QUESTION 2
Your network contains an on-premises Active Directory forest.

You are evaluating the implementation of Microsoft 365 and the deployment of an authentication strategy.

You need to recommend an authentication strategy that meets the following requirements:

- Allows users to sign in by using smart card-based certificates
- Allows users to connect to on-premises and Microsoft 365 services by using SSO

Which authentication strategy should you recommend?

A. password hash synchronization and seamless SSO
B. federation with Active Directory Federation Services (AD FS)
C. pass-through authentication and seamless SSO

Section: (none)
Explanation

Explanation/Reference:
Explanation:
Federation with Active Directory Federation Services (AD FS) is required to allow users to sign in by using smart card-based certificates.

Federated authentication
When you choose this authentication method, Azure AD hands off the authentication process to a separate trusted authentication system, such as on-premises Active Directory Federation Services (AD FS), to validate the user's password.
The authentication system can provide additional advanced authentication requirements. Examples are smartcard-based authentication or third-party multifactor authentication.

Reference:
https://docs.microsoft.com/en-us/azure/security/azure-ad-choose-authn

QUESTION 3
Your network contains an Active Directory domain named adatum.com that is synced to Microsoft Azure Active Directory (Azure AD).

The domain contains 100 user accounts.

The city attribute for all the users is set to the city where the user resides.

You need to modify the value of the city attribute to the three-letter airport code of each city.

What should you do?

A. From Active Directory Administrative Center, select the Active Directory users, and then modify the Properties settings.
B. From the Microsoft 365 admin center, select the users, and then use the Bulk actions option.
C. From Azure Cloud Shell, run the `Get-AzureADUser` and `Set-AzureADUser` cmdlets.
D. From Azure portal, select all the Azure AD users, and then use the User settings blade.

Section: (none)
Explanation

Explanation/Reference:
Explanation:
The user accounts are synced from the on-premise Active Directory to the Microsoft Azure Active Directory (Azure AD). Therefore, the city attribute must be changed in the on-premise Active Directory.
You can modify certain attributes of multiple user accounts simultaneously by selecting them in Active Directory Administrative Center or Active Directory Users and Computers, right clicking then selecting Properties.
The other three options all suggest modifying the city attribute of the users in the Azure Active Directory which is incorrect.

Reference:
https://blogs.technet.microsoft.com/canitpro/2015/11/25/step-by-step-managing-multiple-user-accounts-via-active-directory-admin-center/

QUESTION 4
You have a Microsoft 365 subscription that contains a Microsoft Azure Active Directory (Azure AD) tenant named contoso.com. The tenant includes a user named User1.

You enable Azure AD Identity Protection.

You need to ensure that User1 can review the list in Azure AD Identity Protection of users flagged for risk. The solution must use the principle of least privilege.

To which role should you add User1?

A. Security reader
B. User administrator
C. Owner
D. Global administrator

Section: (none)
Explanation

Explanation/Reference:
Explanation:
  The risky sign-ins reports are available to users in the following roles:
  ▪ Security Administrator
  ▪ Global Administrator
  ▪ Security Reader

Of the three roles listed above, the Security Reader role has the least privilege.

Reference:
https://docs.microsoft.com/en-us/azure/active-directory/reports-monitoring/concept-risky-sign-ins

QUESTION 5
Your network contains three Active Directory forests.

You create a Microsoft Azure Active Directory (Azure AD) tenant.

You plan to sync the on-premises Active Directory to Azure AD.

You need to recommend a synchronization solution. The solution must ensure that the synchronization can complete successfully and as quickly as possible if a single server fails.

What should you include in the recommendation?

A. three Azure AD Connect sync servers and three Azure AD Connect sync servers in staging mode
B. one Azure AD Connect sync server and one Azure AD Connect sync server in staging mode
C. three Azure AD Connect sync servers and one Azure AD Connect sync server in staging mode
D. six Azure AD Connect sync servers and three Azure AD Connect sync servers in staging mode

Section: (none)
Explanation

Explanation/Reference:
Explanation:
Azure AD Connect can be active on only one server. You can install Azure AD Connect on another server for redundancy but the additional installation would need to be in Staging mode. An Azure AD connect installation in Staging mode is configured and ready to go but it needs to be manually switched to Active to perform directory synchronization.

Reference:
https://docs.microsoft.com/en-us/azure/active-directory/hybrid/how-to-connect-install-custom

QUESTION 6
Your company has 10,000 users who access all applications from an on-premises data center.

You plan to create a Microsoft 365 subscription and to migrate data to the cloud.

You plan to implement directory synchronization.

User accounts and group accounts must sync to Microsoft Azure Active Directory (Azure AD) successfully.

You discover that several user accounts fail to sync to Azure AD.

You need to identify which user accounts failed to sync. You must resolve the issue as quickly as possible.

What should you do?

A. From Active Directory Administrative Center, search for all the users, and then modify the properties of the user accounts.
B. Run `idfix.exe`, and then click **Complete**.
C. From Windows PowerShell, run the `Start-AdSyncCycle -PolicyType Delta`

command.
D. Run `idfix.exe`, and then click **Edit**.

Section: (none)
Explanation

Explanation/Reference:
Explanation:
IdFix is used to perform discovery and remediation of identity objects and their attributes in an on-premises Active Directory environment in preparation for migration to Azure Active Directory. IdFix is intended for the Active Directory administrators responsible for directory synchronization with Azure Active Directory.

Reference:
https://docs.microsoft.com/en-us/office365/enterprise/prepare-directory-attributes-for-synch- with-idfix

https://www.microsoft.com/en-gb/download/details.aspx?id=36832

QUESTION 7
Your network contains an Active Directory forest. The forest contains two domains named contoso.com and adatum.com.

Your company recently purchased a Microsoft 365 subscription.

You deploy a federated identity solution to the environment.

You use the following command to configure contoso.com for federation.

`Convert-MsolDomaintoFederated –DomainName contoso.com`

In the Microsoft 365 tenant, an administrator adds and verifies the adatum.com domain name.

You need to configure the adatum.com Active Directory domain for federated authentication.

Which two actions should you perform before you run the Azure AD Connect wizard? Each correct answer presents part of the solution.

NOTE: Each correct selection is worth one point.

A. From Windows PowerShell, run the `Convert-MsolDomaintoFederated –DomainName contoso.com –SupportMultipleDomain` command.
B. From Windows PowerShell, run the `New-MsolFederatedDomain –SupportMultipleDomain –DomainName contoso.com` command.
C. From Windows PowerShell, run the `New-MsolFederatedDomain –DomainName adatum.com` command.
D. From Windows PowerShell, run the `Update-MSOLFederatedDomain –DomainName contoso.com –SupportMultipleDomain` command.
E. From the federation server, remove the Microsoft Office 365 relying party trust.

Explanation/Reference:
Explanation:
When the `Convert-MsolDomaintoFederated –DomainName contoso.com` command was run, a relying party trust was created.
Adding a second domain (adatum.com in this case) will only work if the `SupportMultipleDomain` switch was used when the initial federation was configured by running the `Convert-MsolDomaintoFederated –DomainName contoso.com` command.

Therefore, we need to start again by removing the relying party trust then running the `Convert-MsolDomaintoFederated` command again with the `SupportMultipleDomain` switch.

QUESTION 8
Your network contains a single Active Directory domain and two Microsoft Azure Active Directory (Azure AD) tenants.

You plan to implement directory synchronization for both Azure AD tenants. Each tenant will contain some of the Active Directory users.

You need to recommend a solution for the planned directory synchronization.

What should you include in the recommendation?

- A. Deploy two servers that run Azure AD Connect, and then filter the users for each tenant by using organizational unit (OU)-based filtering.
- B. Deploy two servers that runs Azure AD Connect, and then filter the users for each tenant by using domain-based filtering
- C. Deploy one server that runs Azure AD Connect, and then filter the users for each tenant by using organizational unit (OU)-based filtering.
- D. Deploy one server that runs Azure AD Connect, and then filter the users for each tenant by using domain-based filtering.

Explanation/Reference:
Explanation:
There's a 1:1 relationship between an Azure AD Connect sync server and an Azure AD tenant. For each Azure AD tenant, you need one Azure AD Connect sync server installation. Therefore, we need to deploy two servers that run Azure AD Connect for the two Azure AD tenants.

Each user account can only be synchronized to one Azure AD tenant. Therefore, we need a way of splitting the users between the two Azure AD tenants. Azure AD Connect offers three ways to filter which users get synchronized to an Azure AD tenant. You can use domain-based filtering if you have multiple domains in a forest, attribute-based filtering or OU-based filtering.

Reference:
https://docs.microsoft.com/en-us/azure/active-directory/hybrid/plan-connect-topologies#multiple-azure-ad-tenants

https://docs.microsoft.com/en-us/azure/active-directory/hybrid/how-to-connect-sync-configure-filtering

QUESTION 9
HOTSPOT

Your company has a hybrid deployment of Microsoft 365.

An on-premises user named User1 is synced to Microsoft Azure Active Directory (Azure AD).

Azure AD Connect is configured as shown in the following exhibit.

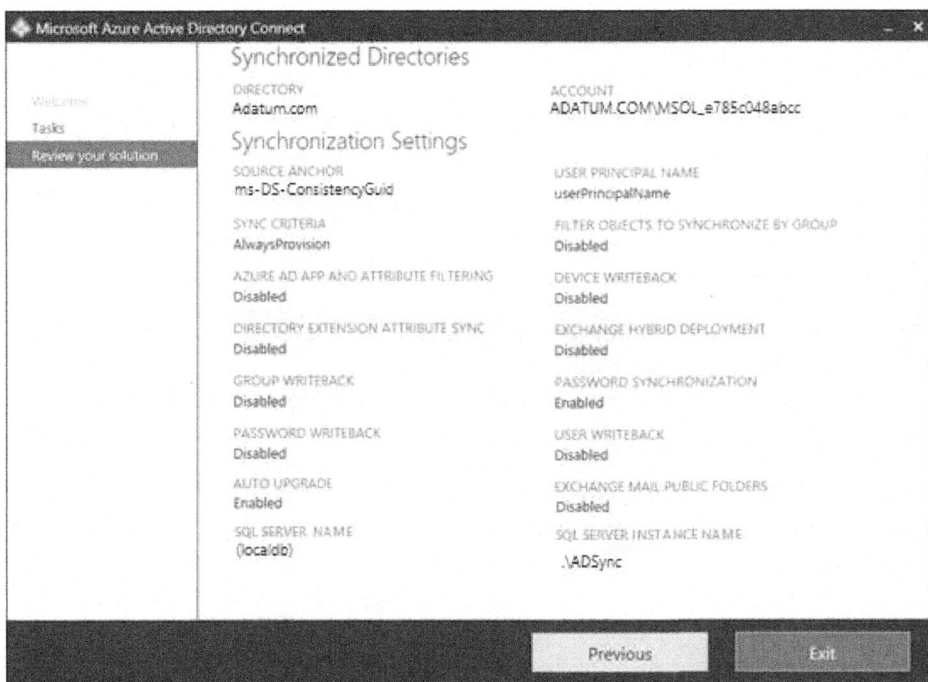

Use the drop-down menus to select the answer choice that completes each statement based on the information presented in the graphic.

NOTE: Each correct selection is worth one point.

Hot Area:

Answer Area

User1 [**answer choice**].

| cannot change her password from any Microsoft portals |
| can change her password by using self-service password reset feature only |
| an change her password from the Office 365 admin center only |

If the password for User1 is changed in Active Directory, [**answer choice**].

| the password will be synchronized to Azure AD |
| a new randomly generated password will be assigned to User1 |
| the password in Azure AD will be unchanged |

Section: (none)
Explanation

Explanation/Reference:
Explanation:

User1 cannot change her password from any Microsoft portals because Password Writeback is disabled in the Azure AD Connect configuration.

If the password for User1 is changed in Active Directory, the password will be synchronized to Azure AD because Password Synchronization is enabled in the Azure AD Connect configuration.

Reference:
https://docs.microsoft.com/en-us/azure/active-directory/hybrid/how-to-connect-install-custom

QUESTION 10
Your company has a Microsoft Azure Active Directory (Azure AD) tenant named contoso.onmicrosoft.com that contains a user named User1.

You suspect that an imposter is signing in to Azure AD by using the credentials of User1.

You need to ensure that an administrator named Admin1 can view all the sign in details of User1 from the past 24 hours.

To which three roles should you add Admin1? Each correct answer presents a complete solution.

NOTE: Each correct selection is worth one point.

A. Security administrator
B. Password administrator
C. User administrator
D. Compliance administrator
E. Reports reader
F. Security reader

Section: (none)
Explanation

Explanation/Reference:
Explanation:
Users in the Security Administrator, Security Reader, Global Reader, and Report Reader roles can view the sign in details.

Reference:
https://docs.microsoft.com/en-us/azure/active-directory/reports-monitoring/concept-sign-ins

QUESTION 11
You have a Microsoft 365 subscription.

You plan to enable Microsoft Azure Information Protection.

You need to ensure that only the members of a group named PilotUsers can protect content.

What should you do?

A. Run the `Add-AadrmRoleBaseAdministrator` cmdlet.
B. Create an Azure Information Protection policy.
C. Configure the protection activation status for Azure Information Protection.
D. Run the `Set-AadrmOnboardingControlPolicy` cmdlet.

Section: (none)
Explanation

Explanation/Reference:
Explanation:
If you don't want all users to be able to protect documents and emails immediately by using Azure Rights Management, you can configure user onboarding controls by using the Set-AadrmOnboardingControlPolicy

Reference:
https://docs.microsoft.com/en-us/azure/information-protection/activate-service

QUESTION 12
Your company has a Microsoft 365 subscription.

You need to identify which users performed the following privileged administration tasks:

- Deleted a folder from the second-stage Recycle Bin if Microsoft SharePoint
- Opened a mailbox of which the user was not the owner
- Reset a user password

What should you use?

A. Microsoft Azure Active Directory (Azure AD) audit logs
B. Microsoft Azure Active Directory (Azure AD) sign-ins
C. Security & Compliance content search

D. Security & Compliance audit log search

Explanation/Reference:
Explanation:
You can view the required information in the audit logs. The Azure AD audit logs provide records of system activities for compliance. To access the audit report, select Audit logs in the Activity section of Azure Active Directory.

Reference:
https://docs.microsoft.com/en-us/azure/active-directory/reports-monitoring/concept-audit-logs

QUESTION 13
You have a Microsoft 365 subscription. You have a user named User1.

You need to ensure that User1 can place a hold on all mailbox content.

What permission should you assign to User1?

A. the User management administrator role from the Microsoft 365 admin center
B. the eDiscovery Manager role from the Security & Compliance admin center
C. the Information Protection administrator role from the Azure Active Directory admin center
D. the Compliance Management role from the Exchange admin center

Explanation/Reference:
Explanation:
To create a query-based In-Place Hold, a user requires both the Mailbox Search and Legal Hold roles to be assigned directly or via membership in a role group that has both roles assigned. To create an In-Place Hold without using a query, which places all mailbox items on hold, you must have the Legal Hold role assigned. The Discovery Management role group is assigned both roles.

Reference:
https://docs.microsoft.com/en-us/Exchange/permissions/feature-permissions/policy-and-compliance-permissions?view=exchserver-2019

QUESTION 14
Your company has a Microsoft Azure Active Directory (Azure AD) tenant named contoso.com.

You sign up for Microsoft Store for Business.

The tenant contains the users shown in the following table.

Name	Microsoft Store for Business role	Azure AD role
User1	Purchaser	*None*
User2	Basic Purchaser	*None*
User3	*None*	Application administrator
User4	*None*	Cloud application administrator
User5	*None*	*None*

Microsoft Store for Business has the following Shopping behavior settings:

- Allow users to shop is set to **On**.
- Make everyone a Basic Purchaser is set to **Off**.

You need to identify which users can install apps from the Microsoft for Business private store.

Which users should you identify?

A. A. user1, User2, User3, User4, and User5
B. User1 only
C. User1 and User2 only
D. User3 and User4 only
E. User1, User2, User3, and User4 only

Section: (none)
Explanation

Explanation/Reference:
Explanation:

Allow users to shop controls the shopping experience in Microsoft Store for Education. When this setting is on, Purchasers and Basic Purchasers can purchase products and services from Microsoft Store for Education.

Reference:
https://docs.microsoft.com/en-us/microsoft-store/acquire-apps-microsoft-store-for-business

QUESTION 15
You have a Microsoft 365 subscription that contains a Microsoft Azure Active Directory (Azure AD) tenant named contoso.com.

In the tenant, you create a user named User1.

You need to ensure that User1 can publish retention labels from the Security & Compliance admin center. The solution must use the principle of least privilege.

To which role group should you add User1?

A. Security Administrator

B. Records Management
C. Compliance Administrator
D. eDiscovery Manager

Section: (none)
Explanation

Explanation/Reference:
Explanation:
Members of your compliance team who will create retention labels need permissions to the Security & Compliance Center. By default, your tenant admin has access to this location and can give compliance officers and other people access to the Security & Compliance Center, without giving them all of the permissions of a tenant admin. To do this, we recommend that you go to the Permissions page of the Security & Compliance Center, edit the Compliance Administrator role group, and add members to that role group.

Reference:
https://docs.microsoft.com/en-us/microsoft-365/compliance/labels#permissions

QUESTION 16
Your company has a Microsoft 365 E5 subscription.

Users in the research department work with sensitive data.

You need to prevent the research department users from accessing potentially unsafe websites by using hyperlinks embedded in email messages and documents. Users in other departments must not be restricted.

What should you do from the Security & Compliance admin center?

A. Create a data loss prevention (DLP) policy that has a Content contains condition.
B. Create a data loss prevention (DLP) policy that has a Content is shared condition.
C. Modify the default safe links policy.
D. Create a new safe links policy.

Section: (none)
Explanation

Explanation/Reference:
Explanation:
ATP Safe Links, a feature of Office 365 Advanced Threat Protection (ATP), can help protect your organization from malicious links used in phishing and other attacks. If you have the necessary permissions for the Office 365 Security & Compliance Center, you can set up ATP Safe Links policies to help ensure that when people click web addresses (URLs), your organization is protected. Your ATP Safe Links policies can be configured to scan URLs in email and URLs in Office documents.

Reference:
https://docs.microsoft.com/en-us/office365/securitycompliance/set-up-atp-safe-links-policies#policies-that-apply-to-specific-email-recipients

QUESTION 17

A user receives the following message when attempting to sign in to https://myapps.microsoft.com:

```
"Your sign-in was blocked. We've detected something unusual about this
sign-in. For example, you might be signing in from a new location,
device, or app. Before you can continue, we need to verify your
identity. Please contact your admin."
```

Which configuration prevents the users from signing in?

A. Security & Compliance supervision policies
B. Security & Compliance data loss prevention (DLP) policies
C. Microsoft Azure Active Directory (Azure AD) conditional access policies
D. Microsoft Azure Active Directory (Azure AD) Identity Protection policies

Section: (none)
Explanation

Explanation/Reference:
Explanation:
The user is being blocked due to a 'risky sign-in'. This can be caused by the user logging in from a device that hasn't been used to sign in before or from an unknown location. Integration with Azure AD Identity Protection allows Conditional Access policies to identify risky sign-in behavior. Policies can then force users to perform password changes or multi-factor authentication to reduce their risk level or be blocked from access until an administrator takes manual action.

Reference:
https://docs.microsoft.com/en-us/azure/active-directory/conditional-access/overview

QUESTION 18
Note: This question is part of a series of questions that present the same scenario. Each question in the series contains a unique solution that might meet the stated goals. Some question sets might have more than one correct solution, while others might not have a correct solution.

After you answer a question in this section, you will NOT be able to return to it. As a result, these questions will not appear in the review screen.

Your network contains an Active Directory domain.

You deploy a Microsoft Azure Active Directory (Azure AD) tenant. Another

administrator configures the domain to synchronize to Azure AD.

You discover that 10 user accounts in an organizational unit (OU) are NOT synchronized to Azure AD. All the other user accounts synchronized successfully.

You review Azure AD Connect Health and discover that all the user account synchronizations completed successfully.

You need to ensure that the 10 user accounts are synchronized to Azure AD.

Solution: From the Synchronization Rules Editor, you create a new outbound synchronization rule.

Does this meet the goal?

A. Yes
B. No

QUESTION 19
Note: This question is part of a series of questions that present the same scenario. Each question in the series contains a unique solution that might meet the stated goals. Some question sets might have more than one correct solution, while others might not have a correct solution.

After you answer a question in this section, you will NOT be able to return to it. As a result, these questions will not appear in the review screen.

Your network contains an Active Directory domain.

You deploy a Microsoft Azure Active Directory (Azure AD) tenant. Another

administrator configures the domain to synchronize to Azure AD.

You discover that 10 user accounts in an organizational unit (OU) are NOT synchronized to Azure AD. All the other user accounts synchronized successfully.

You review Azure AD Connect Health and discover that all the user account synchronizations completed successfully.

You need to ensure that the 10 user accounts are synchronized to Azure AD.

Solution: You run `idfix.exe` and report the 10 user accounts.

Does this meet the goal?

A. Yes
B. No

Section: (none)
Explanation

Explanation/Reference:
Explanation:
The question states that "all the user account synchronizations completed successfully". If there were problems with the 10 accounts that needed fixing with idfix.exe, there would have been synchronization errors in Azure AD Connect Health.
It is likely that the 10 user accounts are being excluded from the synchronization cycle by a filtering rule.

Reference:
https://docs.microsoft.com/en-us/azure/active-directory/hybrid/how-to-connect-sync-configure-filtering

QUESTION 20
Note: This question is part of a series of questions that present the same scenario. Each question in the series contains a unique solution that might meet the stated goals. Some question sets might have more than one correct solution, while others might not have a correct solution.

After you answer a question in this section, you will NOT be able to return to it. As a result, these questions will not appear in the review screen.

Your network contains an Active Directory domain.

You deploy a Microsoft Azure Active Directory (Azure AD) tenant. Another

administrator configures the domain to synchronize to Azure AD.

You discover that 10 user accounts in an organizational unit (OU) are NOT synchronized to Azure AD. All the other user accounts synchronized successfully.

You review Azure AD Connect Health and discover that all the user account synchronizations completed successfully.

You need to ensure that the 10 user accounts are synchronized to Azure AD.

Solution: From Azure AD Connect, you modify the Azure AD credentials.

Does this meet the goal?

A. Yes
B. No

Explanation/Reference:
Explanation:
The question states that "all the user account synchronizations completed successfully".
Therefore, the Azure AD credentials are configured correctly in Azure AD Connect. It is likely
that the 10 user accounts are being excluded from the synchronization cycle by a filtering rule.

Reference:
https://docs.microsoft.com/en-us/azure/active-directory/hybrid/how-to-connect-sync-configure-
filtering

QUESTION 21
HOTSPOT

You have a Microsoft Azure Active Directory (Azure AD) tenant that contains the users shown in
the following table.

Name	Role
User1	Global administrator
User2	Billing administrator
User3	None

You enable self-service password reset for all users. You set Number of methods required to
reset to 1, and you set Methods available to users to Security questions only.

What information must be configured for each user before the user can perform a self-service
password reset? To answer, select the appropriate options in the answer area.

NOTE: Each correct selection is worth one point.

Hot Area:

Answer Area

User1:

Email address only
Phone number only
Security questions only
Phone number and email address

User2:

Email address only
Phone number only
Security questions only
Phone number and email address

User3:

Email address only
Phone number only
Security questions only
Phone number and email address

Section: (none)
Explanation

Explanation/Reference:
Explanation:

Microsoft enforces a strong default two-gate password reset policy for any Azure administrator

role. This policy may be different from the one you have defined for your users and cannot be changed. You should always test password reset functionality as a user without any Azure administrator roles assigned.
With a two-gate policy, administrators don't have the ability to use security questions.
The two-gate policy requires two pieces of authentication data, such as an email address, authenticator app, or a phone number.

User3 is not assigned to an Administrative role so the configured method of Security questions only applies to User3.

Reference:
https://docs.microsoft.com/en-us/azure/active-directory/authentication/concept-sspr-policy#administrator-password-policy-differences

QUESTION 22

You have a Microsoft 365 subscription that uses an Azure Active Directory (Azure AD) tenant named contoso.com. The tenant contains the users shown in the following table.

Name	Role
User1	Exchange administrator
User2	User administrator
User3	Global administrator
User4	None

You add another user named User5 to the User administrator role. You

need to identify which two management tasks User5 can perform.

Which two tasks should you identify? Each correct answer presents a complete solution.

NOTE: Each correct selection is worth one point.

A. Delete User2 and User4 only.
B. Reset the password of User2 and User4 only.
C. Delete User1, User2, and User4 only.
D. Delete any user in Azure AD.
E. Reset the password of any user in Azure AD.
F. Reset the password of User4 only.

Section: (none)
Explanation

Explanation/Reference:
Explanation:
Users with the User Administrator role can create users and manage all aspects of users with some restrictions (see below).

Only on users who are non-admins or in any of the following limited admin roles:
- Directory Readers
- Guest Inviter
- Helpdesk Administrator
- Message Center Reader
- Reports Reader
- User Administrator

Reference:
https://docs.microsoft.com/en-us/azure/active-directory/users-groups-roles/directory-assign-admin-roles#available-roles

QUESTION 23
Note: This question is part of a series of questions that present the same scenario. Each question in the series contains a unique solution that might meet the stated goals. Some question sets might have more than one correct solution, while others might not have a correct solution.

After you answer a question in this section, you will NOT be able to return to it. As a result, these questions will not appear in the review screen.

Your network contains an Active Directory domain.

You deploy a Microsoft Azure Active Directory (Azure AD) tenant. Another

administrator configures the domain to synchronize to Azure AD.

You discover that 10 user accounts in an organizational unit (OU) are NOT synchronized to Azure AD. All the other user accounts synchronized successfully.

You review Azure AD Connect Health and discover that all the user account synchronizations completed successfully.

You need to ensure that the 10 user accounts are synchronized to Azure AD.

Solution: From Azure AD Connect, you modify the filtering settings.

Does this meet the goal?

A. Yes
B. No

Section: (none)
Explanation

Explanation/Reference:
Explanation:
The question states that "all the user account synchronizations completed successfully". Therefore, we know that Azure AD Connect is working and configured correctly. The only thing that would prevent the 10 user accounts from being synchronized is that they are being excluded from the synchronization cycle by a filtering rule.

Reference:
https://docs.microsoft.com/en-us/azure/active-directory/hybrid/how-to-connect-sync-configure-filtering

QUESTION 24
Note: This question is part of a series of questions that present the same scenario. Each question in the series contains a unique solution that might meet the stated goals. Some question sets might have more than one correct solution, while others might not have a correct solution.

After you answer a question in this section, you will NOT be able to return to it. As a result, these questions will not appear in the review screen.

Your company has 3,000 users. All the users are assigned Microsoft 365 E3 licenses.

Some users are assigned licenses for all Microsoft 365 services. Other users are assigned licenses for only certain Microsoft 365 services.

You need to determine whether a user named User1 is licensed for Exchange Online only.

Solution: You run the `Get-MsolUser` cmdlet.

Does this meet the goal?

A. Yes
B. No

Section: (none)
Explanation

Explanation/Reference:
Explanation:
The `Get-MsolUser` cmdlet will tell you if a user is licensed for Microsoft 365 but it does not tell you which licenses are assigned.

Reference:
https://docs.microsoft.com/en-us/powershell/module/msonline/get-msoluser?view=azureadps-1.0

QUESTION 25
Note: This question is part of a series of questions that present the same scenario. Each question in the series contains a unique solution that might meet the stated goals. Some question sets might have more than one correct solution, while others might not have a correct solution.

After you answer a question in this section, you will NOT be able to return to it. As a result, these questions will not appear in the review screen.

Your company has 3,000 users. All the users are assigned Microsoft 365 E3 licenses.

Some users are assigned licenses for all Microsoft 365 services. Other users are assigned licenses for only certain Microsoft 365 services.

You need to determine whether a user named User1 is licensed for Exchange Online only.

Solution: You run the `Get-MsolAccountSku` cmdlet.

Does this meet the goal?

A. Yes
B. No

Section: (none)
Explanation

Explanation/Reference:
Explanation:
The Get-MsolAccountSku cmdlet returns all the SKUs that the company owns. It does not tell you which licenses are assigned to users.

Reference:
https://docs.microsoft.com/en-us/powershell/module/msonline/get-msolaccountsku?view=azureadps-1.0

QUESTION 26
Note: This question is part of a series of questions that present the same scenario. Each question in the series contains a unique solution that might meet the stated goals. Some question sets might have more than one correct solution, while others might not have a correct solution.

After you answer a question in this section, you will NOT be able to return to it. As a result, these questions will not appear in the review screen.

Your company has 3,000 users. All the users are assigned Microsoft 365 E3 licenses.

Some users are assigned licenses for all Microsoft 365 services. Other users are assigned licenses for only certain Microsoft 365 services.

You need to determine whether a user named User1 is licensed for Exchange Online only.

Solution: You launch the Azure portal, and then review the Licenses blade.

Does this meet the goal?

A. Yes
B. No

Section: (none)
Explanation

Explanation/Reference:

Explanation:

In the Licenses blade, click All Products then select the E3 License. This will display a list of all users assigned an E3 license. Select User1. You'll see how many services are assigned in the Enabled Services column. Click on the number in the Enabled Services column for User1 and you'll be taken to the licenses page for that user. Click on the number in the Enabled Services column for User1 again and a page will open which shows you exactly which services are enabled or disabled.

Alternatively, you can go into the user account properties directly then select Licenses. This will display the licenses blade for that user. You can then click on the number in the Enabled Services column for the user and a page will open which shows you exactly which services are enabled or disabled.

QUESTION 27

You have a Microsoft 365 subscription.

You view the service advisories shown in the following exhibit.

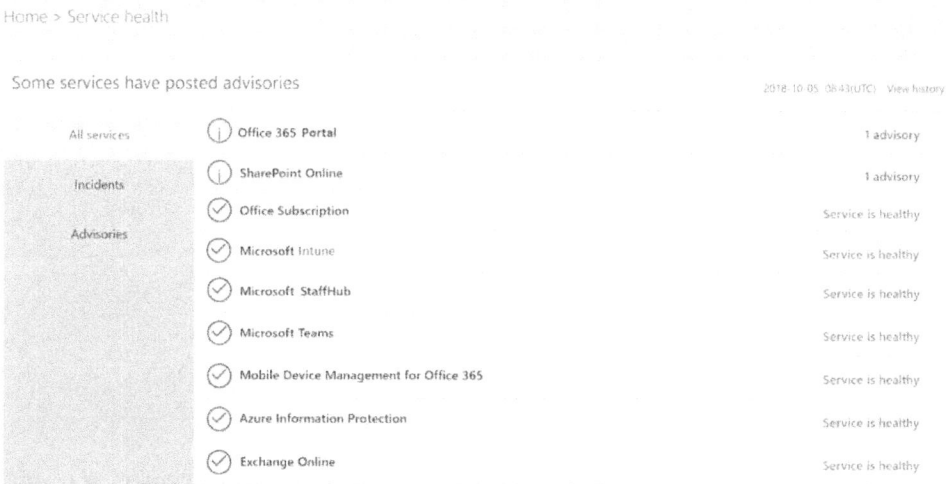

Home > Service health

Some services have posted advisories   2018-10-05 08:43(UTC)   View history

All services	(i) Office 365 Portal	1 advisory
Incidents	(i) SharePoint Online	1 advisory
	(✓) Office Subscription	Service is healthy
Advisories	(✓) Microsoft Intune	Service is healthy
	(✓) Microsoft StaffHub	Service is healthy
	(✓) Microsoft Teams	Service is healthy
	(✓) Mobile Device Management for Office 365	Service is healthy
	(✓) Azure Information Protection	Service is healthy
	(✓) Exchange Online	Service is healthy

You need to ensure that users who administer Microsoft SharePoint Online can view the advisories to investigate health issues.

Which role should you assign to the users?

A. SharePoint administrator
B. Message Center reader
C. Reports reader
D. Service administrator

Explanation/Reference:
Explanation:
People who are assigned the global admin or service administrator role can view service health. To allow Exchange, SharePoint, and Skype for Business admins to view service health, they must also be assigned the Service admin role. For more information about roles that can view service health.

Reference:
https://docs.microsoft.com/en-us/office365/enterprise/view-service-health

QUESTION 28
You have a Microsoft 365 subscription that contains a Microsoft Azure Active Directory (Azure AD) tenant named contoso.com. The tenant includes a user named User1.

You enable Azure AD Identity Protection.

You need to ensure that User1 can review the list in Azure AD Identity Protection of users flagged for risk. The solution must use the principle of least privilege.

To which role should you add User1?

A. Reports reader
B. Security administrator
C. Owner
D. Compliance administrator

Explanation/Reference:
Explanation:
Either one of the following three roles can review the list in Azure AD Identity Protection of users flagged for risk:

- Security Administrator
- Global Administrator
- Security Reader

Reference:
https://docs.microsoft.com/en-us/azure/active-directory/reports-monitoring/concept-risky-sign-ins

QUESTION 29
You have a Microsoft 365 subscription that contains a Microsoft Azure Active Directory (Azure AD) tenant named contoso.com. The tenant includes a user named User1.

You enable Azure AD Identity Protection.

You need to ensure that User1 can review the list in Azure AD Identity Protection of users flagged for risk. The solution must use the principle of least privilege.

To which role should you add User1?

A. Security reader
B. User administrator
C. Owner
D. Service administrator

Section: (none)
Explanation

Explanation/Reference:
Explanation:
Either one of the following three roles can review the list in Azure AD Identity Protection of users flagged for risk:

▪ Security Administrator
▪ Global Administrator
▪ Security Reader

Reference:
https://docs.microsoft.com/en-us/azure/active-directory/reports-monitoring/concept-risky-sign-ins

QUESTION 30
You have a Microsoft 365 subscription that contains a Microsoft Azure Active Directory (Azure AD) tenant named contoso.com. The tenant includes a user named User1.

You enable Azure AD Identity Protection.

You need to ensure that User1 can review the list in Azure AD Identity Protection of users flagged for risk. The solution must use the principle of least privilege.

To which role should you add User1?

A. Reports reader
B. Security reader
C. Owner
D. Compliance administrator

Section: (none)
Explanation

Explanation/Reference:
Explanation:
Either one of the following three roles can review the list in Azure AD Identity Protection of users

flagged for risk:

- Security Administrator
- Global Administrator
- Security Reader

Reference:
https://docs.microsoft.com/en-us/azure/active-directory/reports-monitoring/concept-risky-sign-ins

QUESTION 31
Your network contains a single Active Directory domain and two Microsoft Azure Active Directory (Azure AD) tenants.

You plan to implement directory synchronization for both Azure AD tenants. Each tenant will contain some of the Active Directory users.

You need to recommend a solution for the planned directory synchronization.

What should you include in the recommendation?

A. Deploy two servers that run Azure AD Connect, and then filter the users for each tenant by using organizational unit (OU)-based filtering.
B. Deploy one server that runs Azure AD Connect, and then filter the users for each tenant by using attribute-based filtering.
C. Deploy one server that runs Azure AD Connect, and then filter the users for each tenant by using organizational unit (OU)-based filtering.
D. Deploy one server that runs Azure AD Connect, and then filter the users for each tenant by using domain-based filtering.

Section: (none)
Explanation

Explanation/Reference:
Explanation:
There's a 1:1 relationship between an Azure AD Connect sync server and an Azure AD tenant. For each Azure AD tenant, you need one Azure AD Connect sync server installation. Therefore, we need to deploy two servers that run Azure AD Connect for the two Azure AD tenants.

Each user account can only be synchronized to one Azure AD tenant. Therefore, we need a way of splitting the users between the two Azure AD tenants. Azure AD Connect offers three ways to filter which users get synchronized to an Azure AD tenant. You can use domain-based filtering if you have multiple domains in a forest, attribute-based filtering or OU-based filtering.

Reference:
https://docs.microsoft.com/en-us/azure/active-directory/hybrid/plan-connect-topologies#multiple-azure-ad-tenants

https://docs.microsoft.com/en-us/azure/active-directory/hybrid/how-to-connect-sync-configure-filtering

QUESTION 32

You network contains an on-premises Active Directory domain named contoso.com. The domain contains a Microsoft Exchange Server 2019 organization.

You plan to sync the domain to Azure Active Directory (Azure AD) and to enable device writeback and group writeback.

You need to identify which group types will sync from Azure AD.

Which two group types should you identify? Each correct answer presents a complete solution.

NOTE: Each correct selection is worth one point.

- A. an Office 365 group that uses the Assigned membership type
- B. a security group that uses the Dynamic Device membership type
- C. an Office 365 group that uses the Dynamic User membership type
- D. a security group that uses the Assigned membership type
- E. a security group that uses the Dynamic User membership type

Section: (none)
Explanation

Explanation/Reference:
Explanation:
Group writeback in Azure AD Connect synchronizes Office 365 groups only from Azure Active Directory back to the on-premise Active Directory.

Reference:
https://docs.microsoft.com/en-us/azure/active-directory/hybrid/how-to-connect-preview

Testlet 2

This is a case study. **Case studies are not timed separately. You can use as much exam time as you would like to complete each case**. However, there may be additional case studies and sections on this exam. You must manage your time to ensure that you are able to complete all questions included on this exam in the time provided.

To answer the questions included in a case study, you will need to reference information that is provided in the case study. Case studies might contain exhibits and other resources that provide more information about the scenario that is described in the case study. Each question is independent of the other questions in this case study.

At the end of this case study, a review screen will appear. This screen allows you to review your answer and to make changes before you move to the next section of the exam. After you begin a new section, you cannot return to this section.

To start the case study
To display the first question in this case study, click the **Next** button. Use the buttons in the left pane to explore the content of the case study before you answer the questions. Clicking these buttons displays information such as business requirements, existing environment, and problem statements. When you are ready to answer a question, click the **Question** button to return to the question.

Overview
Contoso, Ltd. is a consulting company that has a main office in Montreal and two branch offices in Seattle and New York.

The offices have the users and devices shown in the following table.

Office	Users	Laptops	Desktops	Mobile devices
Montreal	2,500	2,800	300	3,100
Seattle	1,000	1,100	200	1,500
New York	300	320	30	400

Contoso recently purchased a Microsoft 365 E5 subscription.

Existing Environment
The network contains an Active directory forest named contoso.com and a Microsoft Azure Active Directory (Azure AD) tenant named contoso.onmicrosoft.com.

You recently configured the forest to sync to the Azure AD tenant. You

add and then verify adatum.com as an additional domain name. All

servers run Windows Server 2016.

All desktop computers and laptops run Windows 10 Enterprise and are joined to contoso.com.

All the mobile devices in the Montreal and Seattle offices run Android. All the mobile devices in the New York office run iOS.

Contoso has the users shown in the following table.

Name	Role
User1	*None*
User2	*None*
User3	Customer Lockbox access approver
User4	*None*

Contoso has the groups shown in the following table.

Name	Type	Membership rule
Group1	Assigned	*Not applicable*
Group 2	Dynamic	(user.department –eq "Finance")

Microsoft Office 365 licenses are assigned only to Group2.

The network also contains external users from a vendor company who have Microsoft accounts that use a suffix of @outlook.com.

Requirements

Planned Changes
Contoso plans to provide email addresses for all the users in the following domains:

- East.adatum.com
- Contoso.adatum.com
- Humongousinsurance.com

Technical Requirements
Contoso identifies the following technical requirements:

- All new users must be assigned Office 365 licenses automatically.
- The principle of least privilege must be used whenever possible.

Security Requirements
Contoso identifies the following security requirements:

- Vendors must be able to authenticate by using their Microsoft account when accessing Contoso resources.
- User2 must be able to view reports and schedule the email delivery of security and compliance reports.

- The members of Group1 must be required to answer a security question before changing their password.
- User3 must be able to manage Office 365 connectors.
- User4 must be able to reset User3 password.

QUESTION 1
Note: This question is part of a series of questions that present the same scenario. Each question in the series contains a unique solution that might meet the stated goals. Some question sets might have more than one correct solution, while others might not have a correct solution.

After you answer a question in this section, you will NOT be able to return to it. As a result, these questions will not appear in the review screen.

You need to assign User2 the required roles to meet the security requirements.

Solution: From the Office 365 admin center, you assign User2 the Security Administrator role. From the Exchange admin center, you add User2 to the View-Only Organization Management role.

Does this meet the goal?

A. Yes
B. No

Section: (none)
Explanation

Explanation/Reference:
Explanation:
- User2 must be able to view reports and schedule the email delivery of security and compliance reports.

The Security Administrator role can view reports but not schedule the email delivery of security and compliance reports.
The View-Only Organization Management role cannot schedule the email delivery of security and compliance reports.

Reference:
https://docs.microsoft.com/en-us/exchange/permissions-exo/permissions-exo

QUESTION 2
Note: This question is part of a series of questions that present the same scenario. Each question in the series contains a unique solution that might meet the stated goals. Some question sets might have more than one correct solution, while others might not have a correct solution.

After you answer a question in this section, you will NOT be able to return to it. As a result, these questions will not appear in the review screen.

You need to assign User2 the required roles to meet the security requirements.

Solution: From the Office 365 admin center, you assign User2 the Security Reader role. From the Exchange admin center, you assign User2 the Help Desk role.

Does this meet the goal?

A. Yes

B. No

Section: (none)
Explanation

Explanation/Reference:
Explanation:
- User2 must be able to view reports and schedule the email delivery of security and compliance reports.

The Security Reader role can view reports but not schedule the email delivery of security and compliance reports.
The Help Desk role cannot schedule the email delivery of security and compliance reports.

Reference:
https://docs.microsoft.com/en-us/exchange/permissions-exo/permissions-exo

QUESTION 3
Note: This question is part of a series of questions that present the same scenario. Each question in the series contains a unique solution that might meet the stated goals. Some question sets might have more than one correct solution, while others might not have a correct solution.

After you answer a question in this section, you will NOT be able to return to it. As a result, these questions will not appear in the review screen.

You need to assign User2 the required roles to meet the security requirements.

Solution: From the Office 365 admin center, you assign User2 the Records Management role. From the Exchange admin center, you assign User2 the Help Desk role.

Does this meet the goal?

A. Yes

B. No

Section: (none)
Explanation

Explanation/Reference:
Explanation:
- User2 must be able to view reports and schedule the email delivery of security and

compliance reports.

The Records Management role cannot view reports or schedule the email delivery of security and compliance reports.
The Help Desk role cannot schedule the email delivery of security and compliance reports.

Reference:
https://docs.microsoft.com/en-us/exchange/permissions-exo/permissions-exo

QUESTION 4
To which Azure AD role should you add User4 to meet the security requirement?

- A. Password administrator
- B. Global administrator
- C. Security administrator
- D. Privileged role administrator

Section: (none)
Explanation

Explanation/Reference:
Explanation:
- User4 must be able to reset User3 password.

User3 is assigned the Customer Lockbox Access Approver role. Only global admins can reset the passwords of people assigned to this role as it's considered a privileged role.

Reference:
https://techcommunity.microsoft.com/t5/Security-Privacy-and-Compliance/Customer-Lockbox-Approver-Role-Now-Available/ba-p/223393

Manage Access and Authentication

Question Set 1

QUESTION 1
Note: This question is part of a series of questions that present the same scenario. Each question in the series contains a unique solution that might meet the stated goals. Some question sets might have more than one correct solution, while others might not have a correct solution.

After you answer a question in this section, you will NOT be able to return to it. As a result, these questions will not appear in the review screen.

You have a Microsoft 365 subscription.

You need to prevent users from accessing your Microsoft SharePoint Online sites unless the users are connected to your on-premises network.

Solution: From the Device Management admin center, you a trusted location and compliance policy.

Does this meet the goal?

A. Yes
B. No

Section: (none)
Explanation

Explanation/Reference:
Explanation:
You need to configure a conditional access policy, not a compliance policy.
Conditional Access in SharePoint Online can be configured to use an IP Address white list to allow access.

Reference:
https://techcommunity.microsoft.com/t5/Microsoft-SharePoint-Blog/Conditional-Access-in-SharePoint-Online-and-OneDrive-for/ba-p/46678

QUESTION 2
Note: This question is part of a series of questions that present the same scenario. Each question in the series contains a unique solution that might meet the stated goals. Some question sets might have more than one correct solution, while others might not have a correct solution.

After you answer a question in this section, you will NOT be able to return to it. As a result, these questions will not appear in the review screen.

You have a Microsoft 365 subscription.

You need to prevent users from accessing your Microsoft SharePoint Online sites unless the users are connected to your on-premises network.

Solution: From the Microsoft 365 admin center, you configure the Organization profile settings.

Does this meet the goal?

A. Yes
B. No

Section: (none)
Explanation

Explanation/Reference:
Explanation:
You need to configure a trusted location and a conditional access policy.
Conditional Access in SharePoint Online can be configured to use an IP Address white list to allow access.

Reference:
https://techcommunity.microsoft.com/t5/Microsoft-SharePoint-Blog/Conditional-Access-in-SharePoint-Online-and-OneDrive-for/ba-p/46678

QUESTION 3
Note: This question is part of a series of questions that present the same scenario. Each question in the series contains a unique solution that might meet the stated goals. Some question sets might have more than one correct solution, while others might not have a correct solution.

After you answer a question in this section, you will NOT be able to return to it. As a result, these questions will not appear in the review screen.

You have a Microsoft 365 subscription.

You need to prevent users from accessing your Microsoft SharePoint Online sites unless the users are connected to your on-premises network.

Solution: From the Azure Active Directory admin center, you create a trusted location and a conditional access policy.

Does this meet the goal?

A. Yes
B. No

Section: (none)
Explanation

Explanation/Reference:
Explanation:

Conditional Access in SharePoint Online can be configured to use an IP Address white list to allow access.
With named locations, you can create logical groupings of IP address ranges, for example your office IP range. You can then mark the named location as a trusted location.
Mark as trusted location - A flag you can set for a named location to indicate a trusted location. Typically, trusted locations are network areas that are controlled by your IT department. You would then configure the conditional access policy to allow access only from the trusted location.

Reference:
https://docs.microsoft.com/en-us/azure/active-directory/conditional-access/location-condition

https://techcommunity.microsoft.com/t5/Microsoft-SharePoint-Blog/Conditional-Access-in-SharePoint-Online-and-OneDrive-for/ba-p/46678

QUESTION 4
Your company recently purchased a Microsoft 365 subscription.

You enable Microsoft Azure Multi-Factor Authentication (MFA) for all 500 users in the Azure Active Directory (Azure AD) tenant.

You need to generate a report that lists all the users who completed the Azure MFA registration process.

What is the best approach to achieve the goal? More than one answer choice may achieve the goal. Select the **BEST** answer.

A. From Azure Cloud Shell, run the `Get-AzureADUser` cmdlet.
B. From Azure Cloud Shell, run the `Get-MsolUser` cmdlet.
C. From the Azure Active Directory admin center, use the Multi-Factor Authentication – Server Status blade.
D. From the Azure Active Directory admin center, use Risky sign-ins blade.

Section: (none)
Explanation

Explanation/Reference:
Explanation:
You can use the `Get-MsolUser` cmdlet to generate a report that lists all the users who completed the Azure MFA registration process. The full command would look like this:

```
Get-MsolUser -All | Where-Object {$_.StrongAuthenticationMethods.Count
-eq 0} | Select-Object -Property UserPrincipalName
```

Reference:
https://docs.microsoft.com/en-us/azure/active-directory/authentication/howto-mfa-reporting

QUESTION 5
You have a Microsoft 365 Enterprise subscription.

You have a conditional access policy to force multi-factor authentication when accessing Microsoft SharePoint from a mobile device.

You need to view which users authenticated by using multi-factor authentication.

What should you do?

A. From the Microsoft 365 admin center, view the Security & Compliance reports.
B. From the Azure Active Directory admin center, view the user sign-ins.
C. From the Microsoft 365 admin center, view the Usage reports.
D. From the Azure Active Directory admin center, view the audit logs.

Section: (none)
Explanation

Explanation/Reference:
Explanation:
With the **sign-ins activity report** in the Azure portal, you can get the information you need to determine how your environment is doing.
The sign-ins report can provide you with information about the usage of managed applications and user sign-in activities, which includes information about multi-factor authentication (MFA) usage. The MFA data gives you insights into how MFA is working in your organization. It enables you to answer questions like:
 • Was the sign-in challenged with MFA?
 • How did the user complete MFA?
 • Why was the user unable to complete MFA?
 • How many users are challenged for MFA?
 • How many users are unable to complete the MFA challenge?
 • What are the common MFA issues end users are running into?

Reference:
https://docs.microsoft.com/en-us/azure/active-directory/authentication/howto-mfa-reporting

QUESTION 6
You have a Microsoft 365 Enterprise E5 subscription.

You need to enforce multi-factor authentication on all cloud-based applications for the users in the finance department.

What should you do?

A. Create a sign-in risk policy.
B. Create a new app registration.
C. Create an app permission policy.
D. Assign an Enterprise Mobility + Security E5 license to the finance department users.

Section: (none)
Explanation

Explanation/Reference:
Explanation:
You can configure a sign-in risk policy that applies to the Finance department users. The policy can be configured to 'Allow access' but with multi-factor authentication as a requirement.

Reference:
https://docs.microsoft.com/en-us/azure/active-directory/identity-protection/howto-sign-in-risk-policy

QUESTION 7

Your network contains an on-premises Active Directory domain named contoso.local. The domain contains five domain controllers.

Your company purchases Microsoft 365 and creates a Microsoft Azure Active Directory (Azure AD) tenant named contoso.onmicrosoft.com.

You plan to implement pass-through authentication.

You need to prepare the environment for the planned implementation of pass-through authentication.

Which three actions should you perform? Each correct answer presents part of the solution.

NOTE: Each correct selection is worth one point.

A. Modify the email address attribute for each user account.
B. From the Azure portal, add a custom domain name.
C. From Active Directory Domains and Trusts, add a UPN suffix.
D. Modify the User logon name for each user account.
E. From the Azure portal, configure an authentication method.
F. From a domain controller, install an Authentication Agent.

Section: (none)
Explanation

Explanation/Reference:
Explanation:
To implement pass-through authentication, you need to install and configure Azure AD Connect.

The on-premise Active Directory domain is named contoso.local. Before you can configure Azure AD Connect, you need to purchase a routable domain, for example, contoso.com. You then need to add the domain contoso.com to Microsoft as a custom domain name.

The user accounts in the Active Directory domain need to be configured to use the domain name contoso.com as a UPN suffix. You need to add contoso.com to the Active Directory first by using Active Directory Domains and Trusts to add contoso.com add a UPN suffix. You can then configure each account to use the new UPN suffix.

An Authentication Agent is required on a domain controller to perform the authentication when pass-through authentication is used. When the custom domain and user accounts are configured, you can install and configure Azure AD Connect. An Authentication Agent is installed when you select the pass-through authentication option in the Azure AD Connect configuration or you can install the Authentication Agent manually.

Reference:
https://docs.microsoft.com/en-us/azure/active-directory/hybrid/how-to-connect-pta-quick-start

QUESTION 8
Note: This question is part of a series of questions that present the same scenario. Each question in the series contains a unique solution that might meet the stated goals. Some question sets might have more than one correct solution, while others might not have a correct solution.

After you answer a question in this section, you will NOT be able to return to it. As a result, these questions will not appear in the review screen.

Your company plans to deploy several Microsoft Office 365 services.

You need to design an authentication strategy for the planned deployment. The solution must meet the following requirements:

- Users must be able to authenticate during business hours only.
- Authentication requests must be processed successfully if a single server fails.
- When the password for an on-premises user account expires, the new password must be enforced the next time the user signs in.
- Users who connect to Office 365 services from domain-joined devices that are connected to the internal network must be signed in automatically.

Solution: You design an authentication strategy that contains a pass-through authentication model. The solution contains two servers that have an Authentication Agent installed and password hash synchronization configured.

Does this meet the goal?

A. Yes
B. No

Section: (none)
Explanation

Explanation/Reference:
Explanation:
This solution meets the following goals:
- Users must be able to authenticate during business hours only.
- Authentication requests must be processed successfully if a single server fails.
- When the password for an on-premises user account expires, the new password must be enforced the next time the user signs in.

However, the following goal is not met:
- Users who connect to Office 365 services from domain-joined devices that are connected to

the internal network must be signed in automatically.

You would need to configure Single-sign on (SSO) to meet the last requirement.

Reference:
https://docs.microsoft.com/en-us/azure/security/azure-ad-choose-authn

QUESTION 9
Note: This question is part of a series of questions that present the same scenario. Each question in the series contains a unique solution that might meet the stated goals. Some question sets might have more than one correct solution, while others might not have a correct solution.

After you answer a question in this section, you will NOT be able to return to it. As a result, these questions will not appear in the review screen.

Your company plans to deploy several Microsoft Office 365 services.

You need to design an authentication strategy for the planned deployment. The solution must meet the following requirements:

- Users must be able to authenticate during business hours only.
- Authentication requests must be processed successfully if a single server fails.
- When the password for an on-premises user account expires, the new password must be enforced the next time the user signs in.
- Users who connect to Office 365 services from domain-joined devices that are connected to the internal network must be signed in automatically.

Solution: You design an authentication strategy that contains a pass-through authentication model. You install an Authentication Agent on three servers and configure seamless SSO.

Does this meet the goal?

A. Yes
B. No

Section: (none)
Explanation

Explanation/Reference:
Explanation:
This solution meets all the requirements:
- Users must be able to authenticate during business hours only. (This can be configured by using Logon Hours in Active Directory. Pass-through authentication passes authentication to the on-premise Active Directory)
- Authentication requests must be processed successfully if a single server fails. (We have Authentication Agents running on three servers)
- When the password for an on-premises user account expires, the new password must be enforced the next time the user signs in. (This can be configured in Active Directory. Pass-through authentication passes authentication to the on-premise Active Directory)
- Users who connect to Office 365 services from domain-joined devices that are connected to

the internal network must be signed in automatically. (This goal is met by seamless SSO)

Reference:
https://docs.microsoft.com/en-us/azure/security/azure-ad-choose-authn

QUESTION 10
Note: This question is part of a series of questions that present the same scenario. Each question in the series contains a unique solution that might meet the stated goals. Some question sets might have more than one correct solution, while others might not have a correct solution.

After you answer a question in this section, you will NOT be able to return to it. As a result, these questions will not appear in the review screen.

Your company plans to deploy several Microsoft Office 365 services.

You need to design an authentication strategy for the planned deployment. The solution must meet the following requirements:

- Users must be able to authenticate during business hours only.
- Authentication requests must be processed successfully if a single server fails.
- When the password for an on-premises user account expires, the new password must be enforced the next time the user signs in.
- Users who connect to Office 365 services from domain-joined devices that are connected to the internal network must be signed in automatically.

Solution: You design an authentication strategy that uses password hash synchronization and seamless SSO. The solution contains two servers that have an Authentication Agent installed.

Does this meet the goal?

A. Yes
B. No

Section: (none)
Explanation

Explanation/Reference:
Explanation:
This solution meets the following requirements:
- Users who connect to Office 365 services from domain-joined devices that are connected to the internal network must be signed in automatically.
- Authentication requests must be processed successfully if a single server fails.

The following requirements are not met:
- Users must be able to authenticate during business hours only.
- When the password for an on-premises user account expires, the new password must be enforced the next time the user signs in.

To meet these two requirements, you would have to configure pass-through authentication.

Reference:
https://docs.microsoft.com/en-us/azure/security/azure-ad-choose-authn

QUESTION 11
HOTSPOT

You have an Azure Active Directory (Azure AD) tenant named contoso.com that contains the users shown in the following table.

Name	Member of	Multi-Factor Auth Status
User1	Group1	Disabled
User2	Group1	Required

Multi-factor authentication (MFA) is configured to use 131.107.50/24 for trusted IPs. The

tenant contains the named locations shown in the following table.

Name	IP address range	Trusted location
Location 1	131.107.20.0/24	Yes
Location 2	131.107.50.0/24	Yes

You create a conditional access policy that has the following configurations:

- Users and groups assignment: All users
- Cloud apps assignment: App1
- Conditions: Include all trusted locations
- Grant access: require multi-factor authentication

For each of the following statements, select Yes if the statement is true. otherwise, select No.

NOTE: Each correct selection is worth one point.

Hot Area:

Answer Area

Statements	Yes	No
When User1 connects to App1 from a device that has an IP address of 131.107.50.10, User1 must use MFA.	○	○
When User2 connects to App1 from a device that has an IP address of 131.107.50.15, User2 must use MFA.	○	○
When User2 connects to App1 from a device that has an IP address of 131.107.5.5, User2 must use MFA.	○	○

Section: (none)
Explanation

Explanation/Reference:
Explanation:

Box 1: Yes
131.107.50.10 is in a Trusted Location so the conditional access policy applies. The policy requires MFA so User1 must use MFA.

Box 2: Yes.
131.107.50.15 is in a Trusted Location so the conditional access policy applies. The policy requires MFA so User2 must use MFA.

Box 3: No.
131.107.5.5 is not in a Trusted Location so the conditional access policy does not apply. Therefore, User2 does not need to use MFA.

Reference:
https://docs.microsoft.com/en-us/azure/active-directory/conditional-access/location-condition

QUESTION 12
You have a Microsoft 365 Enterprise E5 subscription.

You need to enforce multi-factor authentication on all cloud-based applications for the users in the finance department.

What should you do?

A. Create an activity policy.

B. Create a new app registration.
C. Create a conditional access policy.
D. Create a session policy.

Section: (none)
Explanation

Explanation/Reference:
Explanation:
You can configure a conditional access policy that applies to the Finance department users. The policy can be configured to 'Allow access' but with multi-factor authentication as a requirement.

The reference below explains how to create a conditional access policy that requires MFA for all users. To apply the policy to finance users only, you would select Users and Group in the Include section instead of All Users and then specify the finance department group.

Reference:
https://docs.microsoft.com/en-us/azure/active-directory/conditional-access/howto-conditional-access-policy-all-users-mfa

QUESTION 13
You have a Microsoft 365 subscription.

Your company deploys an Active Directory Federation Services (AD FS) solution.

You need to configure the environment to audit AD FS user authentication.

Which two actions should you perform? Each correct answer presents part of the solution.

NOTE: Each correct selection is worth one point.

A. From all the AD FS servers, run `auditpol.exe`.
B. From all the domain controllers, run the `Set-AdminAuditLogConfig` cmdlet and specify the `-LogLevel` parameter.
C. On a domain controller, install Azure AD Connect Health for AD DS.
D. From the Azure AD Connect server, run the `Register-AzureADConnectHealthSyncAgent` cmdlet.
E. On an AD FS server, install Azure AD Connect Health for AD FS.

Section: (none)
Explanation

Explanation/Reference:
Explanation:
To audit AD FS user authentication, you need to install Azure AD Connect Health for AD FS. The agent should be installed on an AD FS server. After the installation, you need to register the agent by running the `Register-AzureADConnectHealthSyncAgent` cmdlet.

Reference:

QUESTION 14

Note: This question is part of a series of questions that present the same scenario. Each question in the series contains a unique solution that might meet the stated goals. Some question sets might have more than one correct solution, while others might not have a correct solution.

After you answer a question in this section, you will NOT be able to return to it. As a result, these questions will not appear in the review screen.

Your network contains an Active Directory forest.

You deploy Microsoft 365.

You plan to implement directory synchronization.

You need to recommend a security solution for the synchronized identities. The solution must meet the following requirements:

- Users must be able to authenticate successfully to Microsoft 365 services if Active Directory becomes unavailable.
- Users passwords must be 10 characters or more.

Solution: Implement password hash synchronization and configure password protection in the Azure AD tenant.

Does this meet the goal?

A. Yes
B. No

Section: (none)
Explanation

Explanation/Reference:
Explanation:
This solution meets the following requirement:
- Users must be able to authenticate successfully to Microsoft 365 services if Active Directory becomes unavailable. (this is because the authentication is performed by Azure Active Directory).

This solution does not meet the following requirement:
- Users passwords must be 10 characters or more.

To meet this requirement, you would need to configure the Default Domain Policy in the on-premise Active Directory.

Azure Password Protection can prevent users from using passwords from a 'banned password' list but it cannot be configured to require that passwords must be 10 characters or more.

Reference:
https://docs.microsoft.com/en-us/azure/active-directory/hybrid/how-to-connect-password-hash-synchronization

QUESTION 15
Note: This question is part of a series of questions that present the same scenario. Each question in the series contains a unique solution that might meet the stated goals. Some question sets might have more than one correct solution, while others might not have a correct solution.

After you answer a question in this section, you will NOT be able to return to it. As a result, these questions will not appear in the review screen.

Your network contains an Active Directory forest.

You deploy Microsoft 365.

You plan to implement directory synchronization.

You need to recommend a security solution for the synchronized identities. The solution must meet the following requirements:

- Users must be able to authenticate successfully to Microsoft 365 services if Active Directory becomes unavailable.
- Users passwords must be 10 characters or more.

Solution: Implement pass-through authentication and configure password protection in the Azure AD tenant.

Does this meet the goal?

A. Yes
B. No

Section: (none)
Explanation

Explanation/Reference:
Explanation:
This solution does not meet the following requirement:
- Users must be able to authenticate successfully to Microsoft 365 services if Active Directory becomes unavailable.
This is because with pass-through authentication, the authentication is performed by the on-premise Active Directory.

This solution does not meet the following requirement:
- Users passwords must be 10 characters or more.
To meet this requirement, you would need to configure the Default Domain Policy in the on-

premise Active Directory.

Azure Password Protection can prevent users from using passwords from a 'banned password' list but it cannot be configured to require that passwords must be 10 characters or more.

Reference:
https://docs.microsoft.com/en-us/azure/active-directory/hybrid/how-to-connect-password-hash-synchronization

QUESTION 16
Your company has three main offices and one branch office. The branch office is used for research.

The company plans to implement a Microsoft 365 tenant and to deploy multi-factor authentication.

You need to recommend a Microsoft 365 solution to ensure that multi-factor authentication is enforced only for users in the branch office.

What should you include in the recommendation?

A. Microsoft Azure Active Directory (Azure AD) conditional access.
B. Microsoft Azure Active Directory (Azure AD) password protection.
C. a Microsoft 365 Device Management device compliance policy.
D. a Microsoft 365 Device Management device configuration profile.

Section: (none)
Explanation

Explanation/Reference:
Explanation:
With Azure Active Directory (Azure AD) Conditional Access, you can control how authorized users can access your cloud apps. The location condition of a Conditional Access policy enables you to tie access controls settings to the network locations of your users.

For this question, we need to configure a location condition in a conditional access policy and apply the policy to users in that location (the branch office). The conditional access policy can be required to 'Allow Access' but 'Required MFA'.

Reference:
https://docs.microsoft.com/en-us/azure/active-directory/conditional-access/location-condition

QUESTION 17
Your network contains an Active Directory domain named contoso.com.

All users authenticate by using a third-party authentication solution.

You purchase Microsoft 365 and plan to implement several Microsoft 365 services.

You need to recommend an identity strategy that meets the following requirements:

- Provides seamless SSO
- Minimizes the number of additional servers required to support the solution
- Stores the passwords of all the users in Microsoft Azure Active Directory (Azure AD)
- Ensures that all the users authenticate to Microsoft 365 by using their on-premises user account

You are evaluating the implementation of federation.

Which two requirements are met by using federation? Each correct answer presents a complete solution.

NOTE: Each correct selection is worth one point.

A. minimizes the number of additional servers required to support the solution
B. provides seamless SSO
C. stores the passwords of all the users in Azure AD
D. ensures that all the users authenticate to Microsoft 365 by using their on-premises user account

Section: (none)
Explanation

Explanation/Reference:
Explanation:
When you choose this federation as the authentication method, Azure AD hands off the authentication process to a separate trusted authentication system, such as on-premises Active Directory Federation Services (AD FS), to validate the user's password. AD FS can use on-premise Active Directory as an authentication provider. AD FS can also provide SSO when using Active Directory as an authentication provider.

Incorrect Answers:
A: Additional servers are required to support the AD FS infrastructure.
C: The passwords are not synchronised to Azure AD.

Reference:
https://docs.microsoft.com/en-us/azure/security/azure-ad-choose-authn

QUESTION 18
Note: This question is part of a series of questions that present the same scenario. Each question in the series contains a unique solution that might meet the stated goals. Some question sets might have more than one correct solution, while others might not have a correct solution.

After you answer a question in this section, you will NOT be able to return to it. As a result, these questions will not appear in the review screen.

Your company plans to deploy several Microsoft Office 365 services.

You need to design an authentication strategy for the planned deployment. The solution must meet the following requirements:

- Users must be able to authenticate during business hours only.
- Authentication requests must be processed successfully if a single server fails.
- When the password for an on-premises user account expires, the new password must be enforced the next time the user signs in.
- Users who connect to Office 365 services from domain-joined devices that are connected to the internal network must be signed in automatically.

Solution: You design an authentication strategy that uses federation authentication by using Active Directory Federation Services (AD FS). The solution contains two AD FS servers and two Web Application Proxies.

Does this meet the goal?

A. Yes
B. No

Section: (none)
Explanation

Explanation/Reference:
Explanation:
This solution meets the following requirements:
- Users must be able to authenticate during business hours only.
- Authentication requests must be processed successfully if a single server fails.
- When the password for an on-premises user account expires, the new password must be enforced the next time the user signs in.

The following requirement is not met:
- Users who connect to Office 365 services from domain-joined devices that are connected to the internal network must be signed in automatically.

To meet this requirement, you would need to configure seamless Single Sign-on (SSO)

Reference:
https://docs.microsoft.com/en-us/azure/security/azure-ad-choose-authn

QUESTION 19
HOTSPOT

You have a Microsoft 365 subscription that contains the users shown in the following table.

Name	Group
User1	Group1
User2	Group1, Group2

You have the named locations shown in the following table.

Named location	IP range
Montreal	133.107.0.0/16
Toronto	193.77.10.0/24

You create a conditional access policy that has the following configurations:

- Users and groups:
- Include: Group1
- Exclude: Group2

Cloud apps: Include all cloud apps

- Conditions:
- Include: Any location
- Exclude: Montreal

Access control: Grant access, Require multi-factor authentication

User1 is on the multi-factor authentication (MFA) blocked users list.

For each of the following statements, select Yes if the statement is true. Otherwise, select No.

NOTE: Each correct selection is worth one point.

Hot Area:

Answer Area

Statements	Yes	No
User1 can access Microsoft Office 365 from a device that has an IP address of 133.107.10.20.	O	O
User1 can access Microsoft Office 365 from a device that has an IP address of 193.77.10.15.	O	O
User2 can access Microsoft Office 365 from a device that has an IP address of 193.77.10.20.	O	O

Section: (none)
Explanation

Explanation/Reference:
Explanation:

The Blocked User list is used to block specific users from being able to receive Multi-Factor Authentication requests. Any authentication attempts for blocked users are automatically denied. Users remain blocked for 90 days from the time that they are blocked.

Box 1: Yes

133.107.10.20 is in the Montreal named location. The conditional access policy excludes Montreal so the policy does not apply. Therefore, User1 can access Microsoft Office 365.

Box 2: No
193.77.10.15 is in the Toronto named location. The conditional access policy applies to Group1 which User1 is a member of and all locations except for Montreal. Therefore, the conditional access policy applies in this case. The policy requires MFA but User1 is on the MFA blocked list so he is unable to use MFA. Therefore, User1 cannot access Microsoft 365.

Box 3: Yes
User2 is in Group1 and Group2. The conditional access policy applies to Group1 but excludes Group2. Therefore, the conditional access policy does not apply in this case so User2 can access Microsoft Office 365.

Reference:
https://docs.microsoft.com/en-us/azure/active-directory/authentication/howto-mfa-mfasettings

QUESTION 20
Your network contains an Active Directory domain named contoso.com. The domain contains five domain controllers.

You purchase Microsoft 365 and plan to implement several Microsoft 365 services.

You need to identify an authentication strategy for the planned Microsoft 365 deployment. The solution must meet the following requirements:

- Ensure that users can access Microsoft 365 by using their on-premises credentials.
- Use the existing server infrastructure only.
- Store all user passwords on-premises only.
- Be highly available.

Which authentication strategy should you identify?

A. pass-through authentication and seamless SSO
B. pass-through authentication and seamless SSO with password hash synchronization
C. password hash synchronization and seamless SSO
D. federation

Section: (none)
Explanation

Explanation/Reference:
Explanation:
Azure AD Pass-through Authentication. Provides a simple password validation for Azure AD authentication services by using a software agent that runs on one or more on-premises servers. The servers validate the users directly with your on-premises Active Directory, which ensures that the password validation doesn't happen in the cloud.

Incorrect Answers:
B: Password hash synchronization replicates passwords to Azure Active Directory. This does not meet the following requirement: Store all user passwords on-premises only

C: Password hash synchronization replicates passwords to Azure Active Directory. This does not meet the following requirement: Store all user passwords on-premises only
D: Federation requires additional servers running Active Directory Federation Services. This does not meet the following requirement: Use the existing server infrastructure only.

Reference:
https://docs.microsoft.com/en-us/azure/security/fundamentals/choose-ad-authn

QUESTION 21
Your network contains an on-premises Active Directory domain.

You have a Microsoft 365 subscription.

You implement a directory synchronization solution that uses pass-through authentication.

You configure Microsoft Azure Active Directory (Azure AD) smart lockout as shown in the following exhibit.

🖫 Save	✗ Discard

Custom smart lockout

Lockout threshold ❶	5

Lockout duration in seconds ❶	60

Custom banned passwords

Enforce custom list ❶	**Yes**	No

Custom banned password list ❶	password PaSSw0rd Pa55w0rd Contoso	⌄

Password protection for Windows Server Active Directory

Enable password protection on Windows Server Active Directory ❶	**Yes**	No

Mode ❶	Enforced	**Audit**

You discover that Active Directory users can use the passwords in the custom banned passwords list.

You need to ensure that banned passwords are effective for all users.

Which three actions should you perform? Each correct answer presents part of the solution.

NOTE: Each correct selection is worth one point.

- A. From a domain controller, install the Azure AD Password Protection Proxy.
- B. From a domain controller, install the Microsoft AAD Application Proxy connector.
- C. From Custom banned passwords, modify the Enforce custom list setting.
- D. From Password protection for Windows Server Active Directory, modify the Mode setting.
- E. From all the domain controllers, install the Azure AD Password Protection DC Agent.
- F. From Active Directory, modify the Default Domain Policy.

Section: (none)
Explanation

Explanation/Reference:
Explanation:
Azure AD password protection is a feature that enhances password policies in an organization. On-premises deployment of password protection uses both the global and custom banned-password lists that are stored in Azure AD. It does the same checks on-premises as Azure AD does for cloud-based changes. These checks are performed during password changes and password reset scenarios.

You need to install the Azure AD Password Protection Proxy on a domain controller and install the Azure AD Password Protection DC Agent on all domain controllers. When the proxy and agent are installed and configured, Azure AD password protection will work.

In the exhibit, the password protection is configured in Audit mode. This is used for testing. To enforce the configured policy, you need to set the password protection setting to Enforced.

Reference:
https://docs.microsoft.com/en-us/azure/active-directory/authentication/howto-password-ban-bad-on-premises-deploy

https://docs.microsoft.com/en-us/azure/active-directory/authentication/concept-password-ban-bad-on-premises

QUESTION 22
You have a Microsoft Azure Active Directory (Azure AD) tenant named contoso.onmicrosoft.com.

An external user has a Microsoft account that uses an email address of user1@outlook.com.

An administrator named Admin1 attempts to create a user account for the external user and receives the error message shown in the following exhibit.

You need to ensure that Admin1 can add the user.

What should you do from the Azure Active Directory admin center?

   A. Add a custom domain name named outlook.com.
   B. Modify the Authentication methods.
   C. Modify the External collaboration settings.
   D. Assign Admin1 the Security administrator role.

Section: (none)
Explanation

Explanation/Reference:
Explanation:
In the External Collaboration settings, you can set the following invitation policies:
   ▪ Turn off invitations
   ▪ Only admins and users in the Guest Inviter role can invite
   ▪ Admins, the Guest Inviter role, and members can invite
   ▪ All users, including guests, can invite
In this question, an Admin user is unable to invite the guest user. This suggests that invitations
are turned off altogether.

Reference:
https://docs.microsoft.com/en-us/azure/active-directory/b2b/delegate-invitations

QUESTION 23
Your company has a Microsoft 365 subscription that has multi-factor authentication configured
for all users.

Users that connect to Microsoft 365 services report that they are prompted for multi-factor
authentication multiple times a day.

You need to reduce the number of times the users are prompted for multi-factor authentication
on their company-owned devices.

What should you do?

   A. Enable the multi-factor authentication trusted IPs setting, and then verify each device as a
       trusted device.

B. Enable the remember multi-factor authentication setting, and then verify each device as a trusted device.
C. Enable the multi-factor authentication trusted IPs setting, and then join all client computers to Microsoft Azure Active Directory (Azure AD).
D. Enable the remember multi-factor authentication setting, and then join all client computers to Microsoft Azure Active Directory (Azure AD).

Section: (none)
Explanation

Explanation/Reference:
Explanation:
The remember Multi-Factor Authentication feature for devices and browsers that are trusted by the user is a free feature for all Multi-Factor Authentication users. Users can bypass subsequent verifications for a specified number of days, after they've successfully signed-in to a device by using Multi-Factor Authentication. The feature enhances usability by minimizing the number of times a user has to perform two-step verification on the same device.

Reference:
https://docs.microsoft.com/en-us/azure/active-directory/authentication/howto-mfa-mfasettings

QUESTION 24
Your company has a Microsoft 365 subscription and a Microsoft Azure Active Directory (Azure AD) tenant named contoso.onmicrosoft.com.

An external vendor has a Microsoft account that has a username of user1@outlook.com. You

plan to provide user1@outlook.com with access to several resources in the subscription.

You need to add the external user account to contoso.onmicrosoft.com. The solution must ensure that the external vendor can authenticate by using user1@outlook.com.

What should you do?

A. From Azure Cloud Shell, run the `New-AzureADUser` cmdlet and specify `-UserPrincipalName user1@outlook.com`.
B. From the Microsoft 365 admin center, add a contact, and then specify user1@outlook.com as the email address.
C. From the Azure portal, add a new guest user, and then specify user1@outlook.com as the email address.
D. From the Azure portal, add a custom domain name, and then create a new Azure AD user and use user1@outlook.com as the username.

Section: (none)
Explanation

Explanation/Reference:
Explanation:
You can invite guest users to the directory, to a group, or to an application. After you invite a user through any of these methods, the invited user's account is added to Azure Active Directory

(Azure AD), with a user type of Guest. The guest user must then redeem their invitation to access resources. An invitation of a user does not expire.
The invitation will include a link to create a Microsoft account. The user can then authenticate using their Microsoft account. In this question, the external vendor already has a Microsoft account (user1@outlook.com) so he can authenticate using that.

Reference:
https://docs.microsoft.com/en-us/azure/active-directory/b2b/add-users-administrator

QUESTION 25
Your company has a hybrid deployment of Microsoft 365.

Users authenticate by using pass-through authentication. Several Microsoft Azure AD Connect Authentication Agents are deployed.

You need to verify whether all the Authentication Agents are used for authentication.

What should you do?

A. From the Azure portal, use the Troubleshoot option on the Pass-through authentication page.
B. From Performance Monitor, use the #PTA authentications counter.
C. From the Azure portal, use the Diagnostics settings on the Monitor blade.
D. From Performance Monitor, use the Kerberos authentications counter.

Section: (none)
Explanation

Explanation/Reference:
Explanation:
On the Troubleshoot page, you can view how many agents are configured. If you click on the agents link, you can view the status of each agent. Each agent will have a status of Active or Inactive.

Reference:
https://docs.microsoft.com/en-us/azure/active-directory/hybrid/tshoot-connect-pass-through-authentication

Manage Access and Authentication

Testlet 2

This is a case study. **Case studies are not timed separately. You can use as much exam time as you would like to complete each case**. However, there may be additional case studies and sections on this exam. You must manage your time to ensure that you are able to complete all questions included on this exam in the time provided.

To answer the questions included in a case study, you will need to reference information that is provided in the case study. Case studies might contain exhibits and other resources that provide more information about the scenario that is described in the case study. Each question is independent of the other questions in this case study.

At the end of this case study, a review screen will appear. This screen allows you to review your answer and to make changes before you move to the next section of the exam. After you begin a new section, you cannot return to this section.

To start the case study
To display the first question in this case study, click the **Next** button. Use the buttons in the left pane to explore the content of the case study before you answer the questions. Clicking these buttons displays information such as business requirements, existing environment, and problem statements. When you are ready to answer a question, click the **Question** button to return to the question.

Overview
Contoso, Ltd. is a consulting company that has a main office in Montreal and two branch offices in Seattle and New York.

The offices have the users and devices shown in the following table.

Office	Users	Laptops	Desktops	Mobile devices
Montreal	2,500	2,800	300	3,100
Seattle	1,000	1,100	200	1,500
New York	300	320	30	400

Contoso recently purchased a Microsoft 365 E5 subscription.

Existing Environment
The network contains an Active directory forest named contoso.com and a Microsoft Azure Active Directory (Azure AD) tenant named contoso.onmicrosoft.com.

You recently configured the forest to sync to the Azure AD tenant. You

add and then verify adatum.com as an additional domain name. All

servers run Windows Server 2016.

All desktop computers and laptops run Windows 10 Enterprise and are joined to contoso.com.

All the mobile devices in the Montreal and Seattle offices run Android. All the mobile devices in the New York office run iOS.

Contoso has the users shown in the following table.

Name	Role
User1	*None*
User2	*None*
User3	Customer Lockbox access approver
User4	*None*

Contoso has the groups shown in the following table.

Name	Type	Membership rule
Group1	Assigned	*Not applicable*
Group 2	Dynamic	(user.department –eq "Finance")

Microsoft Office 365 licenses are assigned only to Group2.

The network also contains external users from a vendor company who have Microsoft accounts that use a suffix of @outlook.com.

Requirements

Planned Changes
Contoso plans to provide email addresses for all the users in the following domains:

- East.adatum.com
- Contoso.adatum.com
- Humongousinsurance.com

Technical Requirements
Contoso identifies the following technical requirements:

- All new users must be assigned Office 365 licenses automatically.
- The principle of least privilege must be used whenever possible.

Security Requirements
Contoso identifies the following security requirements:

- Vendors must be able to authenticate by using their Microsoft account when accessing Contoso resources.
- User2 must be able to view reports and schedule the email delivery of security and compliance reports.

- The members of Group1 must be required to answer a security question before changing their password.
- User3 must be able to manage Office 365 connectors.
- User4 must be able to reset User3 password.

QUESTION 1
You need to meet the security requirement for Group1.

What should you do?

A. Configure all users to sign in by using multi-factor authentication.
B. Modify the properties of Group1.
C. Assign Group1 a management role.
D. Modify the Password reset properties of the Azure AD tenant.

Section: (none)
Explanation

Explanation/Reference:
Explanation:
- The members of Group1 must be required to answer a security question before changing their password.

If SSPR (Self Service Password Reset) is enabled, you must select at least one of the following options for the authentication methods. Sometimes you hear these options referred to as "gates."

Mobile app notification
Mobile app code Email
Mobile phone Office
phone Security
questions

You can specify the required authentication methods in the Password reset properties of the Azure AD tenant. In this case, you should set the required authentication method to be 'Security questions'.

Reference:
https://docs.microsoft.com/en-us/azure/active-directory/authentication/concept-sspr-howitworks

QUESTION 2
You need to meet the security requirement for the vendors.

What should you do?

A. From the Azure portal, add an identity provider.
B. From Azure Cloud Shell, run the `New-AzureADUser` cmdlet and specify the – `UserPrincipalName` parameter.

C. From Azure Cloud Shell, run the `Set-AzureADUserExtension` cmdlet.

D. From the Azure portal, create guest accounts.

Section: (none)
Explanation

Explanation/Reference:
Explanation:
- Vendors must be able to authenticate by using their Microsoft account when accessing Contoso resources.

You can invite guest users to the directory, to a group, or to an application. After you invite a user through any of these methods, the invited user's account is added to Azure Active Directory (Azure AD), with a user type of Guest. The guest user must then redeem their invitation to access resources. An invitation of a user does not expire.
The invitation will include a link to create a Microsoft account. The user can then authenticate using their Microsoft account. In this question, the vendors already have Microsoft accounts so they can authenticate using them.

Reference:
https://docs.microsoft.com/en-us/azure/active-directory/b2b/add-users-administrator

Plan Office 365 Workloads and Applications

Question Set 1

QUESTION 1
You create a Microsoft 365 Enterprise subscription.

You assign licenses for all products to all users.

You need to ensure that all Microsoft Office 365 ProPlus installations occur from a network share. The solution must prevent the users from installing Office 365 ProPlus from the Internet.

Which three actions should you perform? Each correct answer presents part of the solution.

NOTE: Each correct selection is worth one point.

A. From your computer, run `setup.exe /download downloadconfig.xml`.
B. Create an XML download file.
C. From the Microsoft 365 admin center, deactivate the Office 365 licenses for all the users.
D. From each client computer, run `setup.exe /configure installconfig.xml`.
E. From the Microsoft 365 admin center, configure the Software download settings.

Section: (none)
Explanation

Explanation/Reference:
Explanation:
You can use the Office Deployment Tool (ODT) to download the installation files for Office 365 ProPlus from a local source on your network instead of from the Office Content Delivery Network (CDN).

The first step is to create the configuration file. You can download an XML template file and modify that.
The next step to install Office 365 ProPlus is to run the ODT executable in configure mode with a reference to the configuration file you just saved. In the following example, the configuration file is named installconfig.xml. setup.exe /configure installconfig.xml
After running the command, you should see the Office installation start.

To prevent the users from installing Office 365 ProPlus from the Internet, you need to configure the Software download settings (disallow downloads) in the Microsoft 365 admin center.

Reference:
https://docs.microsoft.com/en-us/deployoffice/overview-of-the-office-2016-deployment-tool#download-the-installation-files-for-office-365-proplus-from-a-local-source

QUESTION 2
Your network contains the servers shown in the following table.

Server name	Software	Configuration
Server1	Windows Server 2008	Domain controller
Server2	Windows Server 2012	Domain controller
Server3	Microsoft Exchange Server 2007	*Not applicable*
Server4	Microsoft SharePoint Server 2010	*Not applicable*
Server5	Microsoft Lync Server 2013	*Not applicable*

You purchase Microsoft 365 Enterprise E5 and plan to move all workloads to Microsoft 365 by using a hybrid identity solution and a hybrid deployment for all workloads.

You need to identify which server must be upgraded before you move to Microsoft 365.

What should you identify?

A. Server2
B. Server3
C. Server5
D. Server1
E. Server4

Section: (none)
Explanation

Explanation/Reference:
Explanation:
Exchange Server 2007 is not supported for a hybrid deployment.

Reference:
https://docs.microsoft.com/en-us/exchange/hybrid-deployment-prerequisites

QUESTION 3
Your on-premises network contains five file servers. The file servers host shares that contain user data.

You plan to migrate the user data to a Microsoft 365 subscription.

You need to recommend a solution to import the user data into Microsoft OneDrive.

What should you include in the recommendation?

A. Configure the settings of the OneDrive client on your Windows 10 device.
B. Configure the Sync settings in the OneDrive admin center.
C. Run the SharePoint Hybrid Configuration Wizard.
D. Run the SharePoint Migration Tool.

Section: (none)
Explanation

Explanation/Reference:
Explanation:
The SharePoint Migration Tool lets you migrate content to SharePoint Online and OneDrive from the following locations:

- SharePoint Server 2013
- SharePoint Server 2010
- Network and local file shares

Reference:
https://docs.microsoft.com/en-us/sharepointmigration/introducing-the-sharepoint-migration-tool

QUESTION 4
Your network contains two Active Directory forests. Each forest contains two domains. All client computers run Windows 10 and are domain-joined.

You plan to configure Hybrid Azure AD join for the computers. You

create a Microsoft Azure Active Directory (Azure AD) tenant.

You need to ensure that the computers can discover the Azure AD tenant.

What should you create?

- A. a new computer account for each computer
- B. a new service connection point (SCP) for each domain
- C. a new trust relationship for each forest
- D. a new service connection point (SCP) for each forest

Section: (none)
Explanation

Explanation/Reference:
Explanation:
Your devices use a service connection point (SCP) object during the registration to discover Azure AD tenant information. In your on-premises Active Directory instance, the SCP object for the hybrid Azure AD joined devices must exist in the configuration naming context partition of the computer's forest. There is only one configuration naming context per forest. In a multi-forest Active Directory configuration, the service connection point must exist in all forests that contain domain-joined computers.

Reference:
https://docs.microsoft.com/en-us/azure/active-directory/devices/hybrid-azuread-join-manual

QUESTION 5
You have a Microsoft 365 subscription. All users have client computers that run Windows 10 and have Microsoft Office 365 ProPlus installed.

Some users in the research department work for extended periods of time without an Internet connection.

How many days can the research department users remain offline before they are prevented from editing Office documents?

A. 10
B. 30
C. 90
D. 120

Section: (none)
Explanation

Explanation/Reference:
Explanation:
After 30 days, Microsoft Office 365 ProPlus will go into reduced functionality mode. When this happens, users will be able to open files but they won't be able to edit them.

As part of the installation process, Office 365 ProPlus communicates with the Office Licensing Service and the Activation and Validation Service to obtain and activate a product key. Each day, or each time the user logs on to their computer, the computer connects to the Activation and Validation Service to verify the license status and extend the product key. As long as the computer can connect to the Internet at least once every 30 days, Office remains fully functional. If the computer goes offline for more than 30 days, Office enters reduced functionality mode until the next time a connection can be made.

Reference:
https://docs.microsoft.com/en-us/deployoffice/overview-of-licensing-and-activation-in-office-365-proplus

QUESTION 6
Your network contains an Active Directory domain. The domain contains a server named Server1 that runs Windows Server 2016. Server1 has a share named Share1.

You have a hybrid deployment of Microsoft 365.

You need to migrate the content in Share1 to Microsoft OneDrive.

What should you use?

A. Windows Server Migration Tools
B. Microsoft SharePoint Migration Tool
C. Storage Migration Service

Section: (none)
Explanation

Explanation/Reference:
Explanation:
The SharePoint Migration Tool lets you migrate content to SharePoint Online and OneDrive from the following locations:

- SharePoint Server 2013
- SharePoint Server 2010
- Network and local file shares

Reference:
https://docs.microsoft.com/en-us/sharepointmigration/migrating-content-to-onedrive-for-business

https://docs.microsoft.com/en-us/sharepointmigration/introducing-the-sharepoint-migration-tool

QUESTION 7
Note: This question is part of a series of questions that present the same scenario. Each question in the series contains a unique solution that might meet the stated goals. Some question sets might have more than one correct solution, while others might not have a correct solution.

After you answer a question in this section, you will NOT be able to return to it. As a result, these questions will not appear in the review screen.

Your company has a main office and three branch offices. All the branch offices connect to the main office by using a WAN link. The main office has a high-speed Internet connection. All the branch offices connect to the Internet by using the main office connections.

Users use Microsoft Outlook 2016 to connect to a Microsoft Exchange Server mailbox hosted in the main office.

The users report that when the WAN link in their office becomes unavailable, they cannot access their mailbox.

You create a Microsoft 365 subscription, and then migrate all the user data to Microsoft 365.

You need to ensure that all the users can continue to use Outlook to receive email messages if a WAN link fails.

Solution: You enable Cached Exchange Mode for all the Outlook profiles.

Does this meet the goal?

A. Yes
B. No

Section: (none)
Explanation

Explanation/Reference:
Explanation:
The question states that the branch offices connect to the Internet by using the main office connections. Therefore, all Internet traffic goes over the WAN link between the branch office and main office.
After the migration, the users connect to their mailboxes hosted in Exchange Online over the Internet and therefore over the WAN link.

If the WAN link goes down, the branch office users will not be able to connect to the Internet and therefore will not be able to access their email using Outlook.

Using Cached mode would enable users to access emails that have already been downloaded as they would be cached in Outlook. However, the users would not be able to download new email or send email if the WAN link failed.

The solution is to add a direct connection to the Internet from the branch offices, so their Internet traffic does not go over the WAN link.

QUESTION 8

Your organization has an on-premises Microsoft Exchange Server 2016 organization. The organization is in the company's main office in Melbourne. The main office has a low-bandwidth connection to the Internet.

The organization contains 250 mailboxes.

You purchase a Microsoft 365 subscription and plan to migrate to Exchange Online next month.

In 12 months, you plan to increase the bandwidth available for the Internet connection.

You need to recommend the best migration strategy for the organization. The solution must minimize administrative effort.

What is the best recommendation to achieve the goal? More than one answer choice may achieve the goal. Select the **BEST** answer.

A. network upload
B. cutover migration
C. hybrid migration
D. staged migration

Section: (none)
Explanation

Explanation/Reference:
Explanation:
With a hybrid migration, you can migrate the mailboxes in small batches over a period of time which will help to avoid saturating the bandwidth. With the migration wizard, you can configure a migration batch to start outside office hours which would minimize bandwidth usage during office hours.
With a hybrid migration, you do not need to reconfigure Outlook to connect to the migrated mailbox. Outlook will automatically detect the new mailbox location. This reduces administrative effort.

Incorrect Answers:
A: 'Network upload' is not a defined migration strategy.

B: With a cutover migration, all mailboxes are migrated in one go. This is not suitable for a low bandwidth Internet connection. You would also need to manually reconfigure Outlook for each user which does not meet the requirement of minimizing administrative effort.

D: With a staged migration, mailboxes are migrated in batches. However, Microsoft recommends using a staged migration when you have more than 2000 mailboxes. You would also need to manually reconfigure Outlook for each user which does not meet the requirement of minimizing administrative effort.

Reference:
https://docs.microsoft.com/en-us/exchange/mailbox-migration/mailbox-migration

QUESTION 9
Your company has a Microsoft Azure Active Directory (Azure AD) directory tenant named contoso.onmicrosoft.com.

All users have client computers that run Windows 10 Pro and are joined to Azure AD.

The company purchases a Microsoft 365 E3 subscription.

You need to upgrade all the computers to Windows 10 Enterprise. The solution must minimize administrative effort.

You assign licenses from the Microsoft 365 admin center.

What should you do next?

A. Add a custom domain name to the subscription.
B. Deploy Windows 10 Enterprise by using Windows Autopilot.
C. Create a provisioning package, and then deploy the package to all the computers.
D. Instruct all the users to log off of their computer, and then to log in again.

Section: (none)
Explanation

Explanation/Reference:
Explanation:
With Windows Autopilot the user can set up pre-configure devices without the need consult their IT administrator.

Reference:
https://docs.microsoft.com/en-us/windows/deployment/windows-10-deployment-scenarios

https://docs.microsoft.com/en-us/windows/deployment/windows-autopilot/windows-autopilot

QUESTION 10
Your network contains an Active Directory forest named contoso.local.

You purchase a Microsoft 365 subscription.

You plan to move to Microsoft and to implement a hybrid deployment solution for the next 12 months.

You need to prepare for the planned move to Microsoft 365.

What is the best action to perform before you implement directory synchronization? More than one answer choice may achieve the goal. Select the **BEST** answer.

A. Purchase a third-party X.509 certificate.
B. Rename the Active Directory forest.
C. Purchase a custom domain name.
D. Create an external forest trust.

Section: (none)
Explanation

Explanation/Reference:
Explanation:
The first thing you need to do before you implement directory synchronization is to purchase a custom domain name. This could be the domain name that you use in your on-premise Active Directory if it's a routable domain name, for example, contoso.com.
If you use a non-routable domain name in your Active Directory, for example contoso.local, you'll need to add the routable domain name as a UPN suffix in Active Directory.

Reference:
https://docs.microsoft.com/en-us/office365/enterprise/set-up-directory-synchronization

QUESTION 11
You have a Microsoft Azure Active Directory (Azure AD) tenant named contoso.com.

You add an app named App1 to the enterprise applications in contoso.com.

You need to configure self-service for App1.

What should you do first?

A. Assign App1 to users and groups.
B. Add an owner to App1.
C. Configure the provisioning mode for App1.
D. Configure an SSO method for App1.

Section: (none)
Explanation

Explanation/Reference:
Explanation:
The provisioning mode (manual or automatic) needs to be configured for an app before you can enable self-service application access.

Incorrect Answers:
A: If you're assign App1 to users and groups, the users will not need to use self-service to request access to the App. They would already have access to the app.

B: The app does not need an owner. You would configure an owner to delegate control of the app. Without an owner, a Global Admin could configure self-service.
D: The SSO method depends on the provisioning mode.

Reference:
https://docs.microsoft.com/en-us/azure/active-directory/manage-apps/manage-self-service-access

https://techcommunity.microsoft.com/t5/Azure-Active-Directory-Identity/Employee-Self-Service-App-Access-for-Azure-AD-now-in-preview/ba-p/243966

QUESTION 12
Your on-premises network contains the web applications shown in the following table.

Name	Hosted on server
App1	Web1
App2	Web1
App3	Web2
App4	Web2

You purchase Microsoft 365, and then implement directory synchronization.

You plan to publish the web applications.

You need to ensure that all the applications are accessible by using the My Apps portal. The solution must minimize administrative effort.

What should you do first?

A. Deploy one conditional access policy.
B. Deploy one Application Proxy connector.
C. Create four application registrations.
D. Create a site-to-site VPN from Microsoft Azure to the on-premises network.

Section: (none)
Explanation

Explanation/Reference:
Explanation:
The Application Proxy connector is what connects the on-premises environment to the Azure Application Proxy.

Application Proxy is a feature of Azure AD that enables users to access on-premises web applications from a remote client. Application Proxy includes both the Application Proxy service which runs in the cloud, and the Application Proxy connector which runs on an on-premises server. Azure AD, the Application Proxy service, and the Application Proxy connector work together to securely pass the user sign-on token from Azure AD to the web application.

Reference:
https://docs.microsoft.com/en-us/azure/active-directory/manage-apps/application-proxy

https://docs.microsoft.com/en-us/azure/active-directory/manage-apps/application-proxy-connectors

QUESTION 13
Your network contains an Active Directory domain named contoso.com.

You have a Microsoft 365 subscription.

You have a Microsoft Azure Active Directory (Azure AD) tenant named contoso.onmicrosoft.com.

You implement directory synchronization.

The developers at your company plan to build an app named App1. App1 will connect to the Microsoft Graph API to provide access to several Microsoft Office 365 services.

You need to provide the URL for the authorization endpoint that App1 must use.

What should you provide?

A. https://login.microsoftonline.com/
B. https://contoso.com/contoso.onmicrosoft.com/app1
C. https://login.microsoftonline.com/contoso.onmicrosoft.com/
D. https://myapps.microsoft.com

Section: (none)
Explanation

Explanation/Reference:
Explanation:
In a single tenant application, sign-in requests are sent to the tenant's sign-in endpoint. For example, for contoso.onmicrosoft.com the endpoint would be: https://login.microsoftonline.com/ contoso.onmicrosoft.com. Requests sent to a tenant's endpoint can sign in users (or guests) in that tenant to applications in that tenant.

Reference:
https://docs.microsoft.com/en-us/azure/active-directory/develop/howto-convert-app-to-be-multi-tenant

QUESTION 14
DRAG DROP

Your company has a hybrid deployment of Azure Active Directory (Azure AD).

You purchase a Microsoft 365 subscription.

You plan to migrate the Home folder of each user to Microsoft 365 during several weeks. Each user has a device that runs Windows 10.

You need to recommend a solution to migrate the Home folder of five administrative users as quickly as possible.

Which three actions should you recommend be performed in sequence? To answer, move the appropriate actions from the list of actions to the answer area and arrange them in the correct order.

Select and Place:

Actions	Answer Area
Instruct the users to run gpupdate.exe /force at a command prompt on each device.	
From Group Policy Management Editor, configure the OneDrive settings.	
Copy the OneDrive Administrative Templates to your computer.	
From Group Policy Management Editor, configure the Folder Redirection settings.	
Deploy the Azure File Sync agent to all devices.	
From SharePoint Online, create 10 libraries.	

Section: (none)
Explanation

Explanation/Reference:
Explanation:

You need to configure a Group Policy Object (GPO) with the OneDrive settings required to redirect the Home folder of each user to Microsoft 365.

Before you can configure the Group Policy, you need to download the OneDrive Administrative Templates. These templates add the required OneDrive settings to Group Policy so you can configure the settings as required.

After the OneDrive settings have been configured in Group Policy, you can run the gpupdate / force command on the five computers to apply the new Group Policy settings immediately.

Reference:
https://practical365.com/clients/onedrive/migrate-home-drives-to-onedrive-for-business/

QUESTION 15
Note: This question is part of a series of questions that present the same scenario. Each

question in the series contains a unique solution that might meet the stated goals. Some question sets might have more than one correct solution, while others might not have a correct solution.

After you answer a question in this section, you will NOT be able to return to it. As a result, these questions will not appear in the review screen.

Your company has a main office and three branch offices. All the branch offices connect to the main office by using a WAN link. The main office has a high-speed Internet connection. All the branch offices connect to the Internet by using the main office connections.

Users use Microsoft Outlook 2016 to connect to a Microsoft Exchange Server mailbox hosted in the main office.

The users report that when the WAN link in their office becomes unavailable, they cannot access their mailbox.

You create a Microsoft 365 subscription, and then migrate all the user data to Microsoft 365.

You need to ensure that all the users can continue to use Outlook to receive email messages if a WAN link fails.

Solution: For each device, you configure an additional Outlook profile that uses IMAP.

Does this meet the goal?

A. Yes
B. No

Section: (none)
Explanation

Explanation/Reference:
Explanation:
The question states that the branch offices connect to the Internet by using the main office connections. Therefore, all Internet traffic goes over the WAN link between the branch office and main office.
After the migration, the users connect to their mailboxes hosted in Exchange Online over the Internet and therefore over the WAN link.

If the WAN link goes down, the branch office users will not be able to connect to the Internet and therefore will not be able to access their email using Outlook.

Using IMAP to access the mailboxes would still use the WAN link so this answer does achieve the goal.

The solution is to add a direct connection to the Internet from the branch offices, so their Internet traffic does not go over the WAN link.

QUESTION 16
Note: This question is part of a series of questions that present the same scenario. Each

question in the series contains a unique solution that might meet the stated goals. Some question sets might have more than one correct solution, while others might not have a correct solution.

After you answer a question in this section, you will NOT be able to return to it. As a result, these questions will not appear in the review screen.

Your company has a main office and three branch offices. All the branch offices connect to the main office by using a WAN link. The main office has a high-speed Internet connection. All the branch offices connect to the Internet by using the main office connections.

Users use Microsoft Outlook 2016 to connect to a Microsoft Exchange Server mailbox hosted in the main office.

The users report that when the WAN link in their office becomes unavailable, they cannot access their mailbox.

You create a Microsoft 365 subscription, and then migrate all the user data to Microsoft 365.

You need to ensure that all the users can continue to use Outlook to receive email messages if a WAN link fails.

Solution: In each branch office, you add a direct connection to the Internet.

Does this meet the goal?

A. Yes
B. No

Section: (none)
Explanation

Explanation/Reference:
Explanation:
The question states that the branch offices connect to the Internet by using the main office connections. Therefore, all Internet traffic goes over the WAN link between the branch office and main office.
After the migration, the users connect to their mailboxes hosted in Exchange Online over the Internet and therefore over the WAN link.

If the WAN link goes down, the branch office users will not be able to connect to the Internet and therefore will not be able to access their email using Outlook.

Adding a direct connection to the Internet from the branch offices would mean that the Internet traffic does not go over the WAN link. Therefore, if the WAN link fails, the users would still be able to access their email. Therefore, this solution does ensure that all the users can continue to use Outlook to receive email messages if a WAN link fails.

QUESTION 17
You have an on-premises web application that is published by using a URL of https://app.contoso.local.

You purchase a Microsoft 365 subscription.

Several external users must be able to connect to the web application.

You need to recommend a solution for external access to the application. The solution must support multi-factor authentication.

Which two actions should you recommend? Each correct answer presents part of the solution.

NOTE: Each correct selection is worth one point.

    A. From an on-premises server, install a connector and then publish the app.
    B. From the Azure Active Directory admin center, enable an Application Proxy.
    C. From the Azure Active Directory admin center, create a conditional access policy.
    D. From an on-premises server, install an Authentication Agent.
    E. Republish the web application by using https://app.contoso.com.

Section: (none)
Explanation

Explanation/Reference:
Explanation:
Azure Active Directory (Azure AD) has an Application Proxy service that enables users to access on-premises applications by signing in with their Azure AD account. The application proxy enables you to take advantage of Azure AD security features like Conditional Access and Multi-Factor Authentication.
To use Application Proxy, install a connector on each Windows server you're using with the Application Proxy service. The connector is an agent that manages the outbound connection from the on-premises application servers to Application Proxy in Azure AD.

Reference:
https://docs.microsoft.com/en-us/azure/active-directory/manage-apps/application-proxy-add-on-premises-application

QUESTION 18
You have a Microsoft 365 subscription.

From the Security & Compliance admin center, you create a content search of all the mailboxes that contain the word ProjectX.

You need to export the results of the content search. What

do you need to download the report?

    A. an export key
    B. a password
    C. a user certificate
    D. a certification authority (CA) certificate

Section: (none)
Explanation

Explanation/Reference:
Explanation:
When you export a report, the data is temporarily stored in a unique Azure Storage area in the Microsoft cloud before it's downloaded to your local computer.
To download the report from the Azure Storage Area, you need an export key.

Reference:
https://docs.microsoft.com/en-us/microsoft-365/compliance/export-a-content-search-report

Answers 1

Design and Implement Microsoft 365 Services

Question Set 1

Correct Answer: B

Correct Answer: B

Correct Answer: A

Correct Answer: B

Correct Answer: D

Correct Answer: B

Correct Answer: C

Correct Answer: C

Correct Answer: BD

Correct Answer: C

Correct Answer: C

Correct Answer: A

Correct Answer: B

Correct Answer: D

Correct Answer: C

Correct Answer: AE

Correct Answer: AB

Correct Answer: B

Correct Answer: B

Correct Answer: A

Correct Answer: B

Correct Answer: D

Correct Answer: D

Correct Answer: A

Correct Answer: A

Correct Answer: B

Correct Answer: B

Correct Answer: A

Correct Answer: C

Correct Answer: B

Correct Answer: E

Correct Answer: C

Correct Answer: A

Correct Answer: C

Correct Answer: D

Correct Answer: B

Correct Answer: B

Correct Answer: A

Correct Answer: B

Design and Implement Microsoft 365 Services

Testlet 2

This is a case study. **Case studies are not timed separately. You can use as much exam time as you would like to complete each case**. However, there may be additional case studies and sections on this exam. You must manage your time to ensure that you are able to complete all questions included on this exam in the time provided.

To answer the questions included in a case study, you will need to reference information that is provided in the case study. Case studies might contain exhibits and other resources that provide more information about the scenario that is described in the case study. Each question is independent of the other questions in this case study.

At the end of this case study, a review screen will appear. This screen allows you to review your answer and to make changes before you move to the next section of the exam. After you begin a new section, you cannot return to this section.

To start the case study
To display the first question in this case study, click the **Next** button. Use the buttons in the left pane to explore the content of the case study before you answer the questions. Clicking these buttons displays information such as business requirements, existing environment, and problem statements. When you are ready to answer a question, click the **Question** button to return to the question.

Overview
Contoso, Ltd. is a consulting company that has a main office in Montreal and two branch offices in Seattle and New York.

The offices have the users and devices shown in the following table.

Office	Users	Laptops	Desktops	Mobile devices
Montreal	2,500	2,800	300	3,100
Seattle	1,000	1,100	200	1,500
New York	300	320	30	400

Contoso recently purchased a Microsoft 365 E5 subscription.

Existing Environment
The network contains an Active directory forest named contoso.com and a Microsoft Azure Active Directory (Azure AD) tenant named contoso.onmicrosoft.com.

You recently configured the forest to sync to the Azure AD tenant.

You add and then verify adatum.com as an additional domain name.

All servers run Windows Server 2016.

All desktop computers and laptops run Windows 10 Enterprise and are joined to contoso.com.

All the mobile devices in the Montreal and Seattle offices run Android. All the mobile devices in the New York office run iOS.

Contoso has the users shown in the following table.

Name	Role
User1	*None*
User2	*None*
User3	Customer Lockbox access approver
User4	*None*

Contoso has the groups shown in the following table.

Name	Type	Membership rule
Group1	Assigned	*Not applicable*
Group 2	Dynamic	(user.department –eq "Finance")

Microsoft Office 365 licenses are assigned only to Group2.

The network also contains external users from a vendor company who have Microsoft accounts that use a suffix of @outlook.com.

Requirements

Planned Changes
Contoso plans to provide email addresses for all the users in the following domains:

- East.adatum.com
- Contoso.adatum.com
- Humongousinsurance.com

Technical Requirements
Contoso identifies the following technical requirements:

- All new users must be assigned Office 365 licenses automatically.
- The principle of least privilege must be used whenever possible.

Security Requirements
Contoso identifies the following security requirements:

- Vendors must be able to authenticate by using their Microsoft account when accessing Contoso resources.
- User2 must be able to view reports and schedule the email delivery of security and compliance reports.

- The members of Group1 must be required to answer a security question before changing their password.
- User3 must be able to manage Office 365 connectors.
- User4 must be able to reset User3 password.

Correct Answer: D

Design and Implement Microsoft 365 Services

Testlet 3

This is a case study. **Case studies are not timed separately. You can use as much exam time as you would like to complete each case**. However, there may be additional case studies and sections on this exam. You must manage your time to ensure that you are able to complete all questions included on this exam in the time provided.

To answer the questions included in a case study, you will need to reference information that is provided in the case study. Case studies might contain exhibits and other resources that provide more information about the scenario that is described in the case study. Each question is independent of the other questions in this case study.

At the end of this case study, a review screen will appear. This screen allows you to review your answer and to make changes before you move to the next section of the exam. After you begin a new section, you cannot return to this section.

To start the case study
To display the first question in this case study, click the **Next** button. Use the buttons in the left pane to explore the content of the case study before you answer the questions. Clicking these buttons displays information such as business requirements, existing environment, and problem statements. When you are ready to answer a question, click the **Question** button to return to the question.

Overview
Fabrikam, Inc. is an electronics company that produces consumer products. Fabrikam has 10,000 employees worldwide.

Fabrikam has a main office in London and branch offices in major cities in Europe, Asia, and the United States.

Existing Environment
Active Directory Environment
The network contains an Active Directory forest named fabrikam.com. The forest contains all the identities used for user and computer authentication.

Each department is represented by a top-level organizational unit (OU) that contains several child OUs for user accounts and computer accounts.

All users authenticate to on-premises applications by signing in to their device by using a UPN format of *username@fabrikam.com.*

Fabrikam does **NOT** plan to implement identity federation.

Network Infrastructure

Each office has a high-speed connection to the Internet.

Each office contains two domain controllers. All domain controllers are configured as a DNS server.

The public zone for fabrikam.com is managed by an external DNS server.

All users connect to an on-premises Microsoft Exchange Server 2016 organization. The users access their email by using Outlook Anywhere, Outlook on the web, or the Microsoft Outlook app for iOS. All the Exchange servers have the latest cumulative updates installed.

All shared company documents are stored on a Microsoft SharePoint Server farm.

Requirements
Planned Changes
Fabrikam plans to implement a Microsoft 365 Enterprise subscription and move all email and shared documents to the subscription.

Fabrikam plans to implement two pilot projects:

- Project1: During Project1, the mailboxes of 100 users in the sales department will be moved to Microsoft 365.
- Project2: After the successful completion of Project1, Microsoft Teams & Skype for Business will be enabled in Microsoft 365 for the sales department users.

Fabrikam plans to create a group named UserLicenses that will manage the allocation of all Microsoft 365 bulk licenses.

Technical Requirements
Fabrikam identifies the following technical requirements:

- All users must be able to exchange email messages successfully during Project1 by using their current email address.
- Users must be able to authenticate to cloud services if Active Directory becomes unavailable.
- A user named User1 must be able to view all DLP reports from the Microsoft 365 admin center.
- Microsoft Office 365 ProPlus applications must be installed from a network share only.
- Disruptions to email access must be minimized.

Application Requirements
Fabrikam identifies the following application requirements:

- An on-premises web application named App1 must allow users to complete their expense reports online. App1 must be available to users from the My Apps portal.
- The installation of feature updates for Office 365 ProPlus must be minimized.

Security Requirements
Fabrikam identifies the following security requirements:

- After the planned migration to Microsoft 365, all users must continue to authenticate to their mailbox and to SharePoint sites by using their UPN.
- The memberships of UserLicenses must be validated monthly. Unused user accounts must be removed from the group automatically.
- After the planned migration to Microsoft 365, all users must be signed in to on-premises and cloud-based applications automatically.
- The principle of least privilege must be used.

Correct Answer: D

Correct Answer: B

Manage User Identity and Roles

Question Set 1

Correct Answer: A

Correct Answer: B

Correct Answer: D

Correct Answer: AE

Correct Answer: A

Correct Answer: AEF

Correct Answer: D

Correct Answer: A

Correct Answer: B

Correct Answer: C

Correct Answer: C

Correct Answer: D

Correct Answer: C

Correct Answer: B

Correct Answer: B

Correct Answer: B

Correct Answer: AB

Correct Answer: A

Correct Answer: B

Correct Answer: B

Correct Answer: A

Correct Answer: D

Correct Answer: B

Correct Answer: A

Correct Answer: B

Correct Answer: C

Correct Answer: A

Correct Answer: AC

Correct Answer: D

Correct Answer: C

Correct Answer: B

Correct Answer: B

Correct Answer: E

Correct Answer: B

Correct Answer: A

Correct Answer: A

Correct Answer: A

Correct Answer: A

Correct Answer: D

Correct Answer: A

Correct Answer: A

Manage User Identity and Roles

Testlet 2

This is a case study. **Case studies are not timed separately. You can use as much exam time as you would like to complete each case**. However, there may be additional case studies and sections on this exam. You must manage your time to ensure that you are able to complete all questions included on this exam in the time provided.

To answer the questions included in a case study, you will need to reference information that is provided in the case study. Case studies might contain exhibits and other resources that provide more information about the scenario that is described in the case study. Each question is independent of the other questions in this case study.

At the end of this case study, a review screen will appear. This screen allows you to review your answer and to make changes before you move to the next section of the exam. After you begin a new section, you cannot return to this section.

To start the case study
To display the first question in this case study, click the **Next** button. Use the buttons in the left pane to explore the content of the case study before you answer the questions. Clicking these buttons displays information such as business requirements, existing environment, and problem statements. When you are ready to answer a question, click the **Question** button to return to the question.

Overview
Contoso, Ltd. is a consulting company that has a main office in Montreal and two branch offices in Seattle and New York.

The offices have the users and devices shown in the following table.

Office	Users	Laptops	Desktops	Mobile devices
Montreal	2,500	2,800	300	3,100
Seattle	1,000	1,100	200	1,500
New York	300	320	30	400

Contoso recently purchased a Microsoft 365 E5 subscription.

Existing Environment
The network contains an Active directory forest named contoso.com and a Microsoft Azure Active Directory (Azure AD) tenant named contoso.onmicrosoft.com.

You recently configured the forest to sync to the Azure AD tenant.

You add and then verify adatum.com as an additional domain name.

All servers run Windows Server 2016.

All desktop computers and laptops run Windows 10 Enterprise and are joined to contoso.com.

All the mobile devices in the Montreal and Seattle offices run Android. All the mobile devices in the New York office run iOS.

Contoso has the users shown in the following table.

Name	Role
User1	*None*
User2	*None*
User3	Customer Lockbox access approver
User4	*None*

Contoso has the groups shown in the following table.

Name	Type	Membership rule
Group1	Assigned	*Not applicable*
Group 2	Dynamic	(user.department —eq "Finance")

Microsoft Office 365 licenses are assigned only to Group2.

The network also contains external users from a vendor company who have Microsoft accounts that use a suffix of @outlook.com.

Requirements

Planned Changes
Contoso plans to provide email addresses for all the users in the following domains:

- East.adatum.com
- Contoso.adatum.com
- Humongousinsurance.com

Technical Requirements
Contoso identifies the following technical requirements:

- All new users must be assigned Office 365 licenses automatically.
- The principle of least privilege must be used whenever possible.

Security Requirements
Contoso identifies the following security requirements:

- Vendors must be able to authenticate by using their Microsoft account when accessing Contoso resources.
- User2 must be able to view reports and schedule the email delivery of security and compliance reports.

- The members of Group1 must be required to answer a security question before changing their password.
- User3 must be able to manage Office 365 connectors.
- User4 must be able to reset User3 password.

Correct Answer: A

Correct Answer: B

Correct Answer: B

Correct Answer: B

Correct Answer: B

Correct Answer: DE

Testlet 3

This is a case study. **Case studies are not timed separately. You can use as much exam time as you would like to complete each case**. However, there may be additional case studies and sections on this exam. You must manage your time to ensure that you are able to complete all questions included on this exam in the time provided.

To answer the questions included in a case study, you will need to reference information that is provided in the case study. Case studies might contain exhibits and other resources that provide more information about the scenario that is described in the case study. Each question is independent of the other questions in this case study.

At the end of this case study, a review screen will appear. This screen allows you to review your answer and to make changes before you move to the next section of the exam. After you begin a new section, you cannot return to this section.

To start the case study
To display the first question in this case study, click the **Next** button. Use the buttons in the left pane to explore the content of the case study before you answer the questions. Clicking these buttons displays information such as business requirements, existing environment, and problem statements. When you are ready to answer a question, click the **Question** button to return to the question.

Overview
Fabrikam, Inc. is an electronics company that produces consumer products. Fabrikam has 10,000 employees worldwide.

Fabrikam has a main office in London and branch offices in major cities in Europe, Asia, and the United States.

Existing Environment
Active Directory Environment
The network contains an Active Directory forest named fabrikam.com. The forest contains all the identities used for user and computer authentication.

Each department is represented by a top-level organizational unit (OU) that contains several child OUs for user accounts and computer accounts.

All users authenticate to on-premises applications by signing in to their device by using a UPN format of *username@fabrikam.com.*

Fabrikam does **NOT** plan to implement identity federation.

Network Infrastructure

Each office has a high-speed connection to the Internet.

Each office contains two domain controllers. All domain controllers are configured as a DNS server.

The public zone for fabrikam.com is managed by an external DNS server.

All users connect to an on-premises Microsoft Exchange Server 2016 organization. The users access their email by using Outlook Anywhere, Outlook on the web, or the Microsoft Outlook app for iOS. All the Exchange servers have the latest cumulative updates installed.

All shared company documents are stored on a Microsoft SharePoint Server farm.

Requirements
Planned Changes
Fabrikam plans to implement a Microsoft 365 Enterprise subscription and move all email and shared documents to the subscription.

Fabrikam plans to implement two pilot projects:

- Project1: During Project1, the mailboxes of 100 users in the sales department will be moved to Microsoft 365.
- Project2: After the successful completion of Project1, Microsoft Teams & Skype for Business will be enabled in Microsoft 365 for the sales department users.

Fabrikam plans to create a group named UserLicenses that will manage the allocation of all Microsoft 365 bulk licenses.

Technical Requirements
Fabrikam identifies the following technical requirements:

- All users must be able to exchange email messages successfully during Project1 by using their current email address.
- Users must be able to authenticate to cloud services if Active Directory becomes unavailable.
- A user named User1 must be able to view all DLP reports from the Microsoft 365 admin center.
- Microsoft Office 365 ProPlus applications must be installed from a network share only.
- Disruptions to email access must be minimized.

Application Requirements
Fabrikam identifies the following application requirements:

- An on-premises web application named App1 must allow users to complete their expense reports online. App1 must be available to users from the My Apps portal.
- The installation of feature updates for Office 365 ProPlus must be minimized.

Security Requirements
Fabrikam identifies the following security requirements:

- After the planned migration to Microsoft 365, all users must continue to authenticate to their mailbox and to SharePoint sites by using their UPN.
- The memberships of UserLicenses must be validated monthly. Unused user accounts must be removed from the group automatically.
- After the planned migration to Microsoft 365, all users must be signed in to on-premises and cloud-based applications automatically.
- The principle of least privilege must be used.

Correct Answer: C

Manage Access and Authentication

Question Set 1

Correct Answer: B

Correct Answer: C

Correct Answer: D

Correct Answer: A

Correct Answer: B

Correct Answer: B

Correct Answer: A

Correct Answer: B

Correct Answer: B

Correct Answer: A

Correct Answer: D

Correct Answer: B

Correct Answer: B

Correct Answer: A

Correct Answer: BCF

Correct Answer: B

Correct Answer: A

Correct Answer: B

Correct Answer: C

Correct Answer: DE

Correct Answer: B

Correct Answer: B

Correct Answer: C

Correct Answer: D

Correct Answer: C

Correct Answer: B

Correct Answer: A

Correct Answer: A

Correct Answer: BD

Correct Answer: B

Correct Answer: A

Correct Answer: ACE

Correct Answer: C

Testlet 2

This is a case study. **Case studies are not timed separately. You can use as much exam time as you would like to complete each case**. However, there may be additional case studies and sections on this exam. You must manage your time to ensure that you are able to complete all questions included on this exam in the time provided.

To answer the questions included in a case study, you will need to reference information that is provided in the case study. Case studies might contain exhibits and other resources that provide more information about the scenario that is described in the case study. Each question is independent of the other questions in this case study.

At the end of this case study, a review screen will appear. This screen allows you to review your answer and to make changes before you move to the next section of the exam. After you begin a new section, you cannot return to this section.

To start the case study
To display the first question in this case study, click the **Next** button. Use the buttons in the left pane to explore the content of the case study before you answer the questions. Clicking these buttons displays information such as business requirements, existing environment, and problem statements. When you are ready to answer a question, click the **Question** button to return to the question.

Overview
Contoso, Ltd. is a consulting company that has a main office in Montreal and two branch offices in Seattle and New York.

The offices have the users and devices shown in the following table.

Office	Users	Laptops	Desktops	Mobile devices
Montreal	2,500	2,800	300	3,100
Seattle	1,000	1,100	200	1,500
New York	300	320	30	400

Contoso recently purchased a Microsoft 365 E5 subscription.

Existing Environment
The network contains an Active directory forest named contoso.com and a Microsoft Azure Active Directory (Azure AD) tenant named contoso.onmicrosoft.com.

You recently configured the forest to sync to the Azure AD tenant.

You add and then verify adatum.com as an additional domain name.

All servers run Windows Server 2016.

All desktop computers and laptops run Windows 10 Enterprise and are joined to contoso.com.

All the mobile devices in the Montreal and Seattle offices run Android. All the mobile devices in the New York office run iOS.

Contoso has the users shown in the following table.

Name	Role
User1	*None*
User2	*None*
User3	Customer Lockbox access approver
User4	*None*

Contoso has the groups shown in the following table.

Name	Type	Membership rule
Group1	Assigned	*Not applicable*
Group 2	Dynamic	(user.department –eq "Finance")

Microsoft Office 365 licenses are assigned only to Group2.

The network also contains external users from a vendor company who have Microsoft accounts that use a suffix of @outlook.com.

Requirements

Planned Changes
Contoso plans to provide email addresses for all the users in the following domains:

- East.adatum.com
- Contoso.adatum.com
- Humongousinsurance.com

Technical Requirements
Contoso identifies the following technical requirements:

- All new users must be assigned Office 365 licenses automatically.
- The principle of least privilege must be used whenever possible.

Security Requirements
Contoso identifies the following security requirements:

- Vendors must be able to authenticate by using their Microsoft account when accessing Contoso resources.
- User2 must be able to view reports and schedule the email delivery of security and compliance reports.

- The members of Group1 must be required to answer a security question before changing their password.
- User3 must be able to manage Office 365 connectors.
- User4 must be able to reset User3 password.

Correct Answer: D

Correct Answer: D

Correct Answer: D

Manage Access and Authentication

Testlet 3

This is a case study. **Case studies are not timed separately. You can use as much exam time as you would like to complete each case**. However, there may be additional case studies and sections on this exam. You must manage your time to ensure that you are able to complete all questions included on this exam in the time provided.

To answer the questions included in a case study, you will need to reference information that is provided in the case study. Case studies might contain exhibits and other resources that provide more information about the scenario that is described in the case study. Each question is independent of the other questions in this case study.

At the end of this case study, a review screen will appear. This screen allows you to review your answer and to make changes before you move to the next section of the exam. After you begin a new section, you cannot return to this section.

To start the case study
To display the first question in this case study, click the **Next** button. Use the buttons in the left pane to explore the content of the case study before you answer the questions. Clicking these buttons displays information such as business requirements, existing environment, and problem statements. When you are ready to answer a question, click the **Question** button to return to the question.

Overview
Fabrikam, Inc. is an electronics company that produces consumer products. Fabrikam has 10,000 employees worldwide.

Fabrikam has a main office in London and branch offices in major cities in Europe, Asia, and the United States.

Existing Environment
Active Directory Environment
The network contains an Active Directory forest named fabrikam.com. The forest contains all the identities used for user and computer authentication.

Each department is represented by a top-level organizational unit (OU) that contains several child OUs for user accounts and computer accounts.

All users authenticate to on-premises applications by signing in to their device by using a UPN format of *username@fabrikam.com.*

Fabrikam does **NOT** plan to implement identity federation.

Network Infrastructure

Each office has a high-speed connection to the Internet.

Each office contains two domain controllers. All domain controllers are configured as a DNS server.

The public zone for fabrikam.com is managed by an external DNS server.

All users connect to an on-premises Microsoft Exchange Server 2016 organization. The users access their email by using Outlook Anywhere, Outlook on the web, or the Microsoft Outlook app for iOS. All the Exchange servers have the latest cumulative updates installed.

All shared company documents are stored on a Microsoft SharePoint Server farm.

Requirements
Planned Changes
Fabrikam plans to implement a Microsoft 365 Enterprise subscription and move all email and shared documents to the subscription.

Fabrikam plans to implement two pilot projects:

- Project1: During Project1, the mailboxes of 100 users in the sales department will be moved to Microsoft 365.
- Project2: After the successful completion of Project1, Microsoft Teams & Skype for Business will be enabled in Microsoft 365 for the sales department users.

Fabrikam plans to create a group named UserLicenses that will manage the allocation of all Microsoft 365 bulk licenses.

Technical Requirements
Fabrikam identifies the following technical requirements:

- All users must be able to exchange email messages successfully during Project1 by using their current email address.
- Users must be able to authenticate to cloud services if Active Directory becomes unavailable.
- A user named User1 must be able to view all DLP reports from the Microsoft 365 admin center.
- Microsoft Office 365 ProPlus applications must be installed from a network share only.
- Disruptions to email access must be minimized.

Application Requirements
Fabrikam identifies the following application requirements:

- An on-premises web application named App1 must allow users to complete their expense reports online. App1 must be available to users from the My Apps portal.
- The installation of feature updates for Office 365 ProPlus must be minimized.

Security Requirements
Fabrikam identifies the following security requirements:

- After the planned migration to Microsoft 365, all users must continue to authenticate to their mailbox and to SharePoint sites by using their UPN.
- The memberships of UserLicenses must be validated monthly. Unused user accounts must be removed from the group automatically.
- After the planned migration to Microsoft 365, all users must be signed in to on-premises and cloud-based applications automatically.
- The principle of least privilege must be used.

Correct Answer: ABC

Correct Answer: A

Plan Office 365 Workloads and Applications

Question Set 1

Correct Answer: C

Correct Answer: B

Correct Answer: B

Correct Answer: A

Correct Answer: D

Answers 2

Design and Implement Microsoft 365 Services

Question Set 1

Correct Answer: B

Correct Answer: D

Correct Answer: B

Correct Answer: C

Correct Answer: C

Correct Answer: BD

Correct Answer: C

Correct Answer: C

Correct Answer: B

Correct Answer: D

Correct Answer: C

Correct Answer: AE

Correct Answer: AB

Correct Answer: B

Correct Answer:

Actions

On Server1, run `setup.exe` and specify the /configure parameter.

On Server1, run `setup.exe` and specify the /package parameter.

On every client computer, run `setup.exe` and specify the /download parameter.

Answer Area

On Server1, run `setup.exe` and specify the /download parameter.

Create an XML configuration file.

On every client computer, run `setup.exe` and specify the /configure parameter.

Correct Answer: B

Correct Answer: A

Correct Answer: D

Correct Answer: D

Correct Answer: A

Correct Answer:

Answer Area

You can open File1 from:

App1 only
App1 and App2 only
App1 and App3 only
App1, App2, and App3

An action will be logged when you attempt to open File1 from:

App1 only
App3 only
App1 and App2 only
App2 and App3 only
App1, App2, and App3

Correct Answer: A

Correct Answer: B

Correct Answer: B

Correct Answer: A

Correct Answer: B

Correct Answer: E

Correct Answer: C

Design and Implement Microsoft 365 Services

Testlet 2

This is a case study. **Case studies are not timed separately. You can use as much exam time as you would like to complete each case**. However, there may be additional case studies and sections on this exam. You must manage your time to ensure that you are able to complete all questions included on this exam in the time provided.

To answer the questions included in a case study, you will need to reference information that is provided in the case study. Case studies might contain exhibits and other resources that provide more information about the scenario that is described in the case study. Each question is independent of the other questions in this case study.

At the end of this case study, a review screen will appear. This screen allows you to review your answer and to make changes before you move to the next section of the exam. After you begin a new section, you cannot return to this section.

To start the case study
To display the first question in this case study, click the **Next** button. Use the buttons in the left pane to explore the content of the case study before you answer the questions. Clicking these buttons displays information such as business requirements, existing environment, and problem statements. When you are ready to answer a question, click the **Question** button to return to the question.

Overview
Fabrikam, Inc. is an electronics company that produces consumer products. Fabrikam has 10,000 employees worldwide.

Fabrikam has a main office in London and branch offices in major cities in Europe, Asia, and the United States.

Existing Environment
Active Directory Environment
The network contains an Active Directory forest named fabrikam.com. The forest contains all the identities used for user and computer authentication.

Each department is represented by a top-level organizational unit (OU) that contains several child OUs for user accounts and computer accounts.

All users authenticate to on-premises applications by signing in to their device by using a UPN format of *username@fabrikam.com*.

Fabrikam does **NOT** plan to implement identity federation.

Network Infrastructure

Each office has a high-speed connection to the Internet.

Each office contains two domain controllers. All domain controllers are configured as a DNS server.

The public zone for fabrikam.com is managed by an external DNS server.

All users connect to an on-premises Microsoft Exchange Server 2016 organization. The users access their email by using Outlook Anywhere, Outlook on the web, or the Microsoft Outlook app for iOS. All the Exchange servers have the latest cumulative updates installed.

All shared company documents are stored on a Microsoft SharePoint Server farm.

Requirements
Planned Changes
Fabrikam plans to implement a Microsoft 365 Enterprise subscription and move all email and shared documents to the subscription.

Fabrikam plans to implement two pilot projects:

- Project1: During Project1, the mailboxes of 100 users in the sales department will be moved to Microsoft 365.
- Project2: After the successful completion of Project1, Microsoft Teams & Skype for Business will be enabled in Microsoft 365 for the sales department users.

Fabrikam plans to create a group named UserLicenses that will manage the allocation of all Microsoft 365 bulk licenses.

Technical Requirements
Fabrikam identifies the following technical requirements:

- All users must be able to exchange email messages successfully during Project1 by using their current email address.
- Users must be able to authenticate to cloud services if Active Directory becomes unavailable.
- A user named User1 must be able to view all DLP reports from the Microsoft 365 admin center.
- Microsoft Office 365 ProPlus applications must be installed from a network share only.
- Disruptions to email access must be minimized.

Application Requirements
Fabrikam identifies the following application requirements:

- An on-premises web application named App1 must allow users to complete their expense reports online.
- The installation of feature updates for Office 365 ProPlus must be minimized.

Security Requirements
Fabrikam identifies the following security requirements:

- After the planned migration to Microsoft 365, all users must continue to authenticate to their mailbox and to SharePoint sites by using their UPN.
- The memberships of UserLicenses must be validated monthly. Unused user accounts must be removed from the group automatically.
- After the planned migration to Microsoft 365, all users must be signed in to on-premises and cloud-based applications automatically.
- The principle of least privilege must be used.

Correct Answer: D

Correct Answer: B

Manage User Identity and Roles

Question Set 1

Correct Answer: E

Correct Answer: B

Correct Answer: A

Correct Answer: A

Correct Answer: B

Correct Answer: D

Correct Answer: AE

Correct Answer: A

Correct Answer:

Answer Area

User1 [**answer choice**].

| ▼ |
| cannot change her password from any Microsoft portals |
| can change her password by using self-service password reset feature only |
| an change her password from the Office 365 admin center only |

If the password for User1 is changed in Active Directory, [**answer choice**].

| ▼ |
| the password will be synchronized to Azure AD |
| a new randomly generated password will be assigned to User1 |
| the password in Azure AD will be unchanged |

Correct Answer: AEF

Correct Answer: D

Correct Answer: A

Correct Answer: B

Correct Answer: C

Correct Answer: C

Correct Answer: D

Correct Answer: C

Correct Answer: B

Correct Answer: B

Correct Answer: B

Correct Answer:

Answer Area

User1: [▼]
| Email address only |
| Phone number only |
| Security questions only |
| Phone number and email address |

User2: [▼]
| Email address only |
| Phone number only |
| Security questions only |
| Phone number and email address |

User3: [▼]
| Email address only |
| Phone number only |
| Security questions only |
| Phone number and email address |

Correct Answer: AB

Correct Answer: A

Correct Answer: B

Correct Answer: B

Correct Answer: A

Correct Answer: D

Correct Answer: B

Correct Answer: A

Correct Answer: B

Correct Answer: A

Correct Answer: AC

Testlet 2

This is a case study. **Case studies are not timed separately. You can use as much exam time as you would like to complete each case**. However, there may be additional case studies and sections on this exam. You must manage your time to ensure that you are able to complete all questions included on this exam in the time provided.

To answer the questions included in a case study, you will need to reference information that is provided in the case study. Case studies might contain exhibits and other resources that provide more information about the scenario that is described in the case study. Each question is independent of the other questions in this case study.

At the end of this case study, a review screen will appear. This screen allows you to review your answer and to make changes before you move to the next section of the exam. After you begin a new section, you cannot return to this section.

To start the case study
To display the first question in this case study, click the **Next** button. Use the buttons in the left pane to explore the content of the case study before you answer the questions. Clicking these buttons displays information such as business requirements, existing environment, and problem statements. When you are ready to answer a question, click the **Question** button to return to the question.

Overview
Contoso, Ltd. is a consulting company that has a main office in Montreal and two branch offices in Seattle and New York.

The offices have the users and devices shown in the following table.

Office	Users	Laptops	Desktops	Mobile devices
Montreal	2,500	2,800	300	3,100
Seattle	1,000	1,100	200	1,500
New York	300	320	30	400

Contoso recently purchased a Microsoft 365 E5 subscription.

Existing Environment
The network contains an Active directory forest named contoso.com and a Microsoft Azure Active Directory (Azure AD) tenant named contoso.onmicrosoft.com.

You recently configured the forest to sync to the Azure AD tenant.

You add and then verify adatum.com as an additional domain name.

All servers run Windows Server 2016.

All desktop computers and laptops run Windows 10 Enterprise and are joined to contoso.com.

All the mobile devices in the Montreal and Seattle offices run Android. All the mobile devices in the New York office run iOS.

Contoso has the users shown in the following table.

Name	Role
User1	*None*
User2	*None*
User3	Customer Lockbox access approver
User4	*None*

Contoso has the groups shown in the following table.

Name	Type	Membership rule
Group1	Assigned	*Not applicable*
Group 2	Dynamic	(user.department –eq "Finance")

Microsoft Office 365 licenses are assigned only to Group2.

The network also contains external users from a vendor company who have Microsoft accounts that use a suffix of @outlook.com.

Requirements

Planned Changes
Contoso plans to provide email addresses for all the users in the following domains:

- East.adatum.com
- Contoso.adatum.com
- Humongousinsurance.com

Technical Requirements
Contoso identifies the following technical requirements:

- All new users must be assigned Office 365 licenses automatically.
- The principle of least privilege must be used whenever possible.

Security Requirements
Contoso identifies the following security requirements:

- Vendors must be able to authenticate by using their Microsoft account when accessing Contoso resources.
- User2 must be able to view reports and schedule the email delivery of security and compliance reports.

- The members of Group1 must be required to answer a security question before changing their password.
- User3 must be able to manage Office 365 connectors.
- User4 must be able to reset User3 password.

Correct Answer: B

Correct Answer: B

Correct Answer: B

Correct Answer: B

Manage Access and Authentication

Question Set 1

Correct Answer: B

Correct Answer: B

Correct Answer: A

Correct Answer: B

Correct Answer: B

Correct Answer: A

Correct Answer: BCF

Correct Answer: B

Correct Answer: A

Correct Answer: B

Correct Answer:

Answer Area

Statements	Yes	No
When User1 connects to App1 from a device that has an IP address of 131.107.50.10, User1 must use MFA.	O	O
When User2 connects to App1 from a device that has an IP address of 131.107.50.15, User2 must use MFA.	O	O
When User2 connects to App1 from a device that has an IP address of 131.107.5.5, User2 must use MFA.	O	O

Correct Answer: C

Correct Answer: DE

Correct Answer: B

Correct Answer: B

Correct Answer: A

Correct Answer: BD

Correct Answer: B

Correct Answer:

Answer Area

Statements	Yes	No
User1 can access Microsoft Office 365 from a device that has an IP address of 133.107.10.20.	○	○
User1 can access Microsoft Office 365 from a device that has an IP address of 193.77.10.15.	○	○
User2 can access Microsoft Office 365 from a device that has an IP address of 193.77.10.20.	○	○

Correct Answer: A

Correct Answer: ACE

Correct Answer: C

Correct Answer: B

Correct Answer: C

Correct Answer: A

Manage Access and Authentication

Testlet 2

This is a case study. **Case studies are not timed separately. You can use as much exam time as you would like to complete each case**. However, there may be additional case studies and sections on this exam. You must manage your time to ensure that you are able to complete all questions included on this exam in the time provided.

To answer the questions included in a case study, you will need to reference information that is provided in the case study. Case studies might contain exhibits and other resources that provide more information about the scenario that is described in the case study. Each question is independent of the other questions in this case study.

At the end of this case study, a review screen will appear. This screen allows you to review your answer and to make changes before you move to the next section of the exam. After you begin a new section, you cannot return to this section.

To start the case study
To display the first question in this case study, click the **Next** button. Use the buttons in the left pane to explore the content of the case study before you answer the questions. Clicking these buttons displays information such as business requirements, existing environment, and problem statements. When you are ready to answer a question, click the **Question** button to return to the question.

Overview
Contoso, Ltd. is a consulting company that has a main office in Montreal and two branch offices in Seattle and New York.

The offices have the users and devices shown in the following table.

Office	Users	Laptops	Desktops	Mobile devices
Montreal	2,500	2,800	300	3,100
Seattle	1,000	1,100	200	1,500
New York	300	320	30	400

Contoso recently purchased a Microsoft 365 E5 subscription.

Existing Environment
The network contains an Active directory forest named contoso.com and a Microsoft Azure Active Directory (Azure AD) tenant named contoso.onmicrosoft.com.

You recently configured the forest to sync to the Azure AD tenant.

You add and then verify adatum.com as an additional domain name.

All servers run Windows Server 2016.

All desktop computers and laptops run Windows 10 Enterprise and are joined to contoso.com.

All the mobile devices in the Montreal and Seattle offices run Android. All the mobile devices in the New York office run iOS.

Contoso has the users shown in the following table.

Name	Role
User1	*None*
User2	*None*
User3	Customer Lockbox access approver
User4	*None*

Contoso has the groups shown in the following table.

Name	Type	Membership rule
Group1	Assigned	*Not applicable*
Group 2	Dynamic	(user.department –eq "Finance")

Microsoft Office 365 licenses are assigned only to Group2.

The network also contains external users from a vendor company who have Microsoft accounts that use a suffix of @outlook.com.

Requirements

Planned Changes
Contoso plans to provide email addresses for all the users in the following domains:

- East.adatum.com
- Contoso.adatum.com
- Humongousinsurance.com

Technical Requirements
Contoso identifies the following technical requirements:

- All new users must be assigned Office 365 licenses automatically.
- The principle of least privilege must be used whenever possible.

Security Requirements
Contoso identifies the following security requirements:

- Vendors must be able to authenticate by using their Microsoft account when accessing Contoso resources.
- User2 must be able to view reports and schedule the email delivery of security and compliance reports.

- The members of Group1 must be required to answer a security question before changing their password.
- User3 must be able to manage Office 365 connectors.
- User4 must be able to reset User3 password.

Correct Answer: D

Correct Answer: D

Plan Office 365 Workloads and Applications

Question Set 1

Correct Answer: BDE

Correct Answer: B

Correct Answer: D

Correct Answer: D

Correct Answer: B

Correct Answer: B

Correct Answer: B

Correct Answer: C

Correct Answer: B

Correct Answer: C

Correct Answer: C

Correct Answer: B

Correct Answer: C

Correct Answer:

Actions	Answer Area
	Copy the OneDrive Administrative Templates to your computer.
	From Group Policy Management Editor, configure the OneDrive settings.
	Instruct the users to run gpupdate.exe /force at a command prompt on each device.
From Group Policy Management Editor, configure the Folder Redirection settings.	
Deploy the Azure File Sync agent to all devices.	
From SharePoint Online, create 10 libraries.	

Correct Answer: B **Correct**

Answer: A **Correct Answer:**

AB **Correct Answer:** A

Good Luck in your Exam

Made in the USA
Monee, IL
13 January 2021